Melancholy and the critique of modernity

The book examines the connections between the emergence of modern society and the experience of melancholy. The idea of 'sadness without a cause' has played an important part in human self-understanding throughout the development of Western society. But with the emergence of modernity melancholy has become its most pervasive and significant experience.

The affinity between melancholy and modernity is examined through a comprehensive re-examination of the writings of Søren Kierkegaard. The whole range of Kierkegaard's work is set in the context of a social and historical theory of melancholy. From this perspective Kierkegaard emerges as the most important, and the most typical, psychologist of the modern era.

The book makes Kierkegaard's rich and insightful writings accessible to a new audience and establishes him as a central figure for contemporary debates on the nature of modernity.

Harvie Ferguson is Senior Lecturer in Sociology at Glasgow University.

Contents

For Rex

Sadness

Somewhere in a psalm it tells of the rich man who painstakingly amasses a fortune and 'knows not who will inherit it from him'.

In the same way I will leave behind me, intellectually speaking, a not-so-little capital. Alas, but I know who is going to inherit from me, that character I find so repulsive, he who will keep on inheriting all that is best just as he has done in the past – namely, the assistant professor, the professor.

(marginal note)

And even if 'the professor' happened to read this, it would not stop him, it would not prick his conscience – no, he would lecture on this, too. And even if the professor happened to read this remark, it would not stop him either – no, he would lecture on this, too. For the professor is even longer than the tapeworm which a woman was delivered of recently (200 feet according to her husband, who expressed his gratitude in *Addresseavisen* recently) – a professor is even longer than that – and if a man has this tapeworm 'the professor' in him, no human being can deliver him of it; only God can do it if the man himself is willing.

(Søren Kierkegaard, Journals, 6: 6817–18)

Preface

Prefaces bear the stamp of the accidental.

Nicolaus Notabene, *Prefaces*

I came across Kierkegaard by accident.

As an undergraduate in Sociology it was hardly surprising that no one had mentioned any of his works to me. And for several years after I graduated I knew of him only at second and third hand as a precursor, or possibly even the founder, of existentialism, a philosophical fashion I had felt safe in ignoring on the unassailable grounds of its already being dated. Then a momentary confusion in a darkened corner of Glasgow University Library (cut-backs/unreplaced fluorescent tube) placed *Repetition* in my hands. I had been ill-advisedly searching through 'unclassified philosophy' for works on logic and thought I had discovered a slim volume on 'Refutations'.

Under lustrous neon frustration gave way to bewilderment. A strangely arresting title: better, a hopelessly contradictory subtitle, *An Essay in Experimental Psychology*, and a bizarre pseudonym claimed as the author. I had once abandoned a course in experimental psychology, probably, I reflected, because it was a subject unsuited to essay writing. I borrowed the book. It was unlike anything I had previously read. But I did not understand what it was about, and I could not explain why it was so interesting. Part novel, part philosophical psychology, wholly unclassifiable, I was confident that it was interesting; indeed it was, to a large extent, about the category of the interesting. Uncomprehendingly I read that 'repetition' was the '*interest* of metaphysics, and at the same time the interest upon which metaphysics founders'.

I went back to the library and, rather slowly, read my way through the Kierkegaard section. Or, to be more precise, I quickly read his aesthetic works, rather slowly familiarized myself with his philosophical books, and completely ignored his religious writings. 'Kierkegaard' – the name was quite sufficient to cause an anticipatory *frisson* of intellectual pleasure – became something of a hobby. Remote from my main preoccupations, his works provided the ideal opportunity to indulge an admiration for sheer cleverness as well as, in gaining the acquaintance of a great but not well-known writer, a degree of self-flattery.

I knew well enough that this kind of youthful enthusiasm should pass, to be replaced by a passion for opera or foreign travel. It surely should not have survived the daunting practicalities of helping to bring up three children. But, alarmingly, I seemed to be growing into, rather than out of, an author whose unfailing strangeness continued to unsettle me. Gradually I found ways of introducing him into my own work, and from there it was an easy step to begin to work in areas where his writing could figure more prominently. After all the whole development of modern philosophical psychology could be read in a Kierkegaardian context, albeit one defined by reference to Heidegger rather than to Kierkegaard himself.

In spite of an interest in the sociology of religion I was not tempted by Kierkegaard's religious works. Indeed I was somewhat embarrassed at the thought of the *edifying discourses* which I had never read, a neglect I justified not only on ideological grounds but in the conviction that they could not possibly contain anything more, or anything more exciting, than the extraordinary barrage of insights to which I had exposed myself in reading the pseudonymous works. None the less, in claiming not to be tempted by them, I came to recognize that the discourses represented for me something other than an uninteresting, or even a merely interesting, extension of the authorship, and in this recognition lay a wish to which I could hardly pretend indifference. And once I acknowledged that my denial was nothing but a negative affirmation that the religious writings were a temptation, I could not decently resist but at once gave in.

In fact I found the *edifying discourses* (only much later in the new Princeton edition did they become *upbuilding discourses*) disappointing. Relieved, I returned to the relative conventionality of a sociological study of imprisonment, which, with the satisfaction of settling accounts with an awkward companion, I was able to interpret as a negative form of what he had called *repetition*.

Of course it was much too late, and no such simple act of expiation could free me from a writer who had got so far under my skin. I turned to fiction. But in spite of a robust determination to rid myself of all trace of the melancholic Dane, he intruded, not simply as an idea but as a character, in the story I was trying to write. Later academic studies did nothing to lessen my discomfort. There was every reason, certainly, to include him in the discussions of both pleasure and happiness which I undertook, but in both his presence acted as far more of a conditioning element than I had wished. Thus, much later than I should have done so, I decided to tackle Kierkegaard head on.

I also decided to get some professional help. The Divinity Faculty provided me with everything I most needed; open-minded encouragement, the stimulus of people who knew what they were talking about, and a reckless tolerance of every new idea. A more civilized academic community would be hard to find; not a sign of the 'assistant professors' or of the 'academic managers', which is the most recent metamorphosis of the philistinism that Kierkegaard so much hated. I would like particularly to thank the Dean of the Faculty, Professor Robert Carroll, for encouraging my obsessions; and Dr Joe Houston, who guided me through the Kierkegaard literature, selflessly put his learning at my disposal and never complained when I failed to see things his way. He has read the manuscript in its entirety, and would have immensely improved it had I allowed him the chance his care deserved. As it is the errors and extravagant interpretations are my own.

The result is not a book about Kierkegaard. It is, rather, a book which seeks to explain why sociologists, and anyone else interested in the character of modern life, should read Kierkegaard. Naturally many people read Kierkegaard from quite different perspectives and find in him compelling truths neglected in the following pages. An enormous secondary literature bears eloquent testimony to an interpretative fecundity which condemns every new book on Kierkegaard to the fate of disappointing those most inclined to read it. Equally, there are other sources from which insights I have come to think typically 'Kierkegaardian' might be gleaned. None the less I think what I say about Kierkegaard will be of some interest to sociologists interested in describing the inner character of human experience in modern society, and of some concern to theologians and philosophers interested in finding ways of understanding Kierkegaard's intriguing and allusive writings. Primarily, however, I hope to encourage anyone who might be inclined to read a book which addresses itself to Melancholy to reflect on that pervasive and puzzling phenomenon.

This encouragement would have remained the strangled cry of 'Read Kierkegaard' with which I used to harass my friends had it not been for the tireless efficiency of the staff of the Inter-Library Loan Department of Glasgow University Library. Their resilient friendliness in the face of torrential requests, their uncanny ability to trace items of which I had the most tenuous bibliographical details, and their patience with my handwriting, deserve far more than the thanks that I am happy to record here.

My previous research, already influenced by aspects of Kierkegaard's writings, has shaped my attempt to come to terms with his work as a whole. As a result I have found new studies of the social and intellectual context of Kierkegaard's life and work of great interest. And recent efforts to drag him into the vanguard of postmodernism (as a kind of pre-postmodernist) are both stimulating and relevant to the present approach. Yet I have found myself returning with these new perspectives to older views in which melancholy plays a more definite role. Indeed it is, I believe, in the context of a historical understanding of melancholy that the newer contributions to Kierkegaard studies become most illuminating.

All this, as Kierkegaard remarks in confessing that he was in fact the author of the pseudonymous works, 'can scarcely be of interest to anyone'. It serves only to make the rather obvious point that, as a powerful and genuinely original writer, Kierkegaard's works elicit a very personal response from each reader, but, as a lucid and rigorous thinker, he provides us with the means by which we can together grasp the human possibilities given with the conditions of modern life.

Abbreviations

Longer quotations from the works of Kierkegaard are identified in the text by the abbreviated titles listed below. Wherever possible these are from the Princeton edition of *Kierkegaard's Writings*. This listing also identifies subtitles, appropriate pseudonym, and date of first publication. All other quotations are identified through endnotes.

Polemical	*Early Polemical Writings*; includes *From the Papers of One Still Living: Published Against His Will*, S. Kierkegaard, 7 September 1838
Irony	*The Concept of Irony: with Continual Reference to Socrates*, Søren Kierkegaard, 16 September 1841, thesis submitted for Degree of Master of Arts
Either	*Either/Or: A Fragment of Life*, ed. *Victor Eremita, Part 1, Containing A's Papers*, 20 February 1843
Or	*Either/Or: A Fragment of Life*, ed. *Victor Eremita, Part 2, Containing the Papers of B, Letters to A*, 20 February 1843
Discourses	*Two Edifying Discourses*, S. Kierkegaard, 16 May 1843
Repetition	*Repetition: A Venture in Experimenting Psychology, Constantin Constantius*, October 1843
Fear	*Fear and Trembling: Dialectical Lyric, Johanne de Silentio*, 16 October 1843
Discourses	*Three Edifying Discourses*, S. Kierkegaard, 16 October 1843
Climacus	*Johannes Climacus, or De Omnibus Dubitandum Est: A Narrative*, unpublished, 1843
Discourses	*Four Edifying Discourses*, S. Kierkegaard, 6 December 1843
Discourses	*Two Edifying Discourses*, S. Kierkegaard, 5 March 1844
Discourses	*Three Edifying Discourses*, S. Kierkegaard, 8 June 1844

Fragments	*Philosophical Fragments: or A Fragment of Philosophy,* *Johannes Climacus, ed. S. Kierkegaard,* 13 June 1844
Anxiety	*The Concept of Anxiety: A Simple Psychologically Orienting* *Deliberation on the Dogmatic Issue of Hereditary Sin,* *Vigilius Haufniensis,* 17 June 1844
Prefaces	*Prefaces: Light Reading for Certain Classes as the Occasion* *May Require,* *Nicolaus Notabene,* 17 June 1844
Discourses	*Four Edifying Discourses,* S. Kierkegaard, 31 August 1844
Occasions	*Three Discourses on Imagined Occasions,* S. Kierkegaard, 29 April 1844
Stages	*Stages on Life's Way: Studies by Various Persons, Compiled,* *Forwarded to the Press, and Published by Hilarius Bookbinder,* 30 April 1845
Corsair	Various newspaper articles including 'A Cursory Observation Concerning a Detail in *Don Giovanni*', by A.
Postscript	*Concluding Unscientific Postscript to Philosophical Fragments:* *A Mimical-Pathetical-Dialectical Compilation, an Existential* *Contribution,* *Johannes Climacus, ed. S. Kierkegaard,* 27 February 1846
Two Ages	*Two Ages: The Age of Revolution and the Present Age, A* *Literary Review,* S. Kierkegaard, 30 March 1846
Adler	*On Authority and Revelation: The Book on Adler, or a Cycle of* *Ethico-Religious Essays,* unpublished, 1846–7
Purity	*Purity of Heart is to Will One Thing,* Part One of *Upbuilding* *Discourses in Various Spirits,* S. Kierkegaard, 13 March 1847
Lilies	*Consider the Lilies,* Part Two of *Upbuilding Discourses in* *Various Spirits,* S. Kierkegaard, 13 March 1847
Sufferings	*The Gospel of Sufferings,* Part Three of *Upbuilding Discourses* *in Various Spirits,* S. Kierkegaard, 13 March 1847
Love	*Works of Love: Some Christian Reflections in the Form of* *Discourses,* S. Kierkegaard, 29 September 1847
Christian	*Christian Discourses,* S. Kierkegaard, 26 April 1848
Crisis	*The Crisis and a Crisis in the Life of an Actress, Inter et Inter,* 24–27 July 1848
Point of *View*	*The Point of View for My Work as an Author,* unpublished, 1848
Sickness	*The Sickness Unto Death: A Christian Psychological Exposition* *for Upbuilding and Awakening, Anti-Climacus, ed. S.* Kierkegaard, 30 July 1849

Practice	*Practice in Christianity, Anti-Climacus*, ed. S. Kierkegaard, 27 September 1850
Self-Examination	*For Self-Examination: Recommended to the Present Age, First Series*, S. Kierkegaard, 10 September 1851
Self-Examination	*Judge For Yourself!: For Self-Examination Recommended to the Present Age, Second Series*, S. Kierkegaard, unpublished, 1851–2
Attack	Articles, 1854–5
Journals	*Søren Kierkegaard's Journals and Papers*
Letters	*Kierkegaard: Letters and Documents*

Introduction

> In addition to my other numerous acqaintances, with whom, on the whole, I have a very formal relationship, I do have one intimate confidante – my melancholy, and in the midst of my joy, in the midst of my work, she beckons to me, calls me aside, even though physically I remain on the spot. It is the most faithful mistress I have known – no wonder, then, that I must be prepared to follow at any moment.
>
> (Søren Kierkegaard, *Journals*, 5: 5496)

> Let us simply assume that melancholy has no content at all. He who is melancholy can name many cares which hold him in bondage, but the one which binds him he is unable to name.
>
> (Søren Kierkegaard, *Journals*, 5: 5724)

Søren Kierkegaard's writings continue to exercise a growing and somewhat diffuse influence on contemporary culture. It is, in fact, only recently that his stature as a literary and philosophical figure of major importance has been widely recognized. The publication of an authoritative English translation of his works, which itself indicates his growing reputation, will, doubtless, stimulate a horde of 'assistant professors' to fresh expository efforts. And if the immediate context of their composition – the religious and cultural interests of European intellectuals in the aftermath of Hegel's philosophy – remains a matter of fascination primarily for specialists, the prescience of his 'critique of modernity', the experimental character of his discourse, and the way in which his own experience became central to his understanding of the world, make him relevant to a host of contemporary debates. As a result, and perhaps appropriately for an author who wrote so diversely and whose most famous work is subtitled *A Fragment of Life*, Kierkegaard is read partially and from widely divergent perspectives.

He is, perhaps, best known for his 'aesthetic' works, and for the distinctively personal point of view from which they were written. In this context he occupies a position, chronologically and psychologically, towards the end of a series that begins with Goethe's *The Sorrows of Young Werther* (1774) and ends with Dostoyevsky's *Notes From Underground* (1864). Until recently his influence in philosophy was primarily through these same works, viewed somewhat distantly through the 'mediation' of Heidegger and Sartre.

As a religious writer he has been just as one-sidedly treated, his *Discourses*, ignored as theology, have been read, when at all, primarily within the tradition of homiletic literature. Yet Kierkegaard, fearing (rightly) that in due course he would become famous as a merely 'interesting' writer, always claimed to be a 'religious' author. This claim ought to be taken seriously; and it can be taken seriously without rejecting his singular brilliance as a psychologist, or ignoring the seriousness and originality of his philosophy. Indeed, his psychology is penetrating just because it is religious in nature (and not simply in context); and his philosophy is interesting precisely because it is so highly charged with a realistic sense of life; and both are made possible (rather than merely facilitated), by a supreme mastery of language.

The variety of his literary production is astonishing. Clearly there is some sense in which the disparate elements of the authorship are inter-related. It is less clear that they form a coherent and unified view of the world. Rather than claim some spurious 'totality' for the synthesizing power of his literary art, or his philosophy, or his religious outlook, the connections among his various styles of work should be sought in the character of modern life itself.

This is not to invite biographical speculation. Though there is no doubt his own life, as it is for any writer, was significant to the origin and development of his thought, Kierkegaard is, in fact, rather careful in the way in which he allows his personal experience to intrude into his works. It is not that a narrative of life events could 'explain' his books, but, rather, the general 'feel' of his inner experience which provides a clue to the deliberately fragmented character of his writing. He refers to his own experience as dominated by a feeling of 'melancholy'. And it is by reconstructing the meaning and significance of melancholy that the originality and the comprehensiveness of Kierkegaard's religious psychology of modern life can be appreciated.[1]

Melancholy is something more than a pervasive mood, though it is for modern society, its most widespread and in some sense most characteristic mood. One might say it is its *only* mood; or, to be more precise, that what at one time might have been defined as its transient 'colour' has become the defining tone of its every experience. Kierkegaard seems to recognize something melancholic in the very possibility of experience.

The notion of melancholy has been adapted to describe everything which is peculiar to the modern world. Hence the somewhat diffuse, and at times even contradictory, character it assumes. Melancholy is a modern Proteus, transforming itself with every twist and turn of existence, becoming almost indistinguishable from being itself. Yet, the most diverse schools of modern thought protest in unison against any such identity, and insist, in any number of ways, that melancholy has no substance of its own, that it is 'only' the sombre mirror in which being reflects itself. Thus, of the multiplicity of modern attempts to define melancholy, two apparently unconnected formulations have become canonical; melancholy is both 'sorrow without cause' and 'loss of being'.

The modern, disenchanted, disillusioned, wholly secular individual is expected to be melancholic. The Enlightenment tradition, together with its army of critics eager to go 'beyond' its brutal rejection of all outmoded religious views of the world, speak with a melancholic voice. Yet melancholy itself remains an embarrassment to modern thought. How can there be 'sorrow without cause'? Surely if it is 'real' sorrow' its cause is just as real, but, temporarily, unknown; it is merely 'unexplained sorrow'. And what is the 'loss of being' other than a resilient but dangerously sentimental nostalgia over visions of a 'pre-modern' world that never, in fact, existed? In modern thought every effort is made to overcome melancholy by 'rationalization'. That is, by finding its cause and defining its lost reality, an attempt is made to assimilate it to the otherwise endlessly interlinked field of representations. But the reverse, in fact, has taken place. Melancholy, mute and unassimilable, refuses every flattering advance and continues to hide beyond the reach of every seductively intended conceptualization. Worse than that, it breaks into every chain of reasoning, and thoughtlessly undermines every effort to grasp and control the nature of modern experience.

As an incontrovertible sign of modernity melancholy is strangely equivocal. Its inexplicable character as a primitive experience in which, in spite of everything; 'being' discloses itself as an empty and barren nothingness, makes melancholy the sorrowful drain into which the western religious worldview emptied itself before vomiting forth new and deceptive forms. The Enlightenment project foundered upon melancholy, not upon the 'theory' of melancholy, but upon the 'simple fact' of sorrow. And wretchedness, upon the ruins, awakened to a new religious sensitivity. Melancholy, paradoxically, is the disillusionment which prevents the complete triumph of disillusionment. Modern religion is focused on melancholy, then, less to preserve a dubious claim to console, than to worry (as a dog might a sheep) what remains undomesticated by the modern arts of life.

Religion in modern western society is at once melancholic and the 'cure' for melancholy. For modern society, indeed, melancholy alone has 'depth', and it is its 'presence' which lends expression to the profound unease within, if not disease of, existence.

Part I

The physiognomy of the present age

The present age is essentially a sensible, reflecting age, devoid of passion, flaring up in superficial, short-lived enthusiasm and prudentially relaxing in indolence.

Søren Kierkegaard, *Two Ages*

Spirit has broken with the world it has hitherto inhabited and imagined, and it is of a mind to submerge it in the past, and in the labour of its own transformation. . . . The frivolity and boredom which unsettles the established order, the vague foreboding of something unknown, these are the heralds of approaching change.

G.W.F. Hegel, *Phenomenology of Spirit*

Chapter 1

Melancholy: the depth of modern life

When the low heavy sky weighs like a lid
Upon the spirit aching for the light
And all the wide horizon's line is hid
By a black day sadder than any night. . . .

Charles Baudelaire: 'Spleen'

Whence, did you say, does this strange sadness rise?
Like tides that over naked black rocks flow?
– When here the heart's once trampled-vintage lies,
Living's a curse. A secret all men know. . . .

Charles Baudelaire: 'Semper Eadem'

Søren Kierkegaard claimed to have been deeply melancholic throughout his life. In a *Journal* entry from 1844 headed 'Quiet Despair; A Narrative' he associated melancholy with his earliest recollections, and, lacking nothing in modern sensibility, made both central to his effort to understand himself:

> There was a father and a son. Both were highly endowed intellectually, especially the father. Everyone who knew their home was certain to find a visit entertaining. Usually they discussed only between themselves and entertained each other as two good minds without the distinction between father and son. On one rare occasion when the father looked at the son and saw that he was very troubled, he stood quietly before him and said: Poor child, you live in quiet despair. But he never questioned him more closely – alas, he could not, for he, too, lived in quiet despair. Beyond this not a word was exchanged on the subject. But the father and the son were perhaps two of the most melancholy human beings who ever lived in the memory of man.[1]

(Journal, 1: 745)

Between two melancholy people, each self-absorbed to an extraordinary degree, there could be no real communication. The 'rare occasion' had not really broken their mutual incomprehension:

> And the father believed that he was responsible for his son's melancholy, and the son believed that he was responsible for his father's melancholy; therefore they never raised the subject. That outburst by the father was an outburst of his own melancholy; therefore when he said this, he spoke more to himself than to his son.
>
> (*Journals*, 1: 745)

Melancholy is essentially incommunicable. It might be recognized by interpreting another's reserve, laconic manner and apparent disinterestedness in the world on the basis of one's own self-absorption. But these symptoms should not be mistaken for the condition itself. Lethargy has become a kind of conventional token of melancholy, but just as often it may lie concealed in a normal level of sociability. Kierkegaard's melancholy was of this latter secretive type. Dissimulation became part of his nature, not so much because he wished to spare others the burden of his own inner wretchedness (though, most of the time, he did wish this) as because conventional forms of sorrow were wholly inadequate to express its depth and weight. In his most explicit autobiographical writing, *The Point of View for My Work as an Author*, which was composed in 1848 but not published until after his death, he confessed, but could not adequately describe, his melancholy. In fact he took pride in an uncanny ability to conceal his spontaneous feelings. From the beginning, he claims, he had acted a part:

> From a child I was under the sway of a prodigious melancholy, the depth of which finds its only adequate measure in the equally prodigious dexterity I possessed of hiding it under an apparent gaiety and *joie de vivre*. So far back as I can barely remember, my own joy was that nobody could discover how unhappy I felt.[2]
>
> (*Point of View*, p. 76)

Though 'favoured in every way, so far as intellectual gifts go and outward circumstances', Kierkegaard could not rid himself of melancholy. He lacked nothing in self-confidence; his abilities, he knew, were quite exceptional and he believed himself capable of achieving whatever he set his mind to. This well-founded conceit encompassed everything 'only one thing excepted, all else absolutely, but one thing not, the throwing off of the melancholy from which and from its attendant suffering I was never entirely free even for a day'.[3]

Melancholy had made Kierkegaard prematurely old. His early years, spent under the immediate and powerful influence of a gloomy father, were completely incompatible with the playfulness of childhood. In his father's relentless piety the young Søren was 'travestied as an old man'. He claims that: 'Already in my earliest childhood I broke down under the grave impression which the melancholy old man who laid it upon me himself sank under.'[4] Though he came to regret his 'crazy upbringing' he did not blame his father for his own melancholy. Neither the general atmosphere of a claustrophobic household, nor the early death of all but one of his siblings, nor Søren's discovery of some specific offence at the root of his father's intense guilt-feeling, accounts for the origin of his inward gloom, far less for its literary transformation.[5]

Melancholy isolated him from others, and, again from his earliest recollection, he knew that 'for me there was no comfort or help to be looked for in others'. His melancholy, rather than his talent, made him exceptional; and his talent purified his melancholy. There was, for him, something alluring in this 'lonesome inward torment'. At times he exulted in an 'unlimited freedom of being able to deceive' which allowed him the privilege of being 'absolutely alone with my pain'.[6]

Thus, 'relegated to myself and to a relationship with God', Kierkegaard, from an early age, invested his melancholy with a unique value. Melancholy, for him, was more than a mood, or even the peculiarity of a specific temperament; it was, rather, a particular way of existing as a human being. And more than that it was the way of existing which he came to view as most appropriate to the condition of modern life. There was, in Kierkegaard's view, something uniquely truthful in melancholic self-withdrawal. Such 'inclosing reserve' might even be imagined the authentic inwardness of modern life. What is odd in this is that, while truthful, melancholy contests the very truth it proclaims. It protests, as it were, against itself.[7] To grasp how this is possible, and to understand in just what way he accepted the melancholy he believed to be his inescapable shadow, is, in part at least, the task Kierkegaard set himself in his authorship. Yet it is just their melancholic character that makes these works difficult to understand. Melancholy cannot be directly expressed, so that Kierkegaard was forced into a whole series of experimental forms and literary subterfuges through which something of the meaning and significance of this inner experience might be aroused in an unsuspecting reader. Furthermore, as his works were designed to transform, and not merely to describe, this inner experience, it is hardly surprising that his books appear odd, disjointed and unconnected with the major literary and philosophical traditions which we have come to expect lurk within the covers of any major work.

Kierkegaard, however, was less alone than he claimed, or possibly wished, himself to be. In defining his experience of himself, and of the world, as melancholic, he was in fact exploiting a long and significant tradition of western psychology, as well as implicitly claiming a community of feeling with many of its most illustrious exponents. Melancholy, that is to say, is a constitutive part of his writing, not the adventitious (and unbalancing) mood in which it was created. His work as an author, therefore, can be approached by way of this tradition.

THE PERSPECTIVE OF MELANCHOLY

Melancholy, and reflections upon it, have a long history in western society. This history cannot be reconstructed here; but it is only by alluding to its very different past that the specifically modern character of Kierkegaard's melancholy can be appreciated.

Originally melancholy, or black bile, was identified, along with blood, phlegm and yellow (or red) bile, as one of the four fundamental bodily fluids, or 'spirits'. As such melancholy constituted one of those naturally occurring quaternaries which were associated together as the mode of differentiation common to all created things. Under the influence of Pythagorean and even older mythological thought, the health of the human body was held to be dependent on the maintenance of an equilibrium of these four distinct substances, and illness was conceived as the excess of one humour (*chymoi*: juice or flavour) over the others.[8] Bodily states, mental imagery and characteristic forms of behaviour which had been regarded as symptomatic of illness, and thus of humoral imbalance, were progressively associated together as general dispositions or character types. Humours, thus, came to 'denote either pathological states or constitutional aptitudes'.[9]

The melancholic humour was 'cold and dry' and as warmth and

moisture appeared to be essential to vegetative growth, procreation and interaction with all life-giving substance, the melancholic individual was excessively taciturn, withdrawn and lethargic. Such individuals were also liable to uncontrollable fits of madness. Yet melancholy could also be viewed as the bestowal of spiritual privileges. Plato, in the *Phaedrus*, redefined the melancholic as a highly sensitized soul peculiarly adapted to the reception of the most valued of ecstatic states. 'We receive the greatest benefit through frenzy', he declares, and the melancholic is more fitted than any other to receive this 'divine gift'.[10] Even more significantly for the development of subsequent ideas about melancholy, an Aristotelian text brought together earlier medical notions with the Platonic conception of frenzy. *Problem* XXX.1 established a para-digmatic conception of melancholy in its opening question: 'Why is it that all those who are outstanding in philosophy, poetry or the arts are melancholic?'[11] Likening the effect of black bile to that of wine, the Aristotelian theory proposed a naturalistic-pneumatic theory relating divergent bodily states to the physical condition of bodily fluids. The sensitivity, mobility and quickness of thought of the poet and philosopher depended on the maintenance of a narrow range of predisposing conditions. When bile was too cold and excessive in quantity the person experienced 'numbness, despondency and fear', and if it became overly heated the unfortunate individual would be seized with an uncontrollable mania. It was not only the exceptional example of tragic heroes like Ajax and Bellerophon who suffered melancholic madness as a divine retribution for human defiance, but, more generally, all really outstandingly gifted individuals were visited by melancholia. But however successful this attempted 'naturalization' of Platonic frenzy, for later generations, promiscuously influenced by all preceding traditions, melancholy was rarely regarded in a wholly naturalistic fashion. Melancholy, understood within either interpretative context, represented nobility and sensibility, each confirming in its own terms that 'a man's spiritual greatness was measured by his capacity for experience and, above all, for suffering'.[12]

These ancient ideas persisted and were reabsorbed in a variety of ways in the long development of western medical and philosophical conceptions of the relationship between 'body' and 'temperament'. Most significantly, perhaps, Galen, whose extensive writings on medical matters and on natural history were composed during the second century CE, provided a sophisticated development of the Aristotelian theory. His unique and long-lasting authority brought into prominence two aspects of ancient melancholy which remain of fundamental importance to an understanding of Kierkegaard's insight into its modern form.

Firstly, Galen defined melancholy in terms of an inner experience or feeling, rather than as a set of explicit symptoms: it is 'fear and sadness without a real reason . . . an unnatural dread'.[13] And, secondly, he associated melancholy with darkness: 'the humour, like darkness . . . invades the seat of the soul, where reason is situated'.[14] Galen held that black bile, secreted in the liver, gives rise to a dark vapour which, rising in the body, is responsible for both aspects of this physical/psychic gloom. And, developing the analogy with vision: 'as the crystalline lens of the eye if it is limpid allows a clear view . . . but if it becomes ill and opaque it does not allow a distinct view', he argues that in melancholy an inner fog of sour and acid bile 'envelops the rational parts of the soul, upsetting them so that man necessarily is afraid of what he imagines'.[15] It is as if, being cut off from proper contact with both the world and his or her own rational soul, the melancholic comes to fear self-generated images whose real origin and nature remain mysteriously obscured.

Throughout later developments, and in quite different contexts, two somewhat contradictory notions of melancholy were held together. The melancholic was characterized both by a lethargic and torpid nature and by periodic spasms of furious and uncontrollable passion. These opposed tendencies were taken to be typical of melancholy, whether this condition was to be understood in 'spiritual' Platonic or in 'bodily' Aristotelian terms. Indeed, in relation to melancholy, which was always understood as bearing both a bodily and a spiritual significance, the distinction between 'medicine' and 'religion', in principle, hardly applied. In the medieval period, however, in association with the differentiation of an educated ruling class, the growth of an urban secular culture, and the renovation of monasticism, melancholy itself dissolved into a number of distinct tendencies and conditions.

Under the influence of Arabic writers, and especially of Avicenna, a more specialized medical theory of melancholy emerged. Melancholy was seen as the consequence of the corruption of any of the body's natural humours. In a 'burnt' condition, some or all of the 'symptoms' which had previously been viewed as a consequence of the simple preponderance of black bile within the body could be produced. And in the case of melancholy *adust* or burnt melancholy the whole condition was intensified. An already 'dry' and unresponsive spirit was further desiccated, and melancholy came generally to refer to diseased spirits of any kind rather than to a specific humoral imbalance.[16]

In addition to this medical context melancholy gained wide currency throughout the medieval period as *acedia*. The term has biblical antecedents (particularly as the 'noonday devil' of Psalm 90), but its medieval usage is usually traced to a listing by Evagrius of Pontus towards the end of the fourth century CE of the 'eight evil spirits' or 'vicious thoughts' which assail the solitary monk in his desert cell: 'gluttony, lust, avarice, sadness, anger, spiritual apathy (*akedias*), vainglory and pride'.[17] *Acedia* (without care), in contrast to the Platonic valuation of melancholy, appears as a perversion of, rather than a complement to, the soul's seizure by higher spiritual powers. Evagrius vividly portrays the torpor which is likely to oppress the monk:

> The demon of *acedia*, also called the 'noonday demon', is the most oppressive of all demons. . . . First he makes the sun appear sluggish and immobile, as if the day had fifty hours. . . . Moreover, the demon sends him hatred against the place, against life itself, and against the work of his hands, and makes him think he has lost the love among his brothers and that there is none to comfort him.[18]

But it is John Cassian, the founder of western monasticism, to whom most later writers turned for an authoritative description of 'the sin of sloth':

> Our sixth battle is with what the Greeks call acedia which we might name tedium or anxiety of heart. It is related to sadness, and is especially troublesome to hermits, a dangerous and frequent enemy of desert dwellers. It disturbs the monks especially at noon, like a fever recurring at regular intervals, bringing its burning heat in waves. . . . A kind of unreasonable confusion of mind like some soul-darkness takes hold of him, making him idle and useless for every spiritual work.[19]

Cassian specifically distinguishes the spiritual apathy of *acedia* from the purely secular sorrow of *tristitia* (which was later celebrated as lovesickness), and, by implication, both from the medical condition of melancholy.[20] Yet they remain inextricably linked through the common *topos* of darkness. A cold shadow falls over the hermit's soul even as the burning sun stands directly above him in the sky. The soul becomes both actually and metaphorically opaque, impenetrable to the activating radiance which was the nurturing medium of human physical and spiritual wellbeing. For many ancient and medieval thinkers light was much more than the condition of passive sight, it conveyed directly a life-giving and formative power.[21] The cosmos shone with a penetrating divine light, and it was this radiance which melancholy unnaturally obscured. *Acedia*, therefore, was a sin; a wilful, if unwanted, 'disgust with the spiritual'. Wrapped in its insulating darkness, the monk sank into a kind of waking torpor in which he was liable to be assailed by terrifying visions.[22] And clouded by *acedia*, everything in which the individual should rejoice became a source of renewed sorrow.[23]

Whether as bile, *tristitia*, lovesickness or *acedia*, melancholy enveloped the soul in a dark cloud, isolating its victims from the world, from other people, and from a true understanding of themselves. These various forms of isolation were linked, more systematically, as disturbances in the naturally created order of things. Throughout the medieval period a Christianized version of Greek cosmology provided an intellectual and spiritual context within which the human being was conceived as a *microcosm*. This was understood to mean not only that the human frame, constitution and inner nature were in some way 'modelled' on the structure of the cosmos as a whole (as they had been by Plato in the *Timaeus*), but that human beings were completely integrated into this *macrocosm* as an essential link in the natural hierarchy of creation.[24]

Humoral psychology was absorbed into a Christianized version of the Neoplatonic worldview. The doctrine of four temperaments thus became directly linked to a religious cosmology. Original man, Adam, was a warm and moist creature, but in the Fall was corrupted into variations of cold and dry types. In the twelfth century, for example, William of Conches held that the choleric, phlegmatic and melancholic types were all fundamentally alike in being sinful deviations from the sanguine. It was not, therefore, sensuousness as such, but corrupted sensuality which was essentially related to sin.

Throughout the medieval period melancholy, as a natural quaternary division, was reproduced and could be rediscovered within any realm of created being. Not only the human body, the original *locus* of melancholy, with its variable combination of the four primary constituents of nature (earth, air, fire and water), in their specific bodily forms, but the different orders of living creatures, seasons, hours of the day, ages of man, and, through the development of iatromathematical concepts, the planetary 'signs' were ordered and divided according to their 'humour'. A twelfth-century writer, for example, describes the structure of the mind as follows:

> the mind also makes use of the four humours. In place of blood it has sweetness, in place of red bile bitterness, in place of black bile grief, in place of phlegm equanimity. . . . Thus in contemplation lies sweetness, from remembrance of sin comes bitterness, from its commission grief, from its atonement equanimity.[25]

The persistence of the sanguine – the happy (and rare) combination of warmth and moisture within the body – like the spectacle of nature's undying perfection in the night sky, was seen as an echo of man's paradisiacal origin, and the promise of his redemption. And the more normal melancholic state was, therefore, simply one aspect of the entire corruption of nature within the sublunary sphere, after the Fall. Melancholy, with the other humours, therefore, was a natural disposition of the mind.

The hierarchy of being was a natural order, each 'level' of creation depending for its existence upon the greater being embedded in the level immediately above it. Equally, each level of created being represented the divine presence upon which all rested. Created matter, thus, was a kind of visible symbol of the spiritual reality which supported its temporary and imperfect form. Increasingly, natural and human phenomena were understood in terms of elaborate symbolic homologies and analogies.[26] Importantly, however, the human being was always in continuity with the entire world of being which it symbolized. The part always represented the whole to which it naturally belonged, and to which it was related by an unbreakable tie of solidarity.

The breakdown of feudal societies in the west was associated with the emergence of a new understanding of melancholy. During the transitional period a highly sophisticated use of the notion of symbolic relations between *microcosm* and *macrocosm* formed the context in which Marsilio Ficino revived the Platonic praise of melancholy.[27] For Ficino and a number of his contemporaries the connecting spiritual medium between microcosm and macrocosm was conceived to be a subtle fluid. It was this presumed, underlying but actual, continuity that justified the development of highly elaborate astrological and iatromathematical schemata through which the condition of the human soul could be understood and manipulated. It was this universal animating medium that connected the inner life of the individual with celestial dynamics. The condition of human spirit, 'a vapour of the blood, pure, subtle, hot, and clear', was necessarily linked to the disposition of the planets, as well as to the condition of the 'heart, liver and stomach'.[28] Those born under the influence of Saturn tend towards melancholy, and, according to Ficino, this is by no means always unfortunate. Reviving Plato's views, Ficino regards melancholy as an intellectual gift, which in turn stimulates two other divine frenzies, poetry and philosophy. But a positive interpretation of melancholy did not lead him to underestimate the suffering which is the normal cost extracted for enjoying its privileges. Nor does his attempt to articulate a magical-erotic worldview (which was rooted in ancient paganism, and was shortly to be overtaken by a new scientific rationalism) prevent him from grasping its most significant personal features. Indeed, in treating melancholy within the new social context of a postmedieval civic culture, Ficino provides a strikingly modern depiction of its travails:

> It is astonishing that whenever we are at leisure, we fall into grief like exiles, though we do not know, or certainly do not think of, the cause of our grief. Thus it has come about that man cannot live alone. For we think that we can expel our hidden and continual grief through the society of others and through a manifold variety of pleasures. But we are only too deceived. For in the midst of the plays of pleasure we sigh at times, and when the play is over, we depart even more sorrowful.[29]

The strange grief of melancholy induces an inward, and often outward, restlessness; a perpetual, aimless and tormenting motion which can finally be calmed only by a proper use of the melancholic's gifts for spiritual elevation. 'Rest is judged to be much more perfect than movement', so that the melancholic longs above all for the soothing tranquillity of permanence, and especially for the unalterable inner stillness of a return to a primordial state of spiritual ecstasy.[30] Ficino's therapeutic magic is, thus, more ambitious than Petrarch's secular 'Remedies', which are powerless to console those 'troubled by nostalgia for the celestial fatherland'.[31] The melancholic, estranged from that state of spiritual solidarity with the cosmos in which the promise of happiness is held fast, was condemned to a fruitless wandering which could not be escaped unaided.

Ficino is often credited with celebrating notions of individualism and of artistic genius which anticipated modern dynamic conceptions of the human personality.[32] Yet in the maintenance of an ideal of spiritual rest and cosmic self-communion his worldview remained decisively premodern. Nevertheless Ficino effected a fundamental shift in the traditional conceptions of melancholy towards what was to become a decisively modern view. His originality lay in the view of melancholy as perpetual and useless movement, rather than as lethargic immobility. Equally, and paradoxically, it is conceived as heaviness rather than darkness. The intellectual proclivities of the melancholic have to do with the 'earthy' nature of black bile, which is the sediment left after the more subtle fluids have been evaporated, as it were, from the blood. In thought and speculation the person 'draws in upon itself from external things', and is, therefore, like the earth in its quality of self-adhering cohesion. The melancholic, as it were, compresses the soul within his body, making it more material and weighty.[33] There is here the beginning of 'a new analogy between the force of gravity and mental concentration'.[34]

This, from the viewpoint of medieval thought, contradictory combination of mobility and weightiness quickly came to define not only the temperamentally melancholic individual but the peculiar character of modern life itself. As the notion of the 'dignity of man', it became central to both the Italian Renaissance and northern humanism. This important transformation was associated with the emergence of a new cosmological picture and a revaluation of the significance and worth of human beings within creation.[35]

It is hardly surprising that the breakdown of the traditional world picture, and the gradual emergence of a new 'system of the world' which was understood according to radically new principles, implied equally fundamental changes in the notion of melancholy. It is worth emphasizing, however, that in spite of the emergence of a new interpretative context, the complex of phenomena bound together in the term 'melancholy' to a large extent persisted as a unity. Indeed the Aristotelian equation of melancholy with intellectual and artistic gifts only really came into its own in the Renaissance. Furthermore, older conceptions did not simply wither away but, however anachronistic they might come to appear, persisted alongside quite new ideas.

But melancholy, and not merely ideas about melancholy, did change, and in profound ways. In relation to the emergent cosmological setting new meanings were attached to the traditional affliction. The Elizabethan age was rich in melancholy, and increasingly 'heaviness' replaced 'darkness' as one of its defining characteristics.[36] Over a long period authors from quite different backgrounds agreed and were eventually to retrace a diversity of insights back to this common source. Melancholy is to be 'overwhelmed with heaviness ... heaviness without cause',[37] 'dolour or hevynesse of minde',[38] and 'unwelcome heaviness'.[39] It is 'anguish, dullness, heaviness, and vexation of spirit'.[40] It is a 'devitalized existence ... heavy with daily sorrows'.[41] Inexplicably a multitude of sorrows 'suddenly weighs one down',[42] and the 'frailest memories take on the weight of rocks'.[43]

The formation of the new worldview within which these typifications were to gain currency has been described as a transition 'from the closed world to the infinite universe'.[44] At its most general level this involved 'the geometrisation of space and the dissolution of the Cosmos'.[45] For the ancient and medieval world the cosmos was a closed and finite structure within which the totality of created beings were ordered hierarchically according to their relative degree of perfection. The sublime and changeless substance of celestial beings occupied the outer region of the cosmos, while the lesser, corruptible and changeable being of earthly natures occupied the degraded centre, at the furthest possible distance from God.

The qualitative distinction of place gave way gradually, but in the end completely, to the formless indifference of space. This transition can already be glimpsed in Nicholas of Cusa's 'negative theology'. *On Learned Ignorance*, in opposition to the hylomorphic order of a 'chain of being', insisted not only upon the absolute transcendence of God in relation to His own creation, but, more particularly, on the consequential uncertainty of any humanly conceivable ordering of the natural world. All human judgements were judgements of a relative sort, and as untrustworthy as any other manifestation of human, and thus corrupted, nature. God's absolute simplicity, thus, remained unknowable: 'the infinite as infinite is unknown', Nicholas bluntly declares.[46] And the mere appearance of creation offers us a vision of ourselves, rather than undeniable 'evidence' of a Divine Will:

> We are also unable to understand how God can manifest Himself
> to us through visible creation. . . . Who can understand how all
> things, whilst differing from one another by reason of their finite
> nature, are an image of that unique infinite form?[47]

The radical implication of such a view – that the cosmos is a human
image of nature, rather than the natural structure of creation – was
not immediately apparent. But Cusanus stands at the beginning of
a transformation in the human understanding of the physical world
which, in retrospect at least, unfolded itself over a period of three
centuries with syllogistic necessity.

But this entire movement of thought, internally coherent as the
consecutive steps of a single argument, additionally made sense in
virtue of the still more revolutionary demand for the overthrow of
traditional valuations of human nature and its relation to God. It
was the corrupted and worthless character of man after the Fall
which had condemned him to the ignominy of the central and fixed
place of the cosmos. Both within orthodox Christianity, as in the
case of Cusanus, and outside it, as in the revival of Neoplatonic
mysticism exemplified by Marsilio Ficino and Pico della Mirandola,
human being was dignified in its own right. Consequently the links
in the 'chain of being' began to come apart.

Man, created in the 'image and likeness' of his Creator, could
claim at least the dignity of self-movement, and the motion of the
earth expressed his present worthiness and future perfectibility.
Copernicus, who admired Cusanus, claimed the greater simplicity
and elegance of an astronomy which allowed the earth to rotate.
And long before his supposition gained the force of a physical
demonstration it gained enthusiastic adherents because it was
consonant with newly articulated expressions of human dignity.
Some of his followers, indeed, such as Giordano Bruno and Thomas
Digges, were as bold as Cusanus himself and leapt to the conclusion
that the physical universe was 'in actuality' infinite. The earth, freed
of the dubious distinction of occupying the central place of the
cosmos, was liberated into a boundless space occupied by an infinite
number of other worlds.[48]

The ancient distinction between the sublunary sphere of
changeable and corrupted nature and the superlunary sphere of
more 'perfect' celestial bodies composed of a weightless
'quintessential' element gave way to the uniformity of physical
nature and infinite space. Matter was everywhere the same,

distributed throughout the infinity of space in self-adhering quantities. The new image of the cosmos extended to human beings both a greater intimacy with, and a greater distance from, God. The earth moved, and was no more or less privileged than any other heavenly body; it was, therefore, as close to God as any other point in the universe. But neither God, nor any natural body, occupied a specific 'place' in the cosmos. And because the cosmos was itself infinite, God could not be 'located' as a kind of boundary around His creation. 'Space', as pure extension, had no moral or religious connotation. The earth, endowed with effortless and aimless motion, was liberated into the void: 'something new arose: an empty world'.[49]

This fundamental transformation in human self-understanding was associated with the transformation of traditional societies, from fixed hierarchical communities to the inherent dynamism and freedom of civil society, founded upon the unlimited exchange-ability of commodities. Society, like space and time, became the pure dimensionality of interaction among essentially identical units linked together according to universal 'laws of nature'. Civil society was composed of individuals equally endowed with the capacity to reason, an inner tendency to seek pleasure, and an unchallenge-able privilege of knowing their own interests. The cosmos, similarly, was made up of units: 'solid, massy, hard, impenetrable, moveable particles', interacting according to universal laws.[50] Of course there was considerable variety in the way in which the apparent coherence and order of both society and the physical world could be understood. There was a notable and growing difference between accounts which attempted to grasp the 'system of the world' (society) in terms of the inherent properties of particles (individuals) themselves, and those which sought to illuminate larger structures dialectically in terms of the characteristic relationships presupposed in them. However incompatible such approaches might seem to us now, they are both fundamentally *modern* in character. Neither is conceivable outside the new worldview of which they were a part. However significant the differences between Newton and Leibniz, or Locke and Hegel, the distinctions they represent only appear within a cosmology of 'self-moving' rather than of 'dependent' being.[51]

In this transition new meanings accrued to terms and concepts whose linguistic labels remained unchanged. Melancholy, both as a concept and as an experience, was transformed in somewhat complex and unpredictable ways. At first sight, in fact, it might seem that modernity, as both a social and cosmological liberation from a closed world, was a decisive break with the tradition of melancholy. In the context of the decline of feudalism, the intellectual and cultural vitality of both northern humanism and the Italian Renaissance appears contrary to any conception of human wretchedness. Is not modernity, by virtue of its self-assertive autonomy, the denial of melancholy?

Deeper reflection put a swift end to all such premature optimism. Nature, rather than being a symbolic intermediary, emerged in the new world picture as an insurmountable obstacle, between man and God. The Creator was removed to an infinitely remote point in space and time; and as this was no point at all He could be conceived in relation to Creation only as an eternally present but impotent *deus absconditus*: as the hidden god of an inner faith. And the very immediacy of this direct confrontation reduced the human person, once again, to wretchedness. Whether viewed 'atomistically' as a naturally given unity, or 'dialectically' as the emergent properties of a specific set of relations, the human individual found himself or herself in a condition of 'unprecedented inner loneliness'.[52] The inner world of human subjectivity, as boundless in its potentiality for experience as was the new cosmos in its capacity to contain matter, felt itself drawn to melancholy as never before.

The seemingly contradictory tendencies which had been traditionally subsumed in the notion of melancholy – spiritless indifference and states of ecstasy – were now intimately bound together as a sense of cosmic dislocation. The feeling of being alone in a void, of isolation in the face of the double infinity of external and internal space, is at the heart of both Bruno's frenzy and Montaigne's sorrow.

Melancholic isolation later became the truth of modernity both for religiously inspired individuals deprived of a meaningful cosmological picture, and for atheists intent upon the hopeless quest for authentic self-actualization. Romantic writers, recognizing this, immodestly claimed for their poetry a heightened spiritual significance as the modern *locus* of spirit. Thus, for example, Jean Paul's melancholy is given a cosmological significance:

No one is so much alone in the universe as an atheist. With an orphaned heart that has lost the greatest of fathers, he mourns by the immeasurable corpse of Nature, which no universal spirit

moves and holds together. . . . The whole world reposes before
him, like the huge Egyptian Sphinx of stone half lying in the
sand; and the universe is the cold iron mask of a shapeless eternity.[53]

The full consciousness of the modern age came to itself as a
depressive mood that deepened and persisted into a new mournful
sensibility. Any sense of contact with an external reality came to
depend, in fact, on a presumed community of melancholic spirits.
Schelling expressed the pervasive sentiment of modernity in a way
that made only too obvious our remoteness from Being:

> A veil of sadness is spread over all nature . . . a deep unappeasable
> melancholy. . . . The darkest and deepest ground in human na-
> ture is . . . melancholy. This is what really creates the sympathy of
> man with nature. For in nature, too, the deepest ground is mel-
> ancholy. Nature also mourns a lost good.[54]

Melancholy, no longer one type or disposition among several, far
less a degenerate and unbalanced spirit, came into its own as the
immediate experience of modern life. If the melancholic 'primarily
suffers from the contradiction between time and infinity' then there
was nothing illusory about such painful incompatibilities, which
resided in the world itself.[55] Thus, while the 'choleric', 'phlegmatic'
and 'sanguine' prolonged their shadowy existence in the quaint
terminology of an outdated psychology, melancholia, the inner
truth of modernity, was accorded the dignity of a palpable reality.

The self-absorption of melancholy was justified in the context of
the new cosmology. The individual was still, in some sense, a
microcosm, but rather than directly reincarnating the structural
pattern of the world within which he or she remained inescapably
embedded, it was in the aimless freedom of a 'self-adhering body'
linked to nature that a universal principle was established. Rather
than look outwards to discover in the pattern of nature and social
life a model for experience, the inner life was itself regarded as a
realm of infinite freedom. The human being thus became a
self-moving and self-determining individual, each one possessed of
the mobility and inner 'weight' which was at the root of the
experience of melancholy. Truth lay within, and introspection
(rather than obedience to a given authority) was recommended to
the spiritually anxious.[56] But if God had hidden Himself in creation,
the inner infinity of human being was no less reticent of the Divine

Will. Melancholy, in the modern world, was the compulsion to fruitless introspection and endless self-preoccupation; and given the double infinity of cosmos and psyche, this proved to be a uniquely truthful mode of being.

THE DISTRACTION OF PHILOSOPHY

The emergence of modernity, in both its social and intellectual aspects, was accompanied, therefore, by a redefinition and revaluation of melancholy. As the 'Elizabethan Malady' it became, rather than a particular disposition or pathological condition, the leading characteristic of the age. In England and on the continent, in Catholic as well as Reformed circles, for secular as well as for religious reflection, melancholy was a central concern.[57]

By the time Burton wrote his *Anatomy of Melancholy* (first edition 1621), he could afford to make his claims rhetorically: 'For who indeed is not a fool, melancholy, mad?'[58] Thomas Nashe and Ben Jonson had already satirized its more self-conscious and affected devotees, while Timothy Bright's *A Treatise of Melancholia* (1586) had established a new medical tradition in its study and treatment.[59] For both literary and medical authors melancholy represented something fundamental to the modern condition. It could not be treated as a set of purely physical symptoms, or as an arbitrary and rare derangement of the sensibilities or of the mind. Melancholy had its roots in the inescapable reality of human existence. Burton, as both a divine and a physician, was, therefore, especially well qualified to be melancholy's anatomist.[60] And although Burton writes of melancholy as a 'humour', such is the self-expanding range of symptoms, forms, variations, subdivisions and characteristics which belong to it that, in fact, this term no longer refers to a particular type of person or human constitution, but seems rather to encompass the entire realm of normal psychic and psycho-somatic possibilities.

Burton's torrential prose, then, is not intended to have, and certainly does not have, the effect of more clearly defining and accounting for the central object of his concern. The impressive analytic apparatus, and even more the welter of authorities he cites and incorporates into his text, is an artifice through which melancholy can expand, unobstructed, to touch every aspect of life.[61]

Indeed, it is not Burton's intention to 'explain' melancholy, nor yet to express the manner in which it gripped him. Like Michel de Montaigne, whose lapse into melancholy might 'rationally' (and partially) be accounted a 'reaction' to the deaths of his father and his great friend Etienne de La Boëtie, Burton was 'enraptured by sadness' and anatomized melancholy to distract himself from its torments: 'to ease my mind by writing'.[62] And readers of Montaigne's *Essays*, like readers of Burton's *Anatomy*, both of which are constructed with extraordinary care and precision, lose their way in these labyrinthine texts because they are as fluid and restless as their authors' symptoms.[63] Burton might well have appended Montaigne's famous and deceptive line to his own work: 'I myself am the subject of my book.' But their authors, in fact, are neither Montaigne nor Burton, but personae conjured from melancholy itself, the writers who call themselves Michel de Montaigne and Democritus Junior. Melancholy is the *subject* of their books. The *authors* of these books are themselves melancholy. But they write to distract themselves from their own wretchedness, and thus in writing about melancholy hope to express something other than melancholy itself. Furthermore, inasmuch as melancholy is touched by rapture and ecstasy its victims are 'beyond themselves' and in seeking distraction seek to 'return' to their proper selves. Thus, inasmuch as their works are successful antidotes to melancholy they are authentic but untruthful, and where they are truly melancholic they are inauthentic. Here the whole problem of 'indirect communication', and its relation to melancholy, which Kierkegaard was to make so peculiarly his own, is introduced into modern western literature.

Burton's choice of pseudonym is significant in a number of respects. It is, first of all, a response to a challenge issued by Erasmus to discover a second Democritus to mock the follies of the world. The *Anatomy* is thus connected with *The Praise of Folly*, and immediately, therefore, with a radical inversion of the scholastic tradition. Christianity is presented as a non-rational faith, analogous to madness, rather than to the ordered result of reflection and contemplation.[64] More generally it links the *Anatomy* with the ancient doctrines of both atomism and melancholy. Democritus of Abdera, 'a little wearish old man, very melancholy by nature, averse from company in his latter day, and much given to solitariness', was said to have been writing a book on melancholy, and to this end anatomized the carcasses of various animals to discover its seat. As the name of Democritus is also associated with the foundation of atomism Burton is able to allude to the revival and transformation of both. In a lengthy and apparently superfluous 'Digression on the Air', Burton, 'rising' through the air, surveys the entire cosmos in his mind's eye. This practical demonstration of the unlimited capacity of the human imagination, far from being incidental to his main topic, is, in fact, central to the entire book.[65]

The causes of melancholy are legion, or at least appear to be. Any illness, misfortune, or circumstance of life may be either a cause or a symptom (or both) of melancholy, but it is the imagination that makes it so. Melancholy is uncontrolled imagination:

> this strong conceit or imagination is *astrum hominis* (a man's guiding star), and the rudder of this our ship, which reason should steer, but, overborne by phantasy, cannot manage, and so suffers itself and this whole vessel of ours to be overruled, and often overturned.[66]

Allowing the imagination its own freedom 'is most pleasant at first' and, indeed, melancholy isolation is powerfully attractive. It is 'a most delightsome humour, to be alone, dwell alone, walk alone, meditate, lie in bed whole days, dreaming awake as it were, and frame a thousand phantastical imaginations'.[67] But even his Greek model was unable to 'moderate his affections', and

> the scene alters upon a sudden, discontent and perpetual anxiety succeed in their place; so by little, by that shoeing-horn of idleness, and voluntary solitariness, melancholy, this feral fiend, is drawn on ... now it is bitter and harsh; a cankered soul macerated with cares and discontents.[68]

And as his 'Digression on the Air' had shown, the imagination becomes 'giddy' even when it is guided by nature. Burton's often repeated and concluding advice, 'be not idle, be not solitary', is not, therefore, a cure for melancholy, but a means only of ameliorating its worst excesses.

Burton devotes an entire book to two specific forms of melancholy, love-melancholy and religious melancholy. This by no means unbalances his work because these are the specific forms through which melancholy has become a general characteristic of modern life. Love, which includes the intimate friendship praised by Montaigne, is a free relationship subversive of community and all fixed and hierarchical social relations. As a 'vehement perturbation of the mind', love touches every aspect of existence and is 'the circle equant of all other affections'.[69] It is the passion in which imagination plays the greatest part, and is, therefore, most vulnerable to melancholic inversion: 'love is plague, a torture, an hell, a bitter-sweet passion' which turns easily to jealousy, hatred and madness.[70] Similarly, the religious anguish he documents is connected to the inner restless freedom of the imagination. Religious freedom, the destruction of the hierarchical cosmos, and the crystallization of modern religious life in the notion of faith as a personal relationship with God, all provoked new forms of religious melancholy. In a typically torrential passage he writes:

> These and the like places terrify the souls of many; election, predestination, reprobation, preposterously conceived, offend divers, with a deal of foolish presumption, curiosity, needless speculation, contemplation, solicitude, wherein they trouble and puzzle themselves about those questions of grace, free will, perseverance, God's secrets: they will know more than is revealed of God in His Word, human capacity or ignorance can apprehend.[71]

If religious thought and feeling had been liberated from the constraint of an authoritarian and hierarchical church, it had not simultaneously freed the individual from the anguish of religious suffering. Indeed, in now conceptualizing such torments as self-imposed, it intensified, rather than reduced, their effects. Religion – which is at the centre of life – is thus both a cause of, and a cure for, melancholy. 'The last and greatest cause of this malady', Burton tells us: 'is our own conscience', and conscience (rather than contemplation or passive ritual) is, for him, the primary modality of religious experience.[72]

The spectacle of modern life is indeed melancholy: a 'vast, infinite ocean of incredible madness and folly' in which all human beings are prey to 'melancholy fears without a cause', and are distinguished by being 'miraculously vain, various and wavering'.[73] Imagination, which is a kind of infinite inward space, has been wrenched free of a fixed cosmological order and places its relentless question mark over every momentarily settled state of being. The modern form of melancholy joins modern cosmology and psychology to the traditional imagery of the Fall. As a divinely cunning punishment for disobedience God has granted man an inner freedom which, finally realized in the modern world, proves to be a torment which individuals cannot help but impose upon themselves.

Burton recommends study and sociable leisure pursuits as antidotes to melancholy. But distraction is proposed as a means of living with, and not of curing, melancholy, which continues to lurk, so to speak, in the heart of every self-generated means of avoiding its wretchedness.

THE PHILOSOPHY OF DISTRACTION

The religious significance of melancholy in modern society is not restricted to the ideology of the Puritan tradition. Montaigne was, in his own eyes at least, an orthodox Catholic, and in Pascal we can find the first fully developed religious psychology of melancholy. Pascal, among the most gifted mathematicians and physicists of the seventeenth century, as well as one of its most incisive moralists, makes explicit the link between cosmos and psyche, between infinite space and inward wretchedness.[74] The unity of his thought is revealed in his uncompromising religious vision of human existence. For him the communal and hierarchical principles of traditional conceptions have lost their inner meaning, and are rejected in favour of 'the totally different concepts of the isolated individual and of infinite space'.[75]

Pascal is fully alive to the post-feudal conception of reason as a purely human faculty. Human greatness lies in the capacity for knowledge, and above all for self-knowledge. In an infinitely extended universe human beings have no option but to fasten upon themselves as the centre of their own existence. We can no longer see ourselves as part of a cosmos, as a division within its divine totality, and inevitably we grieve over this loss of intimacy. We must, rather, look out upon the world at large, and seek within the confines of this standpoint itself for a comprehensible order and meaning in existence. In this perspective human knowledge stands apart from the world which it reconstructs in conceptual form.

The new science conveys a picture of nature as a coherent mechanism. But this does not mean that we now 'understand' nature, which from a deeper viewpoint remains fundamentally incomprehensible:

Why is my stature what it is and the span of my life one hundred and not one thousand years? Why did nature give me this span of life, choosing it rather than any other from out of the infinite number available, where no compelling reason imposed on her this choice rather than another?[76]

The *religious* problem of modernity is that both nature and its personal subjective equivalent, the ego, must be conceived as autonomously functioning, and meaningless, bundles of relations. The spiritual value of existence cannot any longer be revealed by a mind which mirrors God's structural plan of the cosmos. Pascal does believe, however, that this plan is revealed in the spontaneous movement of the heart, in the inner experience of self-affirming and extra-rational activity.

In a strikingly compact formulation Pascal writes that 'Man's greatness comes from knowing he is wretched'.[77] The peculiar privilege of human reason is the knowledge of its own limitation, the fall from the ineffable self-sufficiency of its primordial state. Pascal elaborates the point by way of a celebrated metaphor:

> Man is only a reed, the weakest in nature, but he is a thinking reed. There is no need for the whole universe to take up arms to crush him: a vapour, a drop of water is enough to kill him. But even if the universe were to crush him, man would still be nobler than his slayer, because he knows that he is dying and the advantage the universe has over him. The universe knows nothing of this.[78]

Within the nostalgia for the security of the old cosmology (authority and community) lies a more specific discomfort which is the unease of modern melancholy. It is not just a sense of dislocation and disorientation, but of estrangement. And yet the fact that we find the cosmos to be an alien and comfortless mechanism is in an odd way the only guarantee of our original unspoilt nature. 'If man had never been anything but corrupt', he points out, 'he would have no idea either of truth or bliss.'[79] In fact, however, as science and morality attest, we have a living conception of both. But only a conception, so that 'unhappy as we are (and we should be less so if there were no element of greatness in our condition) we have an idea of happiness but we cannot attain it'.[80] We cannot know God directly, yet neither are we condemned to eternal ignorance of His nature. God is hidden, rather than revealed, in His creation. And though 'God has appointed visible signs in the Church so that he shall be recognized', He has so planted them 'that he will only be perceived by those who seek him with all their heart'.[81] It is, therefore, in sincerity of heart rather than in natural reason that happiness is discovered. Melancholy is, thus, a consequence of the Fall for modern individuated self-consciousness, and a symptom of the unquenchable longing this implies: 'man wants to be happy, only wants to be happy, and cannot help wanting to be happy.'[82]

By reason alone man cannot 'cure death, wretchedness and ignorance' and consequently seeks diversion from naturally gloomy thoughts. People therefore seek 'some novel and agreeable passion which keeps them busy, like gambling, hunting, some absorbing show, in short what is called diversion'. And Pascal, more rigorous but no less human than Burton, does not condemn them for this: 'they are not wrong to want excitement', he admits.[83] The modern world offers as consolation for the wretchedness upon which it is built nothing but the distraction of perpetual and thoughtless activity.

Distraction is a paradox; it is continuous movement in the pursuit of absolute rest: 'We seek rest . . . [but] rest proves intolerable because of the boredom it produces. We must get away from it and crave excitement.'[84] Distraction is a continuous oscillation between energetic ecstasy and lethargic indifference. But these polarities are fundamentally identical. They are merely different forms of boredom. Pascal understands that diversionary activities do not surmount, but carry within them, the boredom which is their immediate cause. And it is firstly as boredom, therefore, that melancholy makes its way in the modern world. Pascal, indeed, is the first to define boredom as the central experience of modernity. Boredom is inherent in the secular individualism which is the only moral foundation of modern (specifically modern capitalist) society. And although it often appears disguised in the particularities of a more specific malady, boredom is the most common of diseases and reveals a boundless spiritual longing:

> Man is so unhappy that he would be bored even if he had no cause for boredom, by the very nature of his temperament, and he is so vain that, though he has a thousand and one reasons for being bored, the slightest thing, like pushing a ball with a billiard cue, will be enough to divert him.[85]

Left to himself man generates, from within his own soul, an image of fulfilment which he cannot reach. It is the persistence of this authentic longing for happiness that renders everything unconnected with it dull and lifeless. It is the sense of loss of, and of longing for, a vanished perfection that repeatedly compels us to futile activity. 'We are full of things that impel us outwards', of 'wants' we unthinkingly attach to external objects whose subsequent possession we vainly hope will secure our lasting happiness. But the 'depth' of human longing is infinite and cannot be thus easily assuaged. 'Man infinitely transcends man' and as, for the modern world, neither nature nor religious 'belief ' in the sense of a morally binding and universally valid account of the significance of human existence provides an intersubjective medium of transcendence, the human soul must fashion it anew from within the resources of each individual psyche. Self-awareness must, therefore, continually stretch beyond itself, and even for those who sense the vanity of wants: 'our instincts make us feel that our Happiness must be sought outside ourselves. Our passions drive us outwards, even without objects to excite them'.[86]

Melancholy, the secular world of endless and fruitless diversions, is, above all, a sign of lost innocence: 'What else does this craving, and this helplessness proclaim', Pascal asks rhetorically: 'but that there was once in man a true happiness, of which all that now remains is the empty print and trace?'[87] The objects that excite our futile and vain passions cannot fill the emptiness of the soul: 'since this infinite abyss can be filled only with an infinite and immutable object; in other words with God himself '.[88] Immediate self-knowledge is the 'unhappy consciousness' of wretchedness and inconsolable cosmic grief. A soul lies within us, and stirs to life as the power of reason, but it gives us no joy. Its presence, rather, is a perpetual irritant, a tormenting reminder of how far we have fallen beneath an ideal state of bliss. The more, therefore, that we use the natural capacity of the soul to direct our own lives the more we obscure our true end and the more firmly we become rooted in its graceless limitations: 'Our soul is cast into the body where it finds number, time, dimensions; it reasons about these things and calls them natural, or necessary, and can believe nothing else.'[89]

Pascal, thus, fully aware of the genuine triumph of human reason in reducing the appearance of nature to a comprehensible system of relations, none the less fastens upon its inherent incapacity to secure human happiness as the true beginning of both self-knowledge and knowledge of God. Melancholy, as distraction and boredom, may be traced to a sense of cosmic estrangement but, at the same time, it is a sign that we have not been abandoned by

God. Our failure fully to comprehend ourselves, or to reduce our passions to the ordered logic of a 'system of nature', signifies (in a way which also remains incomprehensible) God's presence within us.

He therefore rejects out of hand the comforting optimism spread by the more popular forms of modern materialistic psychology. Such approaches, which by implication at least rejoined us to 'nature' by reducing consciousness to an arrangement of particles, in fact utterly fail to jump the abyss between matter and soul which their very theories presupposed. Alluding to radical Cartesian materialism, for example, he remarks:

> When they say that heat is merely the movement of certain glob-ules and light the *conatus recedendi* (centrifugal force) that we feel, we are amazed . . . the feeling of fire . . . the reception of sound and of light, all seem mysterious. . . . It is true that the smallness of the spirits entering the pores touches other nerves, but they are still nerves.[90]

We perceive the world, not the nerves, and for Pascal it is absurd to regard pleasure as simply a 'ballet of spirits'.

Both real knowledge of God and authentic self-knowledge begin in this failure of reason; we cannot conceive of either as an 'object' with definite characteristics, magnitude, position and so on. They are sensed as 'subjects', as infinite and inexhaustible reservoirs of feeling. We know God, therefore, as we know ourselves, in our hearts. In a famous phrase Pascal tells us that 'the heart has its reasons of which the reason knows nothing; we know this in countless ways'.[91] And this is just another expression for faith, which he defines as 'God perceived by the heart, not by the reason'.[92]

It would be just as misleading to view Pascal's thought as a continuation of the medieval mystical tradition as it would be mistaken to see his practice of natural science as a simple development of late medieval scholasticism. Both are new in principle, adapted as they are to post-feudal cosmology and the social logic of emergent capitalism. This is particularly evident in Pascal's own intellectual brand of asceticism. 'We must love God alone and hate ourselves alone', he remarks at one point, the deep paradox of his instruction less evident to us than he might have wished. The point is that 'love of God' and 'love of self ' can, for the first time, become allied together, if not, indeed, identified with each other. Pascal goes even further and deeper in his rationalization of Christian categories than does Calvin. He expressed with unrivalled eloquence and intensity the 'unprecedented inner loneliness' of the individual adrift in the void of modernity: 'the eternal silence of these infinite spaces fills me with dread.'[93] He seeks to resolve this tension by identifying the self with God and God with the self. 'Self-hatred' is only hatred of what the self has become in the secular world. Authentic selfhood requires an ascetic rejection of all diversions as empty and futile gestures as boredom. Pascal, thus, draws an implicit distinction between the self (authentic inner being) and the ego (immediate experience of the social world). There is, thus, nothing negative or life-denying in genuine asceticism. To allow the self to turn towards God, seriously to long for the unique object which is its authentic goal, is to realize the self as well as, or even rather than, to overcome the ego.

Pascal insists that the ego alone is sinful but is so wholly and always: 'denying it, we can never be unhappy: indulging it, never happy.'[94] That this is no ordinary injunction to 'self-denial' emerges in a passage, remarkable even by the standards of the *Pensées*:

> The true and only virtue is therefore to hate ourselves, for our concupiscence makes us hateful, and to seek for a being really worthy of love in order to love him. But as we cannot love what is outside us, we must love a being who is within us but is not our own self. And this is true for every single person. Now only the universal being is of this kind: the kingdom of God is within us, universal good is within us, and is both ourselves and not ourselves.[95]

The deeper meaning of the Reformation is revealed in the discovery of God within the human subject, as an internal relation of self-transcendence. Salvation no longer depends upon man finding his proper 'place' within a cosmic plan through which God reveals Himself. God hides in creation, a concealment which, never quite complete, urges upon the human subject the necessity of completing himself in the external expression of an inward movement of faith. Pascal is deeply conscious of the religious implications of his acceptance of the new cosmology. For him, paradoxically, the infinite is a relation that is discovered within the finite.[96] Human subjectivity tends towards its own spiritual elevation through passionate self-reflection, rather than by a process of reasoning about the natural world. The infinite is not grasped through an inconceivable expansion of the soul through the cosmos, as if, like some sort of spiritual balloon, it becomes puffed up by God's presence. The infinite, rather, is discovered within the limitations and constraints of a particular existence.

The new cosmology need not lead, therefore, to a purely secular psychology.[97] Indeed, the interiorization of God, His presence within the heart, means that the human affections can never be understood in terms of a rational order. And even for those (that is for almost everyone) who do not consciously sense the heart's mysterious presence, and consequently devalue their own passions, human feelings open upon an incomprehensible depth. In every detail of his humanness 'man infinitely transcends man'.

Man is a passionate creature. This follows necessarily from human imperfection and incompleteness, and from God's concealment. We are constantly driven, by externalizing its inner movements, to discover the soul's inwardly hidden aspects. Melancholic self-absorption has, as its corollary, the need for self-awareness. This urge towards self-expression manifests itself as love, in Pascal's view the most general means of connection between the interior self and the world: 'Disguise it, in fact, as we will, we love without intermission . . . we live not a moment exempt from its influence.'[98] In continually seeking that which is hidden we become conscious of the enormous gulf between the immediate experience of ourselves and self-generated images of perfect happiness. It is this disparity which continues to drive our passions outwards. If we truly possessed God, we would dwell happily within ourselves. But 'Man cannot find his satisfactions within himself only; and, as love is essential to him, he must seek the objects of his affections in external objects'.[99] Man seeks 'beautiful' objects to satisfy his longing for happiness, and, 'as he himself is the fairest being that the hand of God has formed, he must look within himself for a model of those beauties which he seeks elsewhere'.[100] It is the power of his own soul, casting about it, as it were, an aura of attractiveness, which confers upon external things their quality of beauty. Only those objects which 'partake of his own resemblance' have the power to attract, and this resemblance is just a consequence of a projective external- ization of our own self-image. All love, in fact, is self-love: 'all possess in themselves the original of that beauty which they look for externally'.[101]

'Man is full of wants', of deficiencies rather than wishes, and he 'loves only those who can satisfy them'.[102] And what we love in others are just those qualities we feel lacking in ourselves: 'we never love anyone, but only qualities', those 'borrowed qualities' which reflect our own wants.[103] The unique individuality which connects the various qualities of the self is, in itself, incommunicable and cannot be loved directly by another: 'And if someone loves me for my judgement or my memory do they love me? *me* myself? No, for I could lose these qualities without losing myself.'[104]

It is, in fact, to Pascal, rather than to the Puritan divines, that we are indebted for establishing the framework of a new religious psychology. The solitariness of the individual soul, fixed arbitrarily between 'infinity and nullity', is estranged from itself. Christ, 'totally abandoned' and 'alone on earth', was uniquely capable of tolerating authentic spiritual selfhood.[105] In its struggle to free itself from its own limitations the human self projects itself into the social world and seeks to realize its hidden inner value in activity. It fails; and in substituting distraction for happiness discovers the empty pleasure of the ego. In a society apparently held together by mechanical principles (the interaction of individuals motivated by the rational pursuit of their private interests), Christianity, though it retains an institutional presence in public and communal forms, progressively defines itself in terms of private 'conscience'.

The more ardently Pascal sought God, the more completely he felt he discovered himself. After an intense religious experience in 1654 he tried, with increasing desperation, to rid himself of the burden of his own body and its secular appetites. In imitation of forms of asceticism he had himself criticized, he lived in increasing simplicity and austerity. Fearful that the world might ruin the state of heightened spiritual tumescence he longed to make permanent, he withdrew from society, became suspicious of affection, and abandoned the intimacy of friendship which at one time, in common with Montaigne, he had held to be the rarest and most precious of the heart's affections.[106]

The coldness of the intellect overwhelmed his heart and Pascal's introversion deepened into a psychotic withdrawal from the world. None the less he serves as a prototype of the modern religious personality. Melancholy sets in motion, through the deepening self-awareness implied in the failure of distraction to cure us of unhappiness, the specifically modern longing for authentic selfhood. The life-task of modernity is to liberate the unique individuality which lies within us. And however secular the language of self-development became, the fervour with which this universal vocation was embraced marked it unmistakably as a religious quest.

MODERNITY AND THE EXPERIENCE OF MELANCHOLY

'That our age is an age of mental depression, there is no doubt and no question'; its ubiquity rests on the consciousness of the modern world as a set of individuated objects, isolated in space, and set in motion according to universal 'laws of nature' devoid of intention or design, and blind to their consequences.[107] The classical language of melancholy, and its associated network of moral and psychological ideas, has been transformed and adapted to describe the immediate experience of modernity as the consciousness of 'inner loneliness'. Both cosmos and society appear as a meaningless and chaotic background to the emergent ego which, resting on nothing more substantial than its own image, is swept into the turmoil of civil society, or, withdrawing, oscillates between depressed self-absorption and extravagant states of rapture.[108] A remark of Montaigne's anticipates the new perspective: '*being* consists in motion.'[109] The melancholic individual (and in modern society all individuals are more or less melancholic) is self-moving, but, in a world which is a perpetual chaos, this becomes an arbitrary displacement lacking any sense of direction. It is motion productive of disorientation and dizziness, and prolongs the traditional contrariness of melancholy, which is now viewed as both heavy-bodied and light-headed.[110]

After Rousseau, in the literary movements of Romanticism, writers celebrated the absolute freedom of the subject which melancholy, in both its aspects, seemed to represent. The modern hero 'discovered' himself only by going 'beyond' or 'outside' himself. This was a process which began in brooding self-contemplation and ended in ecstasy. A description by Hoffmann, which assumes melancholy to be a commonplace, might serve as representative of many:

> Let me ask you outright, gentle reader, if there have not been hours, indeed whole days and weeks of your life, during which all your usual activities were painfully repugnant . . . your breast was stirred by an obscure feeling that a noble desire for an object surpassing all earthly pleasures must somewhere, sometime be fulfilled . . . this yearning for something unknown obsessed you wherever you went. . . . You crept to and fro with downcast gaze like a rejected lover, and none of humanity's many and varied activities gave you either joy or pain, as though you had ceased to belong to this world.[111]

In the same context Tieck writes that 'existence and torment are one and the same word', and of modern life as 'an unveiling of the madness, the frenzy of all life', as 'sheer nervousness'.[112]

In making of melancholy a starting point for reflecting upon the character of modern life, Kierkegaard could have claimed to be the inheritor of an ancient tradition newly restored and reinvigorated. That he did not, but preferred to write as if from a position of extreme isolation, might be interpreted as symptomatic of his own melancholic temper, but, in fact, had more to do with the tension between this tradition, on the one hand, and theological or philosophical speculation, on the other. Philosophy increasingly defined modernity in terms of the problem of knowledge, or, more generally, of representation. If the world had been emptied of real symbols – if we were no longer part of the world that we sensed beyond ourselves – then how could we be certain what this world was like? Whether sceptical or otherwise, modern philosophy began with the disjunction between knowing subject and unknown object. But this was to accept that which melancholy protested against. The bifurcation of reality, the withdrawal of objects into themselves, to face, uncomprehending, the internal world of the subject, the unbridgeable gulf that marked the antinomies of bourgeois thought, all these *followed* upon an unacknowledged but pervasive melancholy. Modern philosophy, particularly in Descartes, Kant and Hegel, presupposed as a permanent condition the melancholy of modern life, and incorporated this into their reflection, and in doing so domesticated the subversive genius that clung to every real instance of 'sorrow without cause'. To cross swords directly with the tradition of philosophy, or to summon up as its challenger an alternative sequence of 'great thinkers', would be to admit defeat. It would be no better than bad philosophy. The point is not to philosophize at all, but to disarm philosophy with the 'weight' of melancholy which it is powerless to relieve.

Melancholy, unimpressed by philosophical sophistication, none the less had intellectual resources of its own. Modern melancholy, mournful, heavy, and dizzy with infinity, is also charged with the 'metaphysical lucidity of depression'.[113] Like the pictures of Caspar David Friedrich and of Giorgio di Chirico, the impenetrable objectivity of the modern world presents itself to the detached and aimless spectator as a sequence of pure and unconnected appearances, thus with dreamlike clarity.[114]

The lucidity and 'depth' of melancholy are quite distinct from the rigour and 'profundity' of philosophy. The former can never be exhausted, it is sublime because it brings the subject directly into contact with his own free and unbounded nature. The 'zone of melancholy' is a meeting ground between the finite and the infinite, a perilous collapsing in upon itself of the entire human capacity for representation, a 'zero degree of symbolism'.[115] Philosophical discourse, on the other hand, is profoundly beautiful just because it does not issue in conclusions; it is interminable. Kierkegaard realized that, gifted dialectician though he was, his melancholy was deeper than his philosophy, and that systematic reflection, dialectical skill and rational inference would never relieve him of its weight. He began (one is tempted to write 'therefore', but there is no 'reason' here) with melancholy, with his own melancholy, and, in its isolating self-enclosure, could not appeal to his immediate predecessors but had to discover anew the force of their anti-philosophical critique of modernity.[116]

Kierkegaard was, of course, aware of his predecessors. He fought against his own melancholy, and rejected the partial defences offered to it in the traditions of modernity outlined above. He disregarded Burton's and Montaigne's moderate stoicism and sided decisively with Pascal in regarding the wretchedness of melancholy as a sign of spent perfection rather than as the 'natural' condition of modernity. At the same time, however, he rejected the Romantic and mystical elevation of 'rapture' into an image of human freedom and human happiness. But he never used them systematically. For Kierkegaard, the problem posed by modern life is not that of negating 'unhappy consciousness' in favour of 'ecstasy', but of transforming both immanent tendencies of melancholy into real happiness. Kierkegaard, thus, treated the opposed tendencies of melancholy as aspects of *despair* and sought to define the conditions under which despair, in all its guises, might be overcome. It is in this context that he developed a distinctively *religious* psychology of modern life.

Chapter 2

Irony: the romance of distance

Am I not a jarring note
In the heavenly symphony
Since devouring Irony
Gnaws me, shakes me by the throat?
                    Charles Baudelaire, 'Heautontimoroumenos'

Skyward again and again, like the man in Ovid,
Toward an ironic heaven as blank as slate,
And trapped in a ruinous myth, he lifts his head
As if God were the object of his hate.
                    Charles Baudelaire, 'The Swan'

Melancholy is the empty depth of modernity. The sense of simultaneously being in a void and of enclosing a void – of being nothing but an arbitrary division within the formless immensity of space – is reflected in, and reflected upon, by the ironic form in which so much of the progressive literary and artistic culture in which Kierkegaard spent his prolonged student years was cast.[1] Melancholy has become the emblem of modernity primarily because of its sublime self-sufficiency; as 'sorrow without cause', it is indifferent to the world and, therefore, unresponsive to all rational therapeutics. In the modern world this 'holding back from an engagement with existence' seems entirely justified as a primitive understanding of the abyss which has opened in the development of western society between the two opposed worlds of object and subject.[2]

Irony is equally detached and self-absorbed. It is as inconsolable as melancholy. Indeed, both appear to be mysterious diseases. An autobiographical section of *Stages on Life's Way* makes the connection: 'What is my sickness? Melancholy. Where is the seat of this sickness? In the power of imagination.'[3] And, like melancholy, irony has a 'weight' of its own. We talk of 'heavy' irony where its presence becomes too obvious, when it is not 'lightened' by wit. It is not surprising, therefore, that Kierkegaard, as an unusually gifted student and as a supremely melancholic individual, should choose *Irony* as the subject for his dissertation for the degree of Master of Arts.

Kierkegaard himself excludes this elaborate work, together with some earlier polemical essays and reviews, from the authorship proper. If the several separate but related strands of this authorship as an exploration of melancholy are to be fully appreciated, however, *The Concept of Irony* must serve as the essential, if deceptive, starting point.[4] Indeed, prior to November 1842, when he completed *Either/Or*, Kierkegaard had already produced a variety of writings which bear directly on his interpretation of some of the most distinctive features of modern culture. A lengthy article, 'From the Papers of One Still Living', criticizing a novel by Hans Andersen for J.L. Heiberg's literary review, is a somewhat distant anticipation of his later and much more important piece of contemporary literary criticism, *Two Ages*. More significantly, his incomparable *Journals*, which, although not written for immediate publication, unquestionably formed from their inception a major part of his literary work, reveal a number of drafts and writing plans.

There exist in *Journal* form ideas for a series of literary/ philosophical works exploring the nature and significance of a number of primordial character types. He refers most frequently to plans to write on 'The Master Thief', 'Don Juan' and 'The Wandering Jew'. These plans are significant, firstly, in indicating that from his earliest days as a writer Kierkegaard thought primarily in terms of the irreducible character of personal experience rather than in terms of 'ideas', and secondly, in the range and variety of such representations he is evidently preoccupied with the categorical distinctions which appear among them. Don Juan, thus, is conceived to be nothing but pure sensuousness, Faust represents doubt, and Ahasuerus personifies despair. These initial experiments were soon absorbed into a more ambitious 'Faust Project' in which the mythical character would be made to reflect all three primordial forms of 'negation'.[5]

These plans additionally reveal an important feature of Kierkegaard's persona as a writer, namely a powerful and spontaneously 'polyphonic' imagination.[6] Kierkegaard possessed to a high degree a poetic facility for the representation of human types. His artistic genius, characterizing the fullness and inexplicable diversity of life's inner forms in wonderfully plastic images, was from the beginning as essential to him as was his prodigal talent as a dialectician.[7] These early experiments in portraying world-historical characters were later metamorphosed into a series of pseudonyms through which Kierkegaard was able to typify the variety of incompatible forms through which the modern world could be grasped as personal experience. It would be misleading, however, to view Kierkegaard's development as a writer in terms of an unfolding poetic vision of the world. He was both attracted and repelled by his own literary talent, which was, for him, an ideal object of dread, from which he could never completely free himself.[8]

Prior, then, to the delineation of an existential topography of modern life Kierkegaard outlined the central problems of personal existence in terms of irony. In spite of its ambition and intricacy, however, he was soon to dismiss *The Concept of Irony* with the curt and damning remark: 'What a Hegelian fool I was!' Infatuated with what he took to be the philosophical originality of his own age he had been foolish enough to regard it as a 'defect on the part of Socrates to disregard the whole and only consider numerically the individuals'.[9] He quickly reversed this judgement, seeing in Socrates not only the originator of that authentic irony to which its modern exponents had proved unfaithful, but the personality whose presence had somehow insinuated itself into the entire course of western philosophical reflection and, therefore, had become part of its very life. Whatever judgement might finally be made of it, *The Concept of Irony* hardly deserves the neglect its author encouraged.[10]

An early interest in irony, and particularly in its modern literary form, can be seen retrospectively as something of an intellectual temptation for Kierkegaard. The fear that he later expressed – that for subsequent generations his works would become 'merely interesting' – might be applied to his first major book in relation to his own mature work. In *The Concept of Irony*, intellectual brilliance and the poetic capacity to form images were freed from ethical considerations and the more distant religious goal which conditioned all the works of the authorship. The rather harsh judgement which he formed of it shortly after its completion was the product of a fundamental shift in his conception of the purpose of writing. Yet it remains an invaluable clue, both to Kierkegaard's own development as a writer and as a personality, and, more importantly, to the meaning of his authorship as a whole. It remains, however, a clue that is difficult to interpret. The complexity of the language makes it difficult to follow the argument. Worse, there is the suspicion, forced on any reader acquainted with Kierkegaard's pseudonymous works, that this is not only a work on irony, but an ironic work. So much was clear, indeed, to its academic examiners who voted unanimously for its acceptance for the degree of MA (the equivalent of a modern doctorate), and were equally unanimous in their criticism of its style.[11] The difficulties associated with the pseudonymous works are, therefore, already present in his academic dissertation. The author's words can never quite be taken at face-value, even when they are published under his own name.

Irony is no arbitrary or accidental starting point for Kierkegaard's sustained reflection on the character of modern existence. It is, so to speak, the most general solution to the problem of melancholy, the cure which is rooted in the same conditions which produced the sickness. It is, for this very reason, a false beginning, which lacks the discriminatory power Kierkegaard required to mount a genuinely critical analysis of the contemporary world.

One of the most striking features of *The Concept of Irony* is, thus, that it exhibits powerful influences from, though not slavish devotion to, two sources which shortly thereafter were to become polemical targets for Kierkegaard's own writings: Romanticism and the philosophy of Hegel. Irony, indeed, had emerged in the Romantic movement, among creative writers, literary critics and philosophers, as a term held to be descriptive of the most general and fundamental characteristics of modern life. For Friedrich Schlegel, Solger, Tieck and many others, including Kierkegaard, inspired by the subjective turn in modern philosophy, irony was far more than a literary technique. For them the possibility of irony – of communicating a meaning or intention quite distinct from the explicit meaning of the words used (most readily, in fact, an opposite meaning) – raised the more general problem of the possibility and limitations of human communication as such.[12] In irony the privileged status of a single cosmologically valid perspective is abandoned in favour of an infinite multiplicity of equally plausible, and equally unconvincing, points of view. And this was a problem that, after he had rejected both Romanticism and Hegelianism, remained central to Kierkegaard's life and work.

In its distinctively modern form, indeed, irony seemed to have infected every life-relation. Every aspect of life had become charged with its corrosive freedom so that nothing could be taken at face-value, and in every communication there seemed to lurk some other, and perhaps sinister, message. Irony, in fact, seemed to be a fundamental characteristic of modern life, an aspect of the breakdown of a fixed cosmos and a language linked to it. The entire world of symbols, which had been rooted in things themselves, had become transformed into an autonomous domain of arbitrary signs. The entirety of communicative signals had been cut adrift from any necessary order in things themselves, creating, as it were, another world, coherent and well formed in itself, but wholly detached from the world of substance which it claimed to represent. For the Romantics this implied, above all, a new and in principle infinite liberty of human subjectivity. The creative freedom of human imagination had been liberated from the fixed order of nature.

The particular fascination with irony for the Romantic movement can be conveniently traced to the writings of Rousseau, and particularly to the confessional form in which he cast his literary work. The artificiality of social life, the ambiguous and illusory character of everyday language, made impossible any direct communication of an inner truth. It was, thus, upon the reality of modern life, rather than in imitation of an ancient rhetorical device, that the ironist founded a new literary art. The true character of human life as inwardness could be expressed only indirectly, and the ironist, seizing Rousseau's anguish in a new way, accepted this limitation as the binding precondition of a new freedom.

Irony, for all its world-conquering superiority, arrogance and sense of lofty detachment from the 'illusions' of everyday life, is a literary form which begins by admitting its own limitations. Yet it is in this very limitation that its real value is expressed. Embodied in its form – the indirect communication of the hidden truth of inwardness – is the very superficiality and deceptive ease of modern life. Irony, that is to say, does not 'touch' the reality which is of compelling interest to every human being; it must be content, rather, by throwing the reader into a state of frustrated bewilderment, to hint at the existence of such a reality.[13] And in admitting this failure, the writer forces upon the reader a confession of his or her own. In living amidst the superficialities of everyday life – of vanity, ambition and *amour propre* – they are, similarly, living in a world detached from the reality of their own hearts. Irony, thus, is a 'negative philosophy', the main preoccupation of which is to expose the arbitrariness inherent in the apparently fixed order of everyday life. Everything the reader thought to be true, permanent, valuable and proven is, in fact, the figment of a dehumanized imagination. For the Romantics, indeed, irony in the modern era becomes synonymous with the human characteristic of self-consciousness, viewed in the 'negative' perspective of its boundless enthusiasm for subversive self-criticism. For the ironic self-consciousness, that is for the modern age generally, no action or value seems worthwhile; everything has attracted to itself the aura of contingency, doubt and superficiality.

As a student Kierkegaard was attracted by this point of view. Intellectually he found it interesting, and aesthetically he favoured the literary experiments of its leading exponents. He was even more attracted to Hegel, who, in claiming to have 'gone beyond' the Romantic perspective of irony, drew irony itself into the fold of a systematic speculative philosophy. Unsurprisingly, therefore, Kierkegaard was deeply influenced by Hegel's scattered remarks on irony, which form, in fact, the point of departure for his own original analysis of the phenomenon.

HEGEL'S VIEW OF IRONY

The negative character of irony is taken by Hegel to be its defining feature. As such it is a 'moment' in the unfolding of self-consciousness and enters, therefore, as a 'world-historical principle', into the dialectic of the spirit. The lack of seriousness in the ironic is a token of its detachment from the world of actual events, and it is by adopting an ironic pose that the modern Romantic spirit seeks to preserve undimmed within itself the full potentiality of the human: 'Irony knows itself to be master of every possible content; it is serious about nothing, but plays with all forms.'[14] Hegel, developing a phrase of Solger's, furnished Kierkegaard with the most general formulation of modern irony (or the irony of modernity) as 'infinite absolute negativity'.[15] Kierkegaard expounds Hegel's formula as follows:

> It is negativity, because it only negates; it is infinite, because it does not negate this or that phenomenon; it is absolute, because that by virtue of which it negates is a higher something that still is not. The irony establishes nothing, because that which is to be established lies behind it.
>
> (*Irony*, p. 261)

Irony, that is, presupposes, but at the same time obscures, something positive which lies 'beyond' the field of consciousness. And in escaping, as it were, from all immediately given experience, irony preserves for us a corrupted sense of the greater totality to which both it, and the actuality from which it departs, really belong.

The truly human, that is to say, cannot be positively defined or limited in advance, and cannot be bound to any fixed order. Rather, as a constantly malleable spirit, it continually creates and finds new forms into which to empty itself. These forms, which are at any moment only the temporary evanescence of the spirit, should not be taken to be exhaustive of the human potential which carries them forward in the world.

Hegel also provided Kierkegaard with an important critique of Romantic irony as the *illusion*, rather than as the intuition (far less the realization), of human freedom. He contrasts the specifically modern form of ironic detachment and lack of steadfast seriousness with a properly religious subjectivity:

> The other side of this, that subjectivity has cast itself into religious subjectivity. The utter despair in respect of thought, of truth, and absolute objectivity, as also the incapacity to give oneself any settled basis or spontaneity of action, induced the noble soul to abandon itself to feeling, and to seek in Religion something fixed and steadfast; this steadfast basis, this inward satisfaction, is to be found in religious sentiments and feelings.[16]

The freedom, perversity and infinitizing character of irony is no more than a glimpse of the ultimate and abiding reality of spirit. Irony is not a reflection upon spirit, so much as the spiritual element in life playing, so to speak, with its own creation. Hegel criticizes the Romantics just because they identify the spirit's power to manifest itself in human self-creation with the ego's capacity to project itself into the world. This tendency towards egoism, which Hegel sees as the consequence of an enthusiastic but hasty reading of Kant, is exemplified in the radical subjectivism of Fichte. From the proposition that 'all knowledge is only images, representations', Fichte had proclaimed the inner life of the individual human subject to be a realm of total freedom. The godlike independence of the ego, once it has grasped itself as the source of consciousness, destroys every possible boundary to its own freedom. In Hegel's view the realization of such freedom, were it to be possible, would result in a curious loss of reality, the world would become no more substantial than a dream:

this virtuosity of an ironical artistic life apprehends itself as a divine creative genius for which anything and everything is only an unsubstantial creature, to which the creator, knowing himself to be disengaged and free from everything, is not bound, because he is just as able to destroy it as to create it.[17]

It is, in fact, just this dream-like quality into which Fichte and the Romantics wish to plunge. Their ideal is of an immediately responsive world which has become identical with our image of it:

Images are: they are the only things which exist, and they know of themselves after the fashion of images; images which float past without there being anything past which they float. . . . I myself am one of these images; nay, I am not even this, but merely a confused image of the images. All reality is transformed into a strange dream.[18]

For the Romantic ironist nothing can have value for itself, nothing can be earnest. Consequently, melancholy, which is the oppressive weight of an arbitrary and unassimilated exteriority, is turned, ironically, into sheer playfulness. Romantic irony, in other words, is nothing but a 'concentration of the *ego* into itself, for which all bonds are snapped and which can live only in the bliss of self-enjoyment'.[19] But, for Hegel, this is not only a mistaken view of human experience; it fails properly to appreciate the essentially transcending character of irony, which always points towards a 'higher' and as yet undisclosed reality.

Kierkegaard's decisive break with Hegel, and with Romanticism, both of which were connected with the formulation of his literary project as a specifically Christian endeavour, should not blind us to the significance of his early infatuation with both. These enthusiasms not only play a vital part in his analysis of the phenomenon of irony, their subterranean and never wholly exorcized presence charge the entire authorship with aesthetic and philosophical tensions, and, therefore, remain relevant to any adequate understanding of his religious psychology. Kierkegaard's initially excited reaction to both Romanticism, and to Hegel's philosophy which he approached first as an argument against Romanticism, was, however, far from being uncritical. It is with some justification that Kierkegaard's view of irony has been called 'Hegelian and anti-Hegelian at one and the same time'.[20] Equally it might be said to be Romantic and anti-Romantic at one and the same time. To define his relationship to both he set the analysis of irony in a much broader historical and cultural perspective.

SOCRATIC IRONY

The subtitle of Kierkegaard's thesis, 'with constant reference to Socrates', is highly instructive. It makes clear his intention to expose the root of irony in western thought and to uncover the hidden source of both Romantic irony and the Hegelian rejection of it, in the uniquely personal contribution of Socrates to the foundation of the dialectical imagination.

Kierkegaard found in Socrates, in the words of a more recent academic commentator, 'a man who is full of paradox'.[21] Socrates was an individual who was apparently driven by the most passionate commitment to right conduct while, at the same time, admitting that he could not know, unambiguously and certainly, in what such conduct must necessarily exist. Confronted with the painful difficulty of finding a right path, 'it appeared to me as if one ought to seek refuge in the *Logoi*, and perceive through them the true nature of being'.[22] Yet, to suppose this were possible is to admit that 'above this world of being towers that which is beyond everything and, therefore, cannot be grasped even by the *Logoi*'.[23] The Socratic paradox – that the *Logoi* are the only keys to that which is ineffably beyond being and which, therefore, remains incommunicable through the *Logoi* – is seized upon by Kierkegaard as paradigmatic of the human need for, but inability fully to realize, spontaneous and direct communication.

The paradox is made misleadingly more acute by the modern tendency to interpret *Logos* as abstract, rational and systematic thought. For Socrates, however, as Friedländer has made clear, the *Logos* is the permanent representation of the *eidos* – the intuited plastic forms of reality in its most comprehensive sense – and has not yet been crystallized into a self-sufficient realm of concepts.[24] 'Ideas' are, for Socrates, a species of 'vision' connected with the bodily function of seeing. They represent a general human power to sense the presence, within the transience of things which pass away, of a permanent reality of form: 'Precisely because it has an intuitive origin we must not begin by defining conceptually what the *Idea* is: for Plato himself, the *Idea*, though the highest object of knowledge, is never entirely definable in conceptual terms.'[25] The Socratic pursuit of 'knowledge', urgent and apparently futile, is not then so paradoxical as it might at first appear. Zeller, many years ago, made the point clearly; for Socrates 'knowledge' did not mean

> a purely theoretical knowledge which needed only to be learnt, but an unshakeable conviction based on the deepest insight into and realisation of what is really valuable in life, a conviction such as he himself possessed. The opposite of this 'knowledge' of the good is therefore not error but self-deception.[26]

Kierkegaard grasped the nature of this inner conviction very well. It was a conviction which he longed to possess and defend as steadfastly as had Socrates, and he despaired of doing so.

Socrates had been called ironic primarily because he had seemed never to take anyone seriously, or, more precisely, because he had been able to undermine every other person's claims to seriousness. In seeking the meaning of 'justice' or 'goodness', for example, he did not pretend to possess any positive knowledge of such things, but professed only a critical method of asking questions which revealed the vacuousness and pretension of the knowledge claimed by others. This does not mean, as the commentators cited above have made clear, that Socrates believed such questions were meaningless, or that it was a practical impossibility to realize any positive value. His dialectical questioning, in fact, was aimed primarily at the Sophists, at teachers who made a living from the pretence of being able to impart such valuable knowledge. It was not simply a matter of exposing their error and ignorance, but amounted to a demonstration of the inappropriateness of conceiving of practical values within the sphere of abstraction at all. It is not a matter of knowledge but of the determination within practical life to act in accordance with values. And values, the plastic forms of an ineffable reality, are bodied forth in a 'cured soul', rather than acted out as a kind of application of some external and universal norm.

'The concept of irony makes its entry into the world through Socrates', claims Kierkegaard, and significantly it does so as an ethical impulse.[27] In its original meaning, therefore, irony cannot be identified with the modern Romantic preoccupation with 'aesthetic' freedom, but reveals, rather, an inherent human demand for self-determination and self-limitation.[28] In Socrates' persistent dialectical questioning the sharpest contrast is drawn between the outer appearance of human actions and their inner meaning: 'the outer was not at all in harmony with the inner', but more than that, the outer 'continually pointed to something other and beyond'.[29] The very generality of this division allowed Socrates to take any 'accidental' observation as his point of departure. A dialogue could begin with a casual observation, there was 'no phenomenon too humble a point of departure from which to work oneself up into the sphere of thought'.[30]

The ironic mode of inquiry, as distinct from any speculative investigation, presupposes the emptiness of the human subject and assimilates it to a purely formal relation. Where a speculative understanding of human subjectivity continually fills out this relation with a content of its own, imputing to it a manifold of tendencies, instincts, values and drives which fall neatly into naturally ordered categories, an ironic understanding succeeds in stripping away all such positive content to leave exposed the 'divine infinity' of the human soul. The true character of human subjectivity can be reached only by the path of negation, by a progressive casting off of its appearance: 'It is Socratic to disparage all actuality and to direct man to a recollection that continually retreats further and further back towards a past that itself retreats.'[31] In the *Symposium*, for example, the aim of life is projected back to its fictive starting point, and subjectivity is endowed with an inner directionality such that it is 'always wanting to go back into the nebulosity from which the soul emerged or, more correctly, into a formless infinite transparency'.[32] In this view 'life is the incomplete, and the formless is that towards which longing aspires':[33]

> Irony is self-propelling and restless. Every positive content which offers it some resistance is swept aside; it is a position that continually cancels itself; it is a nothing that devours everything, and a something one can never grasp hold of, something that is and is not at the same time.
>
> (*Irony*, p. 131)

Kierkegaard seems as inspired as Hoffmann or Kleist with 'the poetic infinity and heedlessness of irony'.[34]

In the course of his analysis Kierkegaard, ironically commenting on academic seriousness, extends to Aristophanes an authority he withholds from every other commentator on Socrates. *Clouds* is chronologically closer to the life of Socrates than are either the earlier dialogues of Plato or Xenophon's memoir.[35] And it is the comic genius of Aristophanes, rather than the incipient abstraction of Plato or the conventional moralizing of Xenophon, that is the more appropriate medium for representing the truth grasped by Socrates. In *Clouds*, a satire on the Sophists with whom Socrates is in fact wrongly associated, the philosopher makes his entrance suspended above the stage in a basket. This literal 'hovering above existence' is a theme that was more fully developed in *Either/Or*, and is, he argues, a supremely apt representation of the power of abstract reasoning which somehow floats above the multiplicity of determinations which constitute a living person.[36]

The negative dialectic of irony does, however, issue in a positive result; the emergence of the personality as distinct from the concepts and virtues through which it had become conventionally represented. For all its lightness and continuous readiness for metamorphosis, irony remains essentially a 'qualification of the personality', rather than a form of thought. It is, therefore, the person of Socrates, rather than any concept, or theory or argument, which makes an impact on those he questions. And however much his individuality might be no more than 'an abbreviation of a complete personality',[37] it is as a personality 'infinitely in suspension'[38] that his endlessly ironic questioning carries with it the imprint of a uniquely human reality.

THE RELIGIOUS TENDENCY OF IRONY

Irony emerges, in Kierkegaard's text, as a specific form of human reflexivity. It is, on the one hand, the tendency towards abstraction, the dissolving power of thought over any position, and, on the other, the origin of authentic personality. It exercises over its practitioner a strange fascination. In relation to the apparent simplicity of an ironic interrogation every positive statement represents no more than a temporary respite fated to dissolve into ignorance. The dialectic of irony grips human subjectivity with a demonic power, insinuating itself into self-consciousness in such a way as to appear to be an external and ineluctable force. It has a 'weight' of its own, a power to 'absorb' the individual personality and preserve it, so to speak, in a frozen state; irony 'is a holding back from an engagement with existence'.[39] There is nothing rhetorical, therefore, in the Socratic profession of ignorance. It is, rather, a uniquely authentic expression of an inward truth, or, rather, of the truth of inwardness. Ignorance, thus, is the first form in which human subjectivity frees itself from the complacent substantiality of god or nature and claims a territory of its own. In attempting to define the boundaries of such a territory Socrates 'infinitely circumnavigated existence'.[40]

It is clear that, far from being a speculative point of view, the truth of existence was, for Socrates, bound up with his own personality, and that his personality was in turn bound up in some way with relations that transcended his immediate experience of the world. Thus, despite his purely individual and limited existence, he was called upon to convince others of this very truth, to communicate the terrifying depth of his own inwardness: 'He had come not to save the world but to judge it.'[41] The 'eternal unrest' of his own soul showed itself in every challenging encounter, and undermined his own, as well as others', comfortable certainty in received wisdom. This 'unrest' cannot be felt as an intention, or as some aspect of a rational purpose. Though it is felt from within, it none the less constitutes an alien and even crippling force, a demonic impulse that is perpetually antagonistic to the claims of actuality. It is this force which communicates itself as irony, which in turn makes people aware in a new way of something 'higher', and brings them to a consciousness of themselves as spirit.

The incipient religiosity of Socrates, and therefore of irony as an existential 'category', lies primarily in this restless negativity, not in the presumption of some 'higher' realm within which it receives a positive meaning. Indeed, the proclaimed agnosticism of Socrates amounts almost to evidence of his genuine religious inwardness. In an unreligious age (the age of antique sophistication as much as the age of modern scepticism), authentic religiosity hides itself in dialectical forms, in ironic detachment, in insistent, subversive questioning and in morally dangerous conduct.[42]

In the context of Kierkegaard's own times, however, there is something deeply ambivalent in this fascination with the figure of Socrates. It might be seen more obviously as an open declaration of modern secularism than as a veiled identification with the original spiritual genius of western culture. By linking himself so closely with Socrates, and himself making ironic comments about all those modern writers who claim to have 'gone beyond' Socrates (his borrowing from Hegel, even at this stage, was not uncritical), he might be seen as reaching back, beyond Christian religious consciousness, to an original and intellectually more potent form of secular self-reflection.

Such a view, however, depends largely on interpreting *The Concept of Irony* in the light of Kierkegaard's subsequent works in which the sharpest distinction is drawn between speculative dialectic and properly religious categories. It was just this development in fact which prompted Kierkegaard's own harsh judgement on his early work. Now, while the theme of *Irony* plays a continuous and significant part in Kierkegaard's development as a writer, it does not do so in the form of a fixed and completed theory. Thus, even from the point of view of his later writing, the Socratic method, which Kierkegaard identifies with irony, is not without religious implications, and it cannot, therefore, be assimilated to the Hegelian speculative system. Socrates inaugurated, that is to say, an existential dialectic which should not be confused with the tradition of abstract dialectical thought.[43] Even more significantly, Kierkegaard's infatuation with Socrates is linked with an equally compelling identification with the person of Jesus. Thus one of the fundamental tensions in the western tradition – the relation between Greek rationalism and Christian faith – is approached initially by Kierkegaard through a double personal identification. The remarkable feature of his work on irony, therefore, is that he finds in it a point of 'mediation' between Socrates and Jesus, and, therefore, a link between philosophy and religion.[44] Irony is an expression of an intuition of the transcendental structure of human existence from which spring both reason and faith. Kierkegaard, without rejecting this insight, was soon to take up the issue of the subsequent development of philosophical and religious consciousness in which not only did each establish itself independently of the other, but the two were increasingly and necessarily thrown into conflict.

This sharp opposition, if present at all, was latent in his early works. Thus while writing on irony 'with constant reference to Socrates', he was simultaneously compiling *From the Papers of One Still Living*, which, while not religious in content, betrays his personal identification with Christ.[45] He became a writer only after (unexpectedly) surviving the symbolic age of Christ. Yet, at this age, having altogether failed to make of such an identification anything more than a fantasy, he simultaneously saw himself as a Socratic gadfly, and hoped perhaps that the urge to write was a species of *daimonion* which, in gripping him, as it had gripped his master, was the first stirring of the religious spirit which Christianity was to introduce more generally into the world. The Greek 'anticipation' of Christian spirituality was seen, therefore, less in terms of the established speculative system – of the divine *Logos* given rational form as philosophy – than as the irrational freedom of Socratic questioning.

IRONY IN MODERN CULTURE

Irony is essentially and inherently a spiritual phenomenon. Arising from it Christianity and philosophy are united in their infinite capacity for negation, and in their endless power of self-destruction. The difficulty with both is the tendency to draw out from the pure nothingness upon which they are founded elaborate and self-sustaining positive doctrines. Kierkegaard, a modern Socrates, sought to return philosophy and religion to their starting points, to empty them of all positive content (moral law, dogmatics, etc.) and to grasp the infinite human inwardness which is this starting point.

Kierkegaard found in the divine 'frenzy' of Giordano Bruno and the equally divine 'folly' of Erasmus the source of a distinctively modern form of the Socratic spirit.[46] This represented for him, in many ways, an alternative source of the modern age in general. He looked to the roots of Romanticism, as well as to the Reformation and to Cartesian intellectual doubt, for the distinctive innovation of the modern religious spirit, a spirit which preserved (just as had Socrates in relation to Sophistical speculation and natural science), the corrosive power of a genuine and primordial religious inwardness in the face of either dogmatic simplification or philosophical abstraction.

This brings irony into the closest relationship to doubt, and therefore to the first of Kierkegaard's pseudonymous writings. To doubt everything is, from one point of view, simply another formulation of the universality of irony.[47] The privilege of irony over doubt, however, is that it is an existential 'category' rather than a conceptual term or relation. And typically Kierkegaard introduces philosophical reflections on Cartesian doubt with the personal 'story' of Johannes Climacus rather than with its conceptual 'analysis'.[48]

Irony, however, for all its negativity, is also an affirmation of life, an expression of the liveliness of life. Irony is essentially playful, and, influenced by Schiller and the radical interpretation of Kantian aesthetics, Kierkegaard seeks in this unrestrained freedom a point in existence which, so to speak, escapes from all the limiting determinants of everyday life.[49] There is something infinite in irony, and therefore something positive in its negativity. It is a direct expression of human freedom and, thus, of the Romantic longing for 'infinite inward freedom'. If religion is an expression of the infinite within the finite of human being, irony, no less surely, points continually away from itself, and ascends effortlessly from the particular to the general before ultimately losing itself in the infinite. Unlike doubt, irony soars within existence without being 'volatilized' beyond it.

To seize the ultimate reality of human existence: that is the first task of the religious life. This means that the inescapable transcendence of actual existence should not be denied or transmuted into an unreal representation of itself. Religious life is life: life itself. But when its transcending character is grasped in a purely abstract fashion as a philosophical principle, or is subsumed within a body of binding rules, then a misleadingly 'positive' religion results.[50] But the ironic is not yet the religious, it is the evidence of human self-understanding as a potential for religiosity, a kind of embryonic religious consciousness.

The problem facing Kierkegaard, therefore, was to discover how this spirituality might be preserved, and how it might be drawn into a form which was, so to speak, made for religion proper. Existing forms of religious life are spiritually dead. This was the inevitable outcome of the breakdown of the medieval worldview, and the reconstruction of human being as an interior cosmos. The Leibnizian response to this situation (that each individual has preserved within it a perfect copy of the cosmological order), or the Spinozist denial of individuality as such, were not even considered by Kierkegaard. Both resolve the difficulty by abstractly cancelling out the fact of the modern world, and thus fail to confront the actual character of human existence. But if this existence is taken as a starting point (and it is his insistence that it must be which makes Kierkegaard the supreme spiritual spokesman of modernity), then religious life must find for itself a form from within the world of presently existing social relations. Neither Hegel nor the Romantics disclose such a form. The Romantic fusion of the infinite and finite as sensuous feeling has been replaced by the Hegelian conceptual fusion of the infinite and finite as abstract concepts, but neither succeeds in preserving the 'actuality' of human existence and thus making of religion an unreal fantasy.

At this stage Kierkegaard makes no attempt to define such a form; he is content with extolling the virtue of irony. Irony has shaken human beings loose, made them aware of their precarious relation to the cosmos, and rendered the immediate world of experience something shadowy and insubstantial. In 'hovering above existence' irony in fact creates for itself a more interesting world than the one from which it has departed. But it is a strange world, a world of 'infinite inward negativity', without foundation and without aim, a ceaseless flux of denial and counter-denial. The human subject expands within this world and becomes coextensive with its own infinitizing power. Irony flees the world and, looking back upon it, discovers it was already bereft of meaning; it reflects, rather than reflects upon, melancholy.

How might the human subject be given back its substance, regain a content without denying itself, without rejecting its hard-won freedom and without negating its own spirit? This is, for Kierkegaard, the fundamental problem of religion in modern life.

IRONY AND RELIGIOUS PSYCHOLOGY

The two ages of irony – periods when its presence in the world was genuinely characteristic of an entire culture and way of life – were in the Athens of Socrates and in the Germany of the Romantics. This is no literary coincidence, but points in Kierkegaard's view to something fundamental about the human reality of those two epochs. Kierkegaard's lifelong flirtation with irony is an aspect of his fascination with (and almost dread of) those great spiritual turning points in entire societies as well as in individual life which he believed it indicated. Irony is, firstly, the self-conscious birth of the spirit, and, secondly, its liberation after a protracted history in association with the development of the Christian church into the ideally individuated and personal categories of the modern world.

The negative starting point for the entire dialectical process, in both its existential and its philosophical aspects, is taken into the self and gives birth to the modern idea of personality as self-generating spirit. Irony finally gains its positive character in the solipsistic personality of the individual, a character anticipated in the uniqueness of Socrates which stands in Kierkegaard's mind for the individual personality as such.

Thomas Mann, almost a century after Kierkegaard wrote his dissertation, called irony 'the most alluring problem of all'. It captures something fundamental in the nature of modern life, and at the same time makes it clear that this something cannot, any more than it could in previously 'religious' ages, be captured in a formula or expressed as a system. The shameless negativity of the spirit symbolized in irony endlessly renews itself, escaping all positive determination.

THE MAIEUTIC ART

Kierkegaard renounced irony, or tried to. In time he drew back from the 'infinite absolute negativity' which was in so many ways the clearest and most obvious vehicle for melancholic self-expression. The abyss of irony proved to be a temporary and inadequate relief of melancholy, whose conquest required a more radical renewal of subjectivity.[51] But he did not renounce the 'maieutic art' which he had learned from Socrates and made peculiarly his own. Yet the maieutic art itself remained an aspect of irony; it is founded on the impossibility of directly communicating a positive human truth. The truth of individual experience can only be suggested, and if it is to be conveyed to another it must borrow objective and conventional forms which are, in fact, inimical to its real nature. Here there is no alternative to artistry, and no means of preserving and conveying the truth other than by its initial falsification.

It is, in part, as a continuation of his analysis of irony, therefore, that Kierkegaard adopted a series of pseudonyms. This device not only preserved the many-sidedness of human experience, it distanced Kierkegaard from the temptation of a 'positive' philosophy, and guarded him against the possibility of being read as an 'authority'. Significantly a continuation of the insights gained from writing *The Concept of Irony* can also be found in the series of *Upbuilding Discourses* which he wrote under his own name and published in conjunction with the pseudonymous, aesthetic, works. These essays were neither doctrinal works, nor were they, eschewing as they did all conventional expressions of piety, sermons in any usual sense. They were, rather, free literary creations aimed at arousing the subjectivity of the reader to the recognition of his or her own inner truth.

The religious aim of the maieutic art is also behind Kierkegaard's final and somewhat reluctant acceptance of Hegel's criticism of Romanticism as egoism. In viewing everything as an adjunct to the ego, rather than in terms of a much more comprehensive conception of human subjectivity, the essential definiteness and concreteness of the individual is lost. Actuality is 'volatilized' by the ego, which is a personal form of irony in modern life. The 'misty' and 'cloudy' consciousness of the Romantic writer is absolutely typical of this lack of distinctness which was antithetical to Kierkegaard's entire vocation as a writer.[52] His task was to define, for the modern age, the nature of religion, and to clarify the character of Christianity, in precise and lucid terms. And it became increasingly obvious to him that, in the modern world at least, Christianity could not merge with consciousness itself, or with the 'life' which was a typically Romantic epithet for the all-inclusive indifference which was, in fact, the death of real feeling. Interestingly, for the ancient world, prior to Socrates, this separation of life and spirit had not yet taken place: 'For the ancients the divine was continually merged with the world; therefore no irony.'[53]

For all their stress on the ego, the Romantics, following Fichte, were in fact imbued with a 'mystical' and 'oriental' spirit of self-negation which Kierkegaard viewed as inimical to the entire development of Christianity. Far more than was the case with Socrates the Romantic temper was 'always wanting to go back into the nebulosity from which the soul emerged or, more correctly, into a formless, infinite transparency'.[54] To 'romanticize' is nothing more than to mystify. Novalis defines his ambition thus:

> The world must be romanticized. Thus will its original meaning be rediscovered. . . . This operation is still quite unknown. When I endow the vulgar with a noble meaning, the common with a mysterious appearance, the known with the dignity of the unknown, the finite with the semblance of infinitude, I romanticize . . . the Philistine and prosaic perception of the world must give way to marvel and wonder at its mysterious magnificence. As a correlate, we ought to infuse everyday life with our sense of the distant, strange, and higher.[55]

Indeed, the all-encompassing subjectivity of the Romantic, the most fully developed form of irony, was not far removed, according to Kierkegaard, from oriental mysticism, in which:

> whatever dying away (*Hendoen*) is to be found there consists in a relaxation of the soul's muscular strength, of the tension that constitutes consciousness, in a disintegration and melancholic relapsing lethargy, whereby one is not volatilized but is chaotically scrambled and then moves with vague motions in a thick fog.
>
> (*Irony*, p. 66)

The mystical/Romantic ideal is for the 'vegetative still life of the plant instead of locomotion. It is wishing for the foggy, drowsy wallowing that an opiate can procure rather than for the sky of thought.' The heady sense of the infinite is without effect. Thus 'the ironist is conservative', and in the end Kierkegaard is decisive in his rejection of any romanticized image of religious life.[56] In sharp contrast he argues that the religious spirit is born under the 'Grecian sky' and 'does not want to be soaked to softness in vague qualifications but to be stretched more and more'.[57] According to Kierkegaard, therefore, Goethe, the most complete Romantic, 'exhausts himself poetically'.[58] Rather than reflecting the subject back into the determinants of a unique personality, Romantic irony removes the indifferent spectator to such a remote distance that individuality loses itself. Within the modern cosmological picture irony is fiercely 'infinitized'; there is no 'relative' detachment, no observational 'platform', and the observer is either at one with his or her own observations, or loses all contact with the observable. In this sense irony 'seems to be a withdrawal of the subject, indeed a void'. Irony is a 'hollowing out' of the person, who 'actually becomes nothingness'.[59] The 'infinitely delicate play with nothingness' could hardly end differently.[60]

The Concept of Irony is in a very real sense not only the beginning of Kierkegaard's prodigious literary production: it represents an abbreviation of what was to be dramatically unfolded in the works that succeeded it.

Yet, even while composing his dissertation, Kierkegaard was in the process of changing his personality and view of life; or, rather, a personality implying a more definite and positive view of life was in process of formation within him. These changes left their mark on his book on irony and, possibly, account for its relative neglect. From it we do not receive, as we do from virtually any of his other works, an immediate and compelling sense of Kierkegaard as an individual. His analysis, indeed, appears inconclusive and even contradictory. Irony appears to be both an implicit affirmation and an explicit rejection of a religious life; both an intuition and an avoidance of reality; both a means and an obstacle to the realization of human freedom. This is certainly not the result of intellectual confusion on Kierkegaard's part, but, rather, an indication of the undifferentiated character of irony itself. Representing as it does all the spiritual forces at work in human consciousness, it cannot furnish a clear model of the spiritual possibilities open to modern individuals. The irony perspective is superseded in Kierkegaard's work, therefore, with a series of differing but related points of view.

The clearest continuation with *The Concept of Irony* can be found, thus, in the first volume of *Either/Or*, and its firmest rejection in the second volume. Irony is an insufficient starting point for an understanding of modern life, and is blind to the spiritual potentialities it contains. Irony fails to distinguish properly between the negative and the positive starting points of religion, nor does it clearly separate intellectual speculation from existential despair. This is true not only of Kierkegaard's analysis, but, more importantly, of the phenomenon itself. It is, perhaps, for this very reason that irony has become a kind of second nature for so many modern writers. Irony is less used now as a means of self-flattery (though this no doubt attracts its less talented exponents) than as a technique of synthesis. The ironic viewpoint draws everything together, and imparts to it a certain sense of wholeness by virtue of withholding any positive value or meaning from any part or instance. While still deeply influenced by Hegel, Kierkegaard also strove for a literary/philosophical/psychological form of expression for the intuition of the wholeness, unity and synthetic plasticity of human subjectivity. He found this first in irony, but in exploring this form became increasingly dissatisfied with its capacity to grasp (and not simply signify) such a unity, and, more profoundly, he became less convinced of the intuition of psychic coherence upon which it rested.

Kierkegaard felt compelled to begin again; not because he thought his analysis of irony incomplete or misleading, but because he had discovered in it, rather than a genuine starting point for a religious psychology of modern life, a premature and false synthesis of the separate perspectives essential to such a project.

Kierkegaard's analysis of irony, while providing a vehicle for passing criticism of Romantic subjectivism and Hegelian rationalism, remained inconclusive. The relations between irony and melancholy are so multifarious and complex that the reality of the latter cannot be explored through an investigation of the former. But melancholy was already Kierkegaard's real problem. Irony does not cure melancholy, it ignores it. Thus melancholy is just as liable to crush an ironist as it is to deflate a philosopher. Melancholy interrupts the interminable Socratic dialogue, just as it stops the systematic philosopher in his tracks, and chokes off the wellsprings of feeling. The loss of interest in the world leaves the melancholic untouched by thought, will or feeling. All those modern enthusiasts, who claim for reason, or the will, or for the realm of feeling, the privilege of an uninterrupted presence, are therefore mistaken. And it is just this unacknowledged assumption of continuity which is used to justify their extravagant claims that once melancholy is, as it were, properly attached to the self-expanding and autonomous development of reason, or will, or feeling, it will be overcome – to be replaced, ultimately, by a reinstated condition of primordial happiness, as absolute knowledge, self-determination and autonomy.

But melancholy is not overcome. It is uncaused sorrow, and wrecks every hope in which the Enlightenment placed its trust. That Kierkegaard launched a fierce attack on the claims of the Hegelian philosophy is well known; what is less often recognized, though it is clearly stated, is his equally determined opposition to any idea that either a permanent refuge from melancholy, or a temporary condition symmetrical with it (this might provisionally be called faith), can be 'reached' (spatial metaphors remain unavoidable) by either 'giving way to' or 'educating' or 'developing' the will or the feelings. All such views begin by disjointing the human subject who, in the fully articulated synthesis of a person and not as an isolated thought, or feeling or action, is crushed by melancholy.[61]

Irony is a weapon against all such optimism, and Kierkegaard's thesis, in one sense, is an attempt to restore irony to the task of critical self-awareness, and to rescue it from its modern *mésalliances*. But irony, or a 'theory' of irony, does not offer itself to the kind of psychological investigation which Kierkegaard needed to perform to clarify the real possibilities inherent in modern life. To do this required, not that he detach himself from his own experience, or the reported experience of other people, but, quite the reverse, that he identify himself as closely as possible with actuality in all its diversity.

Chapter 3

Reflection: on the surface of modernity

Her eyes are formed of emptiness and shade.
Her skull, with flowers so deftly decked about,
Upon her dainty vertebrae is swayed.
Oh what a charm when nullity tricks out!
Charles Baudelaire, 'The Dance of Death'

Existence is a small surface agitation. . . .
Jean-Paul Sartre: 'The Singular Universal'[1]

Modern society emerges as the 'surface' of life, a boundary between melancholy and irony. 'Sorrow without cause' became assimilated to a sense of cosmological dislocation and loss which, though it could not explain the persistence of melancholy, provided it with a modern form. Adrift in boundless space the human subject, withdrawing into itself, discovered a symmetrical infinite inwardness, which, rather than ground the personality in new determinants, cast it into ironic insecurity. Melancholy is a movement inwards, a retreat from the void of external space. Irony is an opposite, boundlessly expansive movement. But the boundary of human existence is permeable to both melancholy and irony which, as it were, threaten directly to connect 'inner' and 'outer' space. Irony seems to 'raise' itself above existence, while melancholy 'sinks' beneath it. The movement of neither melancholy nor irony takes notice of 'real existence', and they even lay claim to a certain arrogance in 'seeing through' every merely human particular. And, in passing through, rather than being reflected from, the surface of modern life, each, thus, discovers the other. The two intermingle and, at times, become indistinguishable. Thomas Mann, thus, can talk of the typical 'melancholy, ironic way' of looking 'through' the modern world.[2]

When both external and internal 'space' is infinitized the qualitative dividing line between them, the dangerously permeable surface to which human life clings, itself becomes boundless. Rather than conceive a world of fixed and enclosed objects confronting a world of equally fixed and enclosed subjects, both object and subject opened on to an inconceivable vastness. The realm of the human cannot, in that case, curl back on itself and 'contain' as 'inwardness' the plenitude of its own subjectivity. More like a sensitive filament than a microcosmic structure, it extends itself as the distinction between two kinds of space. The actuality of modern life is opened out, unbounded, reduced to a flimsy and insubstantial surface which, at any moment, may become transparent.

Kierkegaard, aware of the close kinship between the life-destroying potential of his own melancholy, and the corrosive power of modern irony, sought to 'thicken' and solidify actuality which is, or ought to be, the dividing line between them. Once the implications of the 'Copernican Revolution' in human self-understanding and the understanding of the world become more clearly articulated, it is evident that actuality is sustained primarily by the strength of social conventions. Indeed, being created from nothing other than the act of distinction itself, actuality is both the foundational convention of modern society, upon which all other distinctions depend, and the emergent reality which is, in turn, supported by the vitality of all these other distinctions.[3]

Kierkegaard focuses on the individual as the point at which actuality can become more substantial. It is clear that, in the context of his writings as a whole, an analysis of the individual results in a specifically modern understanding of society, and a decisively social understanding of modernity. Indeed, contrary to a widely held misunderstanding, the individual is, for Kierkegaard, pre-eminently a social category. Certainly the notion of the 'individual' has an equivocal position in Kierkegaard's writings, and this for two main reasons. Firstly, as characterized by a number of pseudonyms, the individual is portrayed in terms of illusory life-views typical of the 'superficial' character of modern society. And, secondly, as the 'single one' of his religious writings the individual is portrayed as an authentic but as yet unrealized potentiality trapped within the insubstantial melancholy of the Present Age. The 'single one' is a rejection of all those social arrangements which support modern individualism, but in neither case is the individual viewed as a 'non-social' being. In either sense the individual is realistically viewed as a social relation.[4]

Kierkegaard's understanding of the character of modern society is, in fact, fundamental to his writing as a whole. Before turning to the 'critique of melancholy' through which a series of Kierkegaardian pseudonyms offer an exploration and account of modern actuality, it is helpful to consider the plain 'criticism' of modern society and culture which Kierkegaard advanced in a number of journalistic works not all of which are usually considered to fall within the authorship. His critical attitude towards modern culture and the possibilities for human experience inherent within it, his antipathy to both conservative and radical political tendencies in Danish society, and his final uncompromising attack on the Danish Church are best viewed as parallel with, rather than as an addendum to, his pseudonymous and direct 'authorship'. The fundamental question of that authorship – how is it possible to become a Christian? – also animates his literary and polemical journalism.

Indeed, just as it is his commentary on his own melancholy and his academic dissertation that can be used more easily than his major works themselves to locate Kierkegaard within an appropriate intellectual and historical context, so his journalistic writing provides, as it were, a preliminary statement of the 'theory of society' which informs his religious psychology.

It would be quite misleading to read *Two Ages*, or the various pamphlets issued under the title of *The Instant*, as 'occasional' pieces, tangential to Kierkegaard's major preoccupations and of little significance in themselves. The much discussed issue of the 'coherence' of Kierkegaard's writing, for example, has been concerned exclusively with his 'serious' works, and usually, in fact, with the pseudonymous works.[5] It is in his journalistic work, however, that Kierkegaard's criticism of modernity is most sharply reflected. The apparent 'superficiality' of these works is a literary device adapted to the conditions of the present. Modern social life is itself 'superficial', so that, quite apart from any interest in gaining a wide readership, and irrespective of any difficult issues surrounding the method of 'indirect communication' and the conditions under which its restrictions might be lifted, Kierkegaard adopted a 'popular' tone to express, in terms most appropriate to it, the fact that contemporary life (in contrast to the depth of his own melancholy, and the distance of his irony) was nothing but a surface upon which was reflected the ceaseless flux of 'public opinion'. Read in this way these works themselves become symptomatic of the condition which they analyse; thus they preserve, in a different way, the hidden identity of their elusive author. More significantly they reveal the importance of a criticism of modern culture to the entirety of the authorship.

DECEPTION AND PUBLIC OPINION

The story of Søren Kierkegaard's broken engagement to Regine Olsen has frequently been cited as the occasion, if not the cause, of the authorship proper. Certainly it was not an isolated event. The period of the engagement was also the period of mourning over the death of his father, and his academic father-figure, Poul Møller, and it was his relationship to his father which, in all probability, underlay his rejection of marriage. The engagement, whatever it reveals of the 'depth' of Kierkegaard's inner life, serves to dramatize his polemical relationship with the superficiality of modern public opinion.

In September 1840 Kierkegaard, then aged 27, became engaged to Regine Olsen, a girl ten years his junior whom he had met over three years earlier at the house of Bolette Rørdam (who may in fact have been his first love).[6] Almost at once he realized he could never marry Regine. The difficulty apparently centred on the incompatibility of his view of marriage as an absolutely open relationship, and the secret which bound him to his dead father. Inconclusive speculation as to the nature of this secret – that his father, as a child, had despaired and cursed God, that he had begun an affair with his housekeeper, who later became his second wife, while his first wife was still alive, that Søren had himself fathered an illegitimate child – is less significant than the known details of the extraordinary way in which he engineered the dissolution of the engagement. Believing that Regine would be heartbroken if he simply terminated the engagement, and that her reputation would suffer to the extent to which she might have appeared a less attractive future bride to any properly bourgeois potential suitor, Kierkegaard preferred to play the role of heartless deceiver who had cynically toyed with her affections without ever intending to go through with the marriage. To create the desired impression he adopted the role of 'playboy'.

Copenhagen was a city whose bourgeois social life was conducted within the strict limits of conventions of 'respectability'. It was relatively easy to create the impression of scandal; the smallness of the Copenhagen bourgeoisie, as well as its newness, meant that gossip was still a basic form of communication and social control. Kierkegaard exploited this 'premodern' aspect of Copenhagen city life. Later he complained that it had been his misfortune to live in a 'market town', which is usually taken to be a complaint against Danish provincialism and, consequently, his own lack of international recognition. Equally, however, it was this semi-rural backwardness that provided him with the possibility of deceiving Regine, her family and the respectable public. Had he lived in the larger and more anonymous milieu of Berlin or Paris, he would not have been tempted to break the engagement in this way. Indeed, he might have felt himself free of these conventions which, intellectually, he rejected as an aspect of 'bourgeois-philistinism', but, in his own life, presented an obstacle to his marriage.

The engagement and its dissolution, in other words, involved Kierkegaard in a rather complex interaction with the public. He created a false impression within respectable society, not, as had Rousseau, to protect himself from its misunderstanding and create a place apart within which to reconstruct his own world, but, rather, as a shield with which to protect Regine from the truth. Much in his authorship has been interpreted as a highly sophisticated covert message, addressed to the public but intended privately for Regine to inform her, none the less, of the truth of their broken relationship. In fact neither the relationship itself nor Kierkegaard's literary 'working through' of its themes fully accounts for the pseudonymous production, but both reveal a deeply ambivalent attitude to the conventions of bourgeois respectability. His rejection of marriage, like his later and equally tortured refusal to take up an official position in the church, was associated with a clear understanding of respectability and its public and domestic institutions as 'bourgeois-philistinism'. Particularly in relation to the engagement he played the part of a literary romantic hero, in solitary revolt against the expectations of public opinion.

During the period immediately after the publication of *Concluding Unscientific Postscript*, and extending through 1846 to 1847 when Kierkegaard's 'second authorship' gathered momentum, his critical relationship to the modern public became an important theme in both his religious and his aesthetic writings.

He was preoccupied throughout this period with the possibility of becoming a rural parson and this interlude might be regarded as a second engagement crisis, which he ended in the same way as the first, by refusing to commit himself to the established institution. In part, perhaps, to delay any decision over his own future, and to make it more difficult for himself to leave Copenhagen, he engineered a 'collision' with the public through the pages of the popular satirical journal, *The Corsair*.

Modern journalism represented, for Kierkegaard, the worst aspects of the public, and *The Corsair*, a satirical magazine that was scandalous for its day, specialized in the worst type of modern journalism. *The Corsair* polemic, therefore, in which he invited a journalistic attack upon his work, appears at first sight to be a perverse distraction from the central design of the authorship. Why should he become involved in a form of literary activity that he so clearly despised?

The immediate occasion for his involvement was a critical, or rather a satirical, review of *Stages on Life's Way* by P.L. Møller, printed not in fact in *The Corsair*, but in *Gaea*, a literary periodical edited by Møller.[7] The pseudonym, Frater Taciturnus, replied in the newspaper *Faedrelandet*, in which Kierkegaard had previously claimed (with literary correctness!) that he was not responsible for the pseudonymous writings. Frater Taciturnus ends his article by directly linking Møller (who may have been an original model for Johannes the Seducer in *Either/Or*) with *The Corsair*, and challenges *The Corsair* to attack the author of the pseudonymous works:

> Would that I might get into *The Corsair* soon. It is really bad for a poor author to be so singled out in Danish literature that he (assuming that we pseudonyms are one) is the only one who is not abused here . . . *ubi* P.L. Moller, *ibi The Corsair*.
>
> (*Corsair*, p. 46)

Møller's connection with *The Corsair* was already known in literary circles (as was Kierkegaard's authorship), but open publicity of this sort was still damaging to an academic with ambitions to succeed to the Chair of Aesthetics at Copenhagen University.

The editor of *The Corsair*, Meïr Goldschmidt, and Kierkegaard respected and admired each other but, as anticipated, *The Corsair* responded with a series of satirical attacks and caricatures, identifying Kierkegaard as the author of the pseudonymous works.[8]

Kierkegaard claimed that 'it is not true that I got into all this by a rash step'.[9] In some ways it was a carefully engineered 'collision' with the public, or with the representatives of the most corrupting tendencies of the public. It was also an effort to 'rescue' Goldschmidt and his unfulfilled literary talent from Møller and *The Corsair*. In this latter ambition he was successful. Møller left Copenhagen, never to return, and Goldschmidt, after a lengthy trip abroad, returned to more serious literary endeavours. This entanglement in the lives and careers of others sits uneasily in the midst of an authorship dedicated to the single individual, and which, at the period of its greatest intensity, magisterially proclaimed the impossibility of one individual helping, or being helped by, another: 'the sufferer must help himself '.[10]

The *Corsair* affair ought, perhaps, to be seen as an attempt by Kierkegaard to test his indifference to the crowd rather than as an effort to intervene against Møller on what he took to be Goldschmidt's behalf. His provocation of the public confirmed, psychologically if not logically, his own more exalted status as the 'single individual', as the sole reader of his own books. Towards the close of *Purity of Heart*, therefore, he warns his reader (himself) that perseverance in the spiritual discipline 'to will one thing', far from bringing any secular benefits, 'will make your life more taxing, and frequently perhaps wearisome . . . it may make you the target of ridicule'. But, viewed correctly, 'Ridicule will even be a help to you. . . . For the judgment of the crowd has its significance.'[11]

Indeed, a collision with the public was implicit in the entire authorship from the beginning. The deceptive method of the aesthetic works, once their true authorship and purpose were revealed, was bound to cause offence. More significantly, however, the reduplication of the *Upbuilding Discourses* was a self-conscious 'working against the self ' which had as its preconception the corruption of established public values, and thus of the superficially socialized personal identity of the 'first self '.[12]

The entire incident, none the less, marks an important development in Kierkegaard's conception of himself as a writer:

> From that moment on, my idea of what it is to be an author changed. Now I believed that I ought to keep on as long as it was in any way possible; to be an author now, to be here, was such a burden to me that there was more asceticism in this than in going out in the country.
>
> (*Journals*, 6: 6843)

In this regard it bears on the production of the religious works in much the same way as the Regine 'affair' had a bearing on the aesthetic works. And where the first phase of his work had dealt with the self-generating illusions of the aesthetic and the philosophical, the latter phase was preoccupied with a systematic critique of the established order as a barrier to the realization of religious values.

Regine had made him a poet. In that particular case an involuntary relationship created so many psychological difficulties that, to dissolve it, he let himself appear to the public as a seducer. He used public opinion to deceive Regine, and everyone else, about himself. And this served as a practical prototype for the aesthetic writers' maieutic art. She had to be deceived into the truth – that they could not marry – because Kierkegaard's reasons for believing this truth were wholly private, and the fact that he had any wholly private reservations was, in itself, a reason not to marry. An indirect method, further, would liberate Regine from the thought of him, and would leave her without any cause for self-reproach.

In the *Corsair* affair he engineered another public attack upon himself, this time with the ostensible purpose of 'disengaging' Goldschmidt from Møller, who was the actual seducer Kierkegaard had once pretended to be. On this occasion, however, he told the truth about himself – that he was the creator of the pseudonyms – so that he would be ridiculed. Furthermore, he revealed another person's secret – Møller's connection with *The Corsair* – in order to ensure that the attack would take place.

In the first case he sought to protect another by falsely representing himself as guilty. And in the second case he represented himself truthfully in order to make himself appear ridiculous. This 'repetition' is no doubt related to a pathological melancholy, to a highly developed need for isolation, and to an unassuaged longing for martyrdom. Neither situation, however, whether taken separately or together, 'explains' the pseudonymous or signed writings to which, in part, they gave rise. The essential element in both lay, in fact, in Kierkegaard's genius for turning his own experience into 'an epigram of the age'.

The provocation of the public through *The Corsair* is associated with a well-defined second stage in his authorship. His writing is resumed in the broader context of a critique of the conventional bourgeois values of respectable society, a society which too loudly proclaimed itself to be Christian. Rather than focus on ways of achieving individuality within the context of a given actuality, the renewed authorship describes the given world of social relations as itself the source of all those self-deceptions which are obstacles to the realization of a deeper Christian selfhood. It would be misleading to view this development as if it were a 'transition' from the aesthetic to the religious. The *Upbuilding Discourses* are simultaneous with the aesthetic works just to prevent (or, at least, try to prevent) such a misreading. Nor is the earlier series 'indirect' while the later writings are 'direct'; the *Upbuilding* is essentially indirect. The difference lies, rather more simply, in the gradual emergence, after the *Postscript*, and in part by way of *The Corsair*, of a clearer conception that the specifically critical task of the authorship remained incomplete.

In one of his *Upbuilding Discourses in Various Spirits*, in spite of being addressed to the 'single individual', Kierkegaard reflected somewhat bitterly on the damaging psychological and spiritual effects of the 'crowd' in modern society:

> The same persons, who singly, as solitary individuals are able to will the Good, are immediately seduced as soon as they associate themselves and become a crowd.
>
> (*Purity*, p. 144)

Indeed, the whole conception of 'double-mindedness' is a sustained attack on the peculiarly modern phenomenon of public opinion. And in *Consider the Lilies* he said of the person who turns in despair towards the crowd that he 'makes of himself but a number, he belongs like an animal . . . to the multitude'.[13]

THE CHURCH AND BOURGEOIS RESPECTABILITY

Kierkegaard's polemical attitude towards the modern public, particularly as it was represented in journalistic literature, was never a straightforward antagonism. He had a dread of the public, a 'sympathetic antipathy and an antipathetic sympathy', which no doubt absorbed and reflected, among much else, his ambivalence towards his father.[14] Thus, the withering attacks he directed at bourgeois institutions culminated in contempt for the hypocrisy and 'doublemindedness' of conventional respectability which utterly failed to embody the real bourgeois values with which Kierkegaard identified himself. He condemned the superficiality, the lack of seriousness, the inconsistency and 'lightness' of respectability; above all he was outraged by the sentimental piety and complacency of the class which his father had so clearly represented without himself being sentimental or complacent.

The physiognomy of the present age failed to express the inner consistency of its values, and significantly Kierkegaard did not reject bourgeois values in themselves. Enlightened rationality, moral individualism and a liberal constitution, he realized, were in tune with the modern age; in fact, they were the modern age that lay, partially obscured, within the superficial flux of the Present Age. Kierkegaard attempted to bring to the surface and make visible these values, and had no intention of rejecting what he took to be the real character of modernity in favour of its inexpressive mask.[15]

Kierkegaard's commitment to the underlying values of bourgeois modernity, throughout the intensifying attack on bourgeois-philistinism, is thrown into sharper relief by his simultaneous rejection of those intellectual, social and religious movements which had their roots in the premodern age.

His powerful attack on Hegelianism, thus, is at the same time a rejection of Copenhagen's outmoded aristocratic culture associated with the court. Hegel's philosophy was introduced into Danish intellectual life through the varied literary and theatrical activities of Heiberg. His celebrity, his aristocratic style of life, and his unchallenged position as the arbiter of Danish high culture associated Hegel with a romantic 'golden age' which had already passed. Kierkegaard, thus, first encountering Hegel through Danish spokesmen (Heiberg and Martensen), saw him, rather oddly, as expressive of aristocratic values. After a brief flirtation with Heiberg's circle, into which he had little chance of being accepted, Kierkegaard turned his back on the trappings of court life, and became the most sophisticated critic of Hegelianism.[16]

Equally he rejected Grundtvig's ecclesiastical populism, rooted as it was in a premodern rural idyll.[17] Grundtvig attempted to merge Christianity with Scandinavian mythology, and attracted a large following in rural areas neglected by the late, and rapid, modernization of Copenhagen:

> when one regards the world of the spirit with Norse eyes in the light of Christianity, one gets the impression of a universal historical development of art and learning that embraces the whole life of man, with all its energies, conditions and achievements.[18]

Not that rural religious and social life was directly anti-bourgeois.

Throughout the eighteenth century Pietism had taken root in the countryside, and a tradition of religious emotionalism, in opposition to both the more formal aspects of orthodox Lutheranism and secular Enlightenment culture. Pietism, integrating religious ideas with a strictly moral conception of everyday life, also stressed the religious significance of individual conversion and its heightened emotional state, and might be viewed as a form of 'ecstatic religion'. Their meetings were imbued with a 'sultry and almost sensuous atmosphere'.[19] But, at the same time, like English Puritanism 'it was essentially a bourgeois religion'.[20] Indeed, the agrarian reforms dating from the second half of the eighteenth century had created, by the time of Kierkegaard's youth, a 'kind of rural bourgeoisie, in place of the premodern peasantry'.[21] Anti-conventicle legislation in the mid-eighteenth century and the growing liberalism of the established Lutheran church helped to create, as a reaction to it, a significant revivalist movement of which Grundtvig became the articulate spokesman. Kierkegaard's elder brother, Peter Christian Kierkegaard, himself a rural priest, became a supporter of Grundtvig's revivalist movement, and, in contrasting his brother's 'practically ecstatic' writings to the 'sober-minded' orthodoxy of the leading academic theologian, Martensen, hinted that Søren was at least a sympathizer with their cause. Kierkegaard, however, in spite of his fierce attack on the Danish church, had no interest in reforming its liturgy or organization. And as for the idiosyncrasy of his own writings he argued that 'the peculiar characteristic of my ecstasy is that it is borne by a sober-mindedness of equal dimensions'.[22]

For Kierkegaard, that is to say, modern religious life, whether as a liberal elitist church open to every enlightened secular tendency, or as the popular revivalism that reflected national feeling, like all other aspects of modern culture, lay on the surface of the 'Present Age'.[23]

Kierkegaard's distrust of the public, his theatrical management of his own public image, and his rejection of contemporary political and religious positions as superficial, constitute a kind of preliminary statement of the more penetrating critique of modernity offered in the authorship itself. It would be misleading to regard his journalistic work as 'social' and 'political', as opposed to the 'aesthetic', 'philosophical' and 'religious' dimensions of reality explored by the pseudonyms and the 'upbuilding' works. These latter works are also, and not merely by implication, critical commentaries on the Present Age. The fundamental difference between the journalistic writings and the authorship is that the former addressed the experience of modernity in its own terms. They are, after all, pieces of journalism, and, therefore, part of the reflective process through which the Present Age views itself. The 'authorship', however, anatomized modernity from a series of eccentric viewpoints.

The serious import of these writings is most easily appreciated, then, by connecting them with those major figures in the development of modern thought who most clearly announced the break between the modern age and everything which lay in the past, and, even more clearly, in terms of the way in which the distinction between 'reality' and 'appearance' came to be understood by them as a conditioning limitation on the experience of 'selfhood'. This can be indicated briefly in relation to views originating with Rousseau and Kant who, themselves located on the edge of the Enlightenment tradition, inspire both the Romantic movement, and the development of German Idealism which together form such an important point of departure for Kierkegaard's most 'serious' works.

THE MASK OF MODERN SELFHOOD

Modern secular psychology, whether as materialist metaphysics or as utilitarian social thought, could not, any more than could the formalism of the natural sciences, reach its proper object. The 'self' eluded the grasp of ego psychology, just as 'nature' continued to evade its mastery by physics. Neither failure was taken seriously. The overwhelming tendency of the 'moral sciences', as of the 'natural sciences', in the century after the publication of Pascal's fundamental insights was a determined commitment to empiricism. At the same time, however, a 'secular theology' of nature and of the self developed, utilizing new scientific language to point to an ineffable 'spirit' as the inner truth of their design.[24]

Secular critics of utilitarianism in ethics and of sensationalism in psychology, while remaining anticlerical, sought a deeper level of reality to account for the otherwise fortuitous coherence of experience. Rousseau, as one of the most unrelenting of eighteenth-century critics of rationalism, and, like Pascal, impatient of all pious, moralizing and sentimental religiosity, provides perhaps the most comprehensive secular equivalent to the new religious psychology of melancholy. In doing so he dwells on the modern experience of the self, and throws into sharp relief just those features of it which were central to Pascal's religious reflections. They were also to become of crucial significance for Kierkegaard.

Rousseau begins his analysis of personal experience in modern society with what is for him the glaring discrepancy between conventional morality and the actual conduct of everyday life. 'We no longer dare seem what we really are', he complains.[25] Everyone appears in society as if performing on a stage, and, thus 'we never know with whom we are to deal', and as a result there is no certain means of divining other people's intentions or feelings.[26] The heart, heavy with melancholy, remains locked up in itself. We become painfully conscious that 'Jealousy, suspicion, fear, coldness, reserve, hatred, and fraud lie constantly concealed under the uniform and deceitful veil of politeness.'[27] The superficial world of appearances, which ought to depend upon and grow naturally out of a deeper and more rational ordering of social relations, had somehow 'escaped' from the supporting medium of these relations to form an illusory realm of its own. And it is the very work of enlightenment that has produced this 'veil of politeness'. The 'boasted candour and urbanity, for which we are indebted to the enlightened spirit of this age' is nothing but a conventional mask, a kind of secular piety emptied of all human content.[28]

It was the 'scandal of deceit' that was Rousseau's initial target. He wished to free himself from all those conventions of social discourse which had become separated from, and thus obscured, the inward truth of human existence. For a genuine secular morality, as well as for any modern religious sensibility, the duty to unmask and unveil, to strip the world of appearances and of its claims to autonomy, was an urgent task. It was a duty that required, first and foremost, that the writer unveil himself. In writing about himself, therefore, and even more in living, or trying to live, in conformity with the image of himself portrayed in his writings, Rousseau became the first Romantic hero of the bourgeois psyche. In attempting to bring into the open the hidden and secret parts of himself Rousseau was acting with fearless honesty. His fault, which was in turn to ruin every 'serious' individual within the bourgeois world, was integrity. He tried to become that very person he believed he ought to be; the sovereign individual proclaimed as the universal phenomenon of bourgeois society. But, in fact, bourgeois society preferred its individuals to be images of each other rather than expressions of a unique inner selfhood.

Rousseau, thus, complains bitterly of public opinion and the hold it has over people's conceptions of themselves and of their conduct. He rejects all complacent, half-hearted and hypocritical restraint, and 'sought to break the shackles of opinion and to *do* with courage what seemed to me good, without giving the slightest thought to the judgment of others'.[29]

Solitude, in the sense of inner autonomy if not actual isolation, is, for the modern world, the most basic of all ethical demands; it is the insistence on 'being free and virtuous, superior to fortune and man's opinion, and independent of all circumstances'.[30] We should disregard the opinion of others, even when (especially when) it seems to coincide with our own immediate inclinations. We must be wary, above all, of virtue. Where Montaigne and Burton had condemned an over-zealous conscience as a cause of melancholy, Rousseau goes further, and neatly subverting Puritan ethics boldly declares that 'conscience is the vice of the soul'.[31]

To pierce the veil of conventional morality it is necessary only to recollect the history of the self, to observe the 'train of secret emotions' which formed the soul into the condition in which it now finds itself. Rousseau's *Confessions* is the first genuinely modern autobiographical work; in it the journey towards self-knowledge becomes identical with the narrative of his inner life. He traces the path through which he himself emerges and becomes real, but the recounting of this story, with its wealth of circumstantial detail, ought not to obscure for its reader the genuinely creative act of recollection which precedes and accompanies it.

As if following an unbroken sequence of effects to their efficient causes, he allows his recollection to recede to its most distant point. There he finds an innocent primal world, a paradise of original experience unclouded by the deceit of society.[32] The unrestrained inner freedom of this world, its magical intersubjective unity, and its 'transparency' to thought affected him deeply. Our entire later life, spent in false and wasteful diversion, is nothing more than a series of failed attempts to recover this lost paradise. The real object of the search instituted in the disclosure of the disparity between appearance and reality is the enraptured primal world. 'True joy defies description', but as the intuition of happiness primal innocence is lodged in our heart and continues to exercise a teleological fascination over all our recollection, and is the real transcending goal of the ego's hectic and misdirected adventures.[33]

Rousseau, thus, absorbs the religious mythology of the Fall into his own biographical history and gives it a purely personal significance. At the origin of his moral history stands the recollection of injustice. He had been falsely accused of breaking a comb. His protestations of innocence were to no avail, he was not believed. Worse than that, as according to an adult assessment of the 'evidence' he was guilty, accusations of lying followed and his reluctance to 'confess' was treated as more reprehensible than the original offence. The transparent world of childhood, in which the inner truth of the heart is directly communicable, became clouded with adult 'rational', expectations.[34] Thereafter Rousseau found himself drawn into a web of deceit. The Fall is reinterpreted as a defensive retreat out of nature. It is experienced primarily in the birth of pride, and the growing power of reflection and self-deception. Thereafter actions become self-regarding in the narrow sense of supporting the pride which feeds upon the expectations and approbation of others. 'Selfishness perverts innocent love of self (*amour de soi-même* as opposed to *amour-propre*), vice is born, and society takes shape.'[35]

It is subordination to appearances (society) which created within him a host of artificial desires:

> For his own advantage he had to make himself appear other than he really was. Appearance and reality became two entirely different things, and from this distinction arose insolent ostentation, deceitful cunning, and all the vices that follow in their train.[36]

It is this distinction, and the subsequent growth of pride that 'explains not only the inner division of civilized man but also his subjugation to limitless desires'.[37] The endless renewal of want is a social artifice which has no counterpart in nature: 'Desire is not a physical need; it is not true that it is a need at all.'[38]

Rousseau espouses the immediacy of the primal world against the mediation (reflection and desire) of society. To inculcate its value in others he withdrew from society to lead a life of exemplary solitude. As society was the negation of authentic selfhood, Jean-Jacques freely abandoned society in order to reclaim the primal world which took precedence over it. He 'made himself a stranger to men in order to protest against the alienation that makes men strangers to one another – a paradox for which he is still criticized'.[39] But it was only after he had freed himself from the 'mournful train' of social passions that he was able to rediscover nature 'in all her charm'.

All that remains of the primal world is the intuition of happiness that lies in the bewildering melancholy of restless passions, a vague unease that is the consciousness of its loss, and the unconscious longing for its return.

> Everything is in constant flux on the earth. Nothing keeps the same unchanging shape, and our affections, being attached to things outside us, necessarily change and pass away as they do. . . . Thus our earthly joys are almost without exception the creatures of the moment. . . . And how can we give the name of happiness to a fleeting state which leaves our hearts still empty and anxious, either regretting something that is past or desiring something that is yet to come.[40]

What in fact we seek in each fleeting pleasure is that deeper and unchanging state of happiness that remains within us as a faint recollection of our first, uncorrupted, experience of the world. For Rousseau there is no original sin, and happiness is consequently a humanly attainable goal. This goal is obstructed by the way we live. While he lived in society 'my entire being was in things that were foreign to me, and in the continual agitation of my heart I felt all the instability of human life'.[41] But in his retreat from society, on the Island of Saint-Pierre, undisturbed by the spectacle of society, he could find

> a state where the soul can find a resting-place secure enough to establish itself and concentrate its entire being there . . . where time is nothing to it . . . and no other feeling of deprivation or enjoyment, pleasure or pain, desire or fear than the simple feeling of existence, a feeling that fills our soul entirely.[42]

In his solitary 'reveries' (literally also 'ravings'), he felt himself to be 'full' of being, 'self-sufficient like God', his heart finally at peace, 'its calm untroubled by any passion'.[43]

'Salvation', that is to say, depends neither upon theological reflection nor conventional virtue, both of which belong to the estranged world of society, but rests simply upon 'giving way' to the prompting of the heart. This is, in fact, more difficult to accomplish than obedience to the strictest rule for life. Everything tends to obstruct such self-surrender. The heart, once joined to the ceaseless flow of secular passions, is never known directly. In patient solitude and reverie, however, the ego is gradually divested of its spurious affections. He claims, thus, that while rigorous conceptual thinking, which is a fully socialized activity, 'has always been for me a disagreeable and thankless occupation', in reveries 'my soul roams and soars through the universe on wings of imagination, in ecstasies which surpass all other pleasures'.[44] In this state of 'blissful self-abandonment' the individual 'loses himself in the intensity of the beautiful order, with which he feels himself at one'.[45] The contemplation of nature's primordial simplicity is really a merging with and participation in its unity in which 'all individual objects escape him; he sees and feels nothing but the unity of all things', and is quite distinct from any deliberative act of conceptualization, which separates and divides consciousness from the world.[46] In blissful indifference 'my ideas are hardly more than sensations, and my understanding cannot transcend the objects which form my surroundings'.[47]

The exemplary solitude of Christ is, for Rousseau, a decisive argument against all theological sophistry. Christ's words are one with his entire being which directly affects the heart, and Christ's presence, unlike the dogmatic works of his modern philosophical 'followers', is effortlessly illuminating. 'The essence of Christianity', he claims, 'lies in the preaching of a truth that is *immediate.*'[48]

THE CONSEQUENCES OF COPERNICANISM

Modernity is a form, or forms, of consciousness inherent in the transformation of society, out of the Christian feudal west and towards the liberated world of a civil society apparently bound together by bonds of mutual self-interest. That such a view is itself 'superficial' does not mean that it is not an accurate characterization of the experience of modernity. Whatever else might be invoked as a 'necessary being' underlying the coherence of modern society as its precondition must remain a theoretical reconstruction of an unconscious mechanism. In terms of 'immediacy' the modern world remains centred on the ego as its undeniably 'given' reality. Indeed, it is the experience of the world from the perspective of the ego which is in fact superficial that fuelled the Romantic longing for self-transcendence, and was the foundation for new aesthetic as well as new religious movements through which the 'deeper' or 'higher' reality of being could, in some fashion, enter consciousness as a direct experience.[49]

A gulf was opened between the experience of the self as an ego, and the world of 'objects' which the ego could disclose to the inner world of experience exclusively as 'pictures' of a reality from which it had itself become detached. The soul no longer penetrated the world of nature, as it had within the medieval cosmos, but stood apart as a spectator. And it is just the suspicion that such a separation has occurred that provoked new understandings of melancholy and irony in terms of a uniquely modern encounter between the isolated self and the incomprehensible otherness of the rest of creation. The one was rationalized as a form of mourning over the loss of an original and fuller experience of creation, while the other was glorified as a seemingly divine capacity for detachment consequent upon this loss.

A self-sufficient domain of subjectivity confronted a world of equally self-sufficient objectivity. The relation between the two remained incomprehensible. But the consequences of Copernicanism went further than that.[50] Kant's revolution in philosophy brought into focus many of the central difficulties in reflecting upon the emergence of modernity.[51] What proved to be most significant, for those who followed him and more directly influenced Kierkegaard, can be briefly summarized.

Rather than clearing the way for a new understanding, and a new form, of religious faith established from the ruins of Hume's attacks, Kant's *Critique of Pure Reason* was often taken to be an affirmative 'Concluding Postscript' to modern scepticism. The fundamental insight, that all human knowledge was confined to a 'sphere' of representation from which the 'thing in itself' had been banished, was taken as an authoritative point of departure for a restrained view of philosophical reflection as a 'theory of knowledge', or, more generally, a 'theory of representation'. Inasmuch as religion was characterized as a species of 'belief' or a form of 'knowledge' (which Kant had refused to do) this had the effect of undermining the certainty with which such beliefs were held as 'faith'.

In the present context, however, the more important implication of Kant's philosophy centred on the possibilities of 'self-knowledge'. The self is hidden from the ego, and remains as unknown to it as does the rest of creation. Knowledge of ourselves is no more perfect than our knowledge of the world. The subject is partitioned, so to speak, between the immediacy of the ego and the 'secret springs of action' without which the ego could not make its appearance. It is this division which makes all knowledge of the self precarious, and leaves us open to self-deception, vanity and flattery:

> We like then to flatter ourselves by falsely taking credit for a more noble motive; whereas in fact we can never, even by the strictest examination, get completely behind the secret springs of action; since when the question is of moral worth, it is not with the actions which we see that we are concerned, but with those inward principles of them which we do not see.[52]

And, again, although Kant's intention was to establish from this insight the autonomy of practical reason and its moral sense, it was often borrowed in support of either revolutionary libertarianism, or conservative authoritarianism.[53] In either event social life became the continuous interplay of appearances, floating, so to speak, on the surface of reality, or rather the surface which was actuality.

> Even as to himself, a man cannot pretend to know what he is in himself from the knowledge he has by internal sensation. . . . For as he does not come by the conception of himself *a priori* but empirically, it naturally follows that he can obtain his knowledge of himself only by the inner sense, and consequently only through the appearance of his nature and the way in which his consciousness is affected.[54]

As a social being an individual became self-aware exclusively as a 'subject made of mere appearances'. The immediate unity of the self, thus, if it exists at all cannot be conceptualized. Kant, in attempting none the less to grasp the inner reality of selfhood, is driven to a near paradoxical formulation. 'Beneath' the incoherence of appearances the self is constituted as an act of will, directed by the autonomy of freely chosen but non-arbitrary moral principles.[55] This, in effect, only emphasizes the surface of selfhood, its shape rather than its depth or inner structure. In a somewhat different way in exercising aesthetic judgements, the individual gave expression, in matters of taste, to the social character of selfhood and thus to the conspiracy of appearances, but in confronting the melancholic distance of the sublime, the ego experiences itself as an empty vessel, or as a mirror into which it reflects an infinite, and thus invisible, depth.

The ego is a surface aware of itself as a dividing line or boundary between two qualitatively different 'spheres'. But as it is an infinity which, so to speak, extends in either direction, outwards and inwards, it can experience itself only as a surface, a surface which, trying to close on itself, hopes to exclude from itself the entire cosmos of extended matter, bound to it through necessary laws, and include within itself the infinite freedom of subjectivity. Neither is conceivable. The 'depth' and 'weight' of melancholy, the infinitude of irony, are alternative expressions which throw into sharper relief, therefore, the literally superficial character of modern life.

Kant describes this superficiality (which is itself a consequence of an unlimited and therefore inconceivable depth) as boredom. Boredom is '*disgust* with our own existence', a melancholic condition in which 'we also feel weighed down by inertia'.[56] And more particularly boredom is *emptiness*, a kind of inner subjective equivalent of the infinite extension of space: 'For boredom means that a man who is used to changing sensations sees a void of sensations in himself, and strains his vital force to fill it up with something or other.'[57]

This 'oppressive, even frightening burden' is not simply the tedium in which 'nothing happens', but is associated, rather, with an ever changing present, with a flux of appearances, that seem unconnected to any inner experience of 'depth'. As life is contained on a depthless filament, is itself just a surface, its ever changing physiognomy cannot be interpreted as an expression of some 'deep' process. Kant feels an acute revulsion against this loss of depth, and thus of meaning, and mounts through his critical philosophy a heroic effort to retrieve for consciousness some link with a structured inner world. But every effort fails, and serves only to disclose the powerlessness of thought to penetrate beneath the surface which has closed off from itself either the sublime indifference of the object, or the authentic inwardness of the subject. For Kant the problem of thought is that it remains too closely bound to life's surface, it can never really detach itself from everyday conventions and overcome the remoteness of the object or the subject.

The self, laminated upon itself, for ever reflecting itself, and others in itself, and itself in others, cannot escape the boredom of the modern age and is reduced to the experience of meaningless duration. And though 'we equate anything that shortens time with enjoyment' each distraction serves only to make more evident the void which presses in upon us from either 'side'. 'The void of sensations we perceive in ourselves arouses horror (*horror vacui*) and, as it were, the presentiment of a slow death, which we find more painful than having fate cut the thread of life quickly.'[58]

REFLECTIONS OF THE PRESENT

In 1846, having completed a major work whose title *Concluding Unscientific Postscript* hinted that it was to be his last, Kierkegaard wrote a long review of a novel, *Two Ages*, that he wrongly believed to have been written by J.L. Heiberg, Denmark's leading literary critic and aesthetician. This wonderfully ironic deception (it was in fact written by Heiberg's mother Thomasine Gyllembourg-Ehrensvard, and Heiberg's claim to having been involved in a limited editorial capacity was perfectly accurate) provided Kierkegaard with the occasion to renew his authorship under the pretence of writing reviews rather than books.[59]

It also provided Kierkegaard with an opportunity to renew, through the medium of literary criticism, the more general analysis of modern culture which he had begun in his student days. The interval between *From the Papers of One Still Living* (1838) and *Two Ages* (1846) is marked not only by a significant intellectual maturation but, even more significantly, by a completely different conception of his task as a writer. The earlier work deals primarily with Hans Andersen as a novelist, an activity for which Kierkegaard believed he (Andersen) had no real vocation. Kierkegaard argued that Andersen, in attempting to write novels, or at least the novel *Only a Fiddler* which is considered in some detail, could not really develop himself as a person and his work consequently lacked inner coherence. His writing is episodic, and depends upon the gratuitous creation of a variety of incidental poetic moods which lack inner connection with each other, with the characters in his stories, or with any deeper 'life-view' which the author might, and indeed should, wish to express.[60] This 'inner emptiness under motley pictures' becomes in *Two Ages* the general characteristic of modern culture as such. In Thomasine Gyllembourg's short novel, and even more clearly in her earlier, longer and better-known work *A Story of Everyday Life*, Kierkegaard finds reflected the characteristic formlessness of contemporary life. The lack of a coherent 'worldview' is no longer seen as evidence of the artistic short-comings of the author, but is viewed rather as itself a sign of novelistic genius in portraying the real conditions of life.

His review turns into a general comparison between the contrasting cultures of an 'Age of Revolution', which 'is essentially passionate, and therefore it essentially has *form*',[61] and of the 'Present Age', which 'is essentially a *sensible, reflecting age*'.[62] There is, in fact, nothing particularly historical in this contrast. He refers to no particular period as an 'Age of Revolution', and when, two years later, Denmark's belated bourgeois revolution did take place he did not feel compelled to alter his judgement of the tendencies of the Present Age. The European-wide social upheavals of 1848, indeed, were typical of the age which contained, rather than was transformed, by them: 'flaring up in superficial short-lived enthusiasms and prudentially relaxing in indolence'.[63]

The 'Present Age' has become an age of publicity, in which nothing real happens. An age of ceaseless chatter and exhibitionism in which members of the public are caught up in perpetually renewed and quite meaningless anticipation of events which never actually occur. In terms reminiscent of his celebrated contemporary Alexis de Tocqueville he draws attention to the *levelling* tendencies of the Present Age.[64] It is, above all, an age of *abstraction* in which medium the 'single individual' cannot live; he 'has not fomented enough passion in himself to tear himself out of the web of reflection and the seductive ambiguity of reflection'.[65] It is clear from Kierkegaard's admittedly rather general discussion that he conceives his ideal 'single individual' as in some way 'defined' through passion:

> So also in the world of individuals. If the essential passion is taken away, the one motivation, and everything becomes meaningless externality, devoid of character, then the spring of ideality stops flowing and life together becomes stagnant water – this is crudeness.
>
> (*Two Ages*, p. 62)

It is equally clear that his notion of 'passion' is quite distinct from either the British empiricist, or the continental metaphysical, traditions in psychology. Where, for the former, passion was viewed almost exclusively as a disturbing element within a rationally conceived and intentional ego, and for the latter passion was conceived in terms of an 'absence' within the ego – and thus as a stimulating desire to possess something that would 'complete' and thus express the self – Kierkegaard regards passion as the multiplicity of differences which give structure and form to human experience. But in the Present Age, we might say, nothing makes a difference. No distinctions can withstand the dissolving tendencies of abstraction. The inner tension and 'colour' are drained from individual experience and, therefore, from social relations:

> The coiled springs of life-relationships, which are what they are
> only because of qualitatively distinguishing passion, lose their
> resilience; the qualitative expression of difference between
> opposites is no longer the law for the relation of inwardness to
> each other in the relation. Inwardness is lacking, and to that
> extent the relation does not exist or the relation is an inert
> cohesion.
>
> (*Two Ages*, p. 78)

The citizen of the Present Age 'does not relate himself in the
relation but is a spectator'. Everything in consequence is trivialized:
'Not even a suicide these days does away with himself in desperation
but deliberates on this step so long and so sensibly that he is
strangled by calculation.'[66] Where a passionate age is united
through 'enthusiasm', '*envy* becomes the *negatively unifying principle*
in a passionless and very reflective age'.[67] Envy, indeed, is a novel
and ingenious means of preserving order: 'Reflection's envy holds
the will and energy in a kind of captivity.' But in 'holding the
individual and the age in a prison', reflective envy is a
self-suppression which has no need of tyrants and secret police, nor
the clergy and aristocracy.[68]

The Present Age annuls passion and the contradictions essential
to passion. It is preoccupied with 'chatter', which is the annulled
passionate distinction between being silent and speaking. Where
silence and speaking are linked in their essential relation to the
person 'chattering gets ahead of essential speaking' and merely
'reflects' inconsequential events; it is nothing but 'the caricaturing
externalization of inwardness'.[69] And as 'loquacity' the modern
thinker, in hastily announcing a new philosophy, too easily elides
the distinction between subjectivity and objectivity. By the same
token it is an age of 'principle', annulling the distinction between
form and content in a high-minded insistence on acting ethically.
But 'one can do anything and everything on principle', because the
principle lies outside the person, who may 'personally be a
non-human nonentity'.[70] It is specifically an age of 'superficiality',
which, as the annulled passionate distinction between hiddenness
and revelation, is 'a revelation of emptiness'. This superficiality
manifests itself most clearly in an 'exhibitionist tendency' which is
caught up in 'the self-infatuation of the conceit of reflection'.[71] The
extensive and ever-changing surface of modern life is nothing but a
kaleidoscope of reflections:

And eventually human speech will become just like the public: pure abstraction – there will no longer be anyone who speaks, but objective reflection will gradually deposit a kind of atmosphere, an abstract noise that will render human speech superfluous, just as machines make workers superfluous.

(*Two Ages*, p. 104)

Also in 1846 Kierkegaard worked on a much larger project addressed to 'the confusion of the Present Age'. Unpublished in his own lifetime, 'The Book on Adler', as he referred to the manuscript, develops his distinctive understanding of the 'superficiality' of modern bourgeois culture as an aspect of passionless 'reflection'.[72] Adler was a young country minister (a role Kierkegaard struggled, but failed, to accept for himself) who prefaced a book of sermons he published in 1843 with the claim that they had been directly inspired by a revelation. Kierkegaard views Adler as a phenomenon of the age: loquacious and deluded, he has mistaken the arcane abstractness of Hegelian dialectics for a vision of the absolute.

The ceaseless and pointless movement of the present is exemplified in Adler's wild flights of fancy. In becoming an author Adler makes use of the very 'sickness of our age'; he lives in and through arbitrary 'premises', which he can turn into books which are 'precisely what the age demands'.[73] An age of 'reflection and intelligence' is all too easily duped by such 'premise-authors' who lack real inner consistency and seek to create a big effect on the basis of appearing to be clever. And as every truth can exist only as a reflection on the surface of life, becoming an image or shadow drained of passion and essential qualities, it is understandable that 'nowadays one takes for a revelation any sort of strong impression'.[74] If the essential difference between revelation and madness has been abolished, then, for the Present Age, no differences are essential, and everything becomes 'characterless'.[75] Thus 'triumphant argumentation' is able to transform 'eternal truth into a hypothesis'.[76] As 'a transparent medium for seeing the confusion of our age', Adler serves as a warning sign, an anticipation of the consequences of living superficially. He has become too responsive to the age, buoyant on its volatile and chaotic turbulence, and as a result has lost touch with actuality. But Adler's madness is the lunacy of the age, which is reflected in him with fearful clarity.

The Present Age has no 'depth'. From *Two Ages* to 'The Book on Adler' Kierkegaard traces a series of connections linking together apparently isolated aspects of modern culture as equivalent 'reflections' on the surface of life. And through the medium of 'reflection' the most disparate of human contents, from the conventions of everyday behaviour to the latest philosophical craze, are reduced to a characterless flux of essentially identical elements. Once 'flattened' into a thin surface, a boundary between the infinites of object and subject, actuality is all too readily pierced. Living images are not reflected back into existence, filling it out so to speak with a real content, but drain themselves into fantastic and empty concepts, and, like water on a hot surface, are 'volatilized' out of existence.

Many of these remarks now seem astonishingly prescient and make yet more remarkable the enigma of Kierkegaard's authorship, one of the least likely places, perhaps, in which to have discovered a premature critique of the 'condition of postmodernism'.[77]

Part II

Despair: critical perspectives on modern society

My pseudonymity or polyonymity has not had an *accidental* basis in my *person* . . . but an *essential* basis in the *production* itself. . . . Thus in the pseudonymous books there is not a single word by me.

Søren Kierkegaard, 'A First and Last Explanation'
appended to *Postscript*

Poetry is not the imitation of a reality which already exists prior to it; nor is it the adornment of truths or spiritual meanings which could have been expressed independently. The aesthetic capacity is a creative power for the production of a meaning that transcends reality and that could never be found in abstract thought. Indeed, it is a way or mode of viewing the world.

Wilhelm Dilthey, *Poetry and Experience*

Chapter 4

Revolution of the spheres: a topological fantasy

> Sceptical self-consciousness . . . is in fact nothing but a purely casual, confused medley, the dizziness of a perpetually self-engendered disorder. It is itself aware of this; for itself maintains and creates this restless confusion.
>
> G.W.F. Hegel, *The Phenomenology of Spirit*

The authorship proper begins with a 'topological' analysis of the characteristic forms of personal experience in modern society. Its starting point, that is to say, is with aspects of the Present Age rather than with the pretension of an 'unthematized' or 'universal' human nature. It might be suspected that such an apparently modest descriptive programme would amount to little more than an apologetics of 'bourgeois-philistinism'. But Kierkegaard's intention is explicitly critical. Without departing from the 'surface' of modern life, or rather from the surface that is modern life, he outlines the possibilities for unified and coherent personal experience immanent within its chaotic appearance.

In several senses this approach is 'aesthetic'. Firstly, many of these works bear the unmistakable mark of a highly developed literary art. To appreciate the distinctive features of life's current possibilities, each must be recreated as a fully embodied character into whose life-view the reader can enter imaginatively in a way that would be impossible in relation to any purely conceptual representation. To this end Kierkegaard indulged a prodigious literary talent, inventing a whole series of 'young men' and a coterie of their somewhat older companions. The deliberate evocation of a literary work, rather than a philosophical or theological treatise, served a double purpose. It created an 'aesthetic distance' between the 'real' author, Søren Kierkegaard, and the many books he issued under a variety of pseudonyms. This was, in fact, implied in his initial conviction that 'life-views' could be articulated only through the 'medium' of personal existence. Thus, even if there were only one such view Kierkegaard could not directly express its 'inner nature', as, in conveying its fullness he would, in effect, rather as Marcel Proust was to do in relation to his own Narrator, recreate, and thus in an important sense misrepresent, himself as a fiction. And, as he believed there were several such 'possibilities' he could not even claim to be the author of each of its personae without appearing to be insincere. None, in fact, expressed Kierkegaard's own 'position', and his aesthetic 'method' aimed above all at representing the independence and internal completeness of each of his 'characters'. Significantly it was just this distance and independence which made each character accessible to the reader. In spite of the welter of pseudonyms, however, and Kierkegaard's insistence that 'in the pseudonymous books there is not a single word by me' the aesthetic works are most frequently read, or rather misread, 'as if ' they were directly written by him and, thus, express positions which at one time or another were his own.[1]

Secondly, for modern life, in which all 'depth' and 'distance' had been infinitized, religious thought, which previously had been connected with a structural model of both *cosmos* and *psyche*, lost its inner coherence as an immediately graspable picture or narrative. If religion still dealt with the mysteries of the universe and of the human soul, it could do so only by proclaiming the incomprehensibility of both. And as it was Reason which had dissolved this structural model, it was itself powerless to reconstruct a meaningful totality from the fragments into which it had cast reality. By the close of the eighteenth century art alone seemed capable of offering to the bewildered observer of modern life a form-giving structure into which its chaotic but finite content could be poured. Art, as Schiller, Lessing and the Romantics insisted, provided a new mode of unification for modern experience. The aesthetic provided, in this sense, an 'immediate' unity through which life could be grasped and shaped. Kierkegaard's 'aesthetics' is an extended ironic comment on this premature optimism.

Thirdly, Kierkegaard's reconstructions might be viewed as an aesthetic 'critique' of actuality, as well as a criticism of (illusory) aesthetics. In a Kantian sense the pseudonyms might be viewed as the living 'categories' through which experience, in the sense of consistent life-views, becomes possible. These possibilities, or 'spheres', represent the most far-reaching implications of the

'Copernican Revolution'; they are forms dignified by self-adhering 'gravity' and their own inner movement of 'self-actualization'. They are part of actuality, while at the same time being the 'ground' upon which actuality is based. As the pseudonyms multiply the reader becomes more acutely conscious that actuality may be constituted in a number of mutually exclusive ways. The pseudonyms, by establishing their own life-view as possible forms of existence in modern life, generate powerful relativizing tendencies which expose, more clearly than could any transcendental critique, the entirely conventional character of both modern society and the forms of personal experience it harboured.

The 'aesthetic' works present a 'topology' of modern life-forms. This is not a description of the whole of actuality, but an exploration of the variety of consistent modes of being which can be found, chaotically intermingled, within it. The aesthetic writers present a series of 'stages' or 'spheres' of existence in which the promiscuous disorder of the Present Age is painstakingly recombined in a number of different ways. Each represents, thus, a pure form, an example of personal existence consistently developed from a simple underlying principle. The relation among the pseudonyms almost irresistibly suggests spatial divisions of some sort; hence 'spheres' or 'stages'. But in an important sense this is misleading. Each, in fact, exhausts actuality in its own particular way. They do not coexist by dividing up, so to speak, the 'space' of human experience, each claiming for itself a specific territory. One might imagine, rather than a juxtaposition in space, a succession in time. The 'surface' of modern life might then be represented as the limited number of 'states', each characterized by its specific tension, into which its primitive material can be formed.

There is, indeed, a significant sense in which simply by resorting to the deception of their own authorship, the pseudonyms produce only aesthetic works. Their carefully contrived subterfuge places an awkward question mark over the interpretation of many of the works. Thus, to cite only one of the most obvious difficulties, among the best known of Kierkegaardian themes is the qualitative differentiation of 'aesthetic', 'ethical' and 'religious' spheres or stages in human existence. Yet, as usually presented, and in terms of the most frequently cited texts illustrating such distinctions, each ought more properly to be regarded as 'aesthetic' categories. The 'ethical' and the 'religious' viewed from an 'aesthetic' standpoint – and their characterization in terms of pseudonyms is such a standpoint – may turn out to be rather different from the 'ethical' or 'religious' view of the same distinction, if such a distinction even exists for an authentically 'ethical' or 'religious' view.

The topological perspective, that is to say, is essentially 'aesthetic', however many 'non-aesthetic' 'stages' or 'spheres' are introduced to complicate the picture. And as a result it contains both less and more than is usually included in expositions of the 'Kierkegaardian' theory of the 'stages':[2] less in that it contains only different versions of the aesthetic, and more in according to the aesthetic a more positive and flexible role in the formation of self-identity than most commentators have cared to admit.

THE AESTHETIC

The starting point for Kierkegaard's exploration of modern culture is through a description of the 'aesthetic' *sphere* or *stage* of existence, as a developed position in contrast to either a primordial preconceptual unity, or a purely empirical description of the chaotic present. The point of departure for the authorship proper is to be found, therefore, in the melancholia and refined sensitivity of the 'young man' who is the purported author of *Either*.

Kierkegaard, indeed, begins with the most sophisticated and advanced of positions within modern culture. And in exchanging a singular philosophical starting point for systematic reflection for a multiplicity of actual subjects Kierkegaard was forced to abandon the framework of *The Concept of Irony*. *Either* deals with what he terms 'immediacy', but what is 'immediate' to the young man cannot be the same as it was for either Socrates or an average member of the crowd. It is neither singular nor unchanging; however much it intrudes into our experience as something external, natural and changeless 'immediacy' has a long and tortured history.

What is equally clear is that the 'immediate' is not a purely sensuous category. The aesthetic sphere is organized around the distinction between pleasure and unpleasure, but 'pleasure' is a complex of physical and psychic satisfactions which cannot be reduced to any merely organic imperative.

Kierkegaard's topography of modern existence begins, then, from an already developed position, from the immediate as melancholy.[3] The subject matter of *Either* is, in consequence, no hastily compiled stereotype whose purpose is to flatter the more mature life-view of *Or*, and initiate an insubstantial argument the outcome of which, from the very beginning, the reader could not doubt. Kierkegaard's method, and talent, are more subtle. He presents the 'aesthetic' sphere of existence in its most attractive, refined and alluring form. Through the somewhat baffling diversity of its contents we glimpse the putative author of *Either*, a young man who is not only a highly gifted and sensitive person, but, in Kierkegaard's beautifully written pages, exercises a certain power of attraction, a fascination for and over any moderately sympathetic reader.

In *Either* the Romantic hero of Goethe, Tieck, Novalis, Hoffmann and countless lesser writers steps, fully formed, into the midst of contemporary life and tries to grasp it in all its disillusioned immediacy.[4] Kierkegaard refuses the temptation of beginning 'without presuppositions', because only 'speculation' and 'abstraction' (the characteristic features of the Present Age) begin with nothing.[5] The 'aesthetic' youth is no straw man seeking pleasure in the artificial decoration of reality, or the vain pursuit of some fantastic conception of 'the beautiful'. Aesthetic immediacy means quite the reverse and is grounded in an acceptance of the world as it is. Rather than distancing himself from the reality of life he is determined to find pleasure in its incomprehensible succession of appearances. The 'deeper' meaning of reality for the Romantic hero, therefore, does not lie in interpreting appearances through a network of profound ideas, so much as in discovering within it the private destiny of erotic love. This represents, for the modern world, the first possibility for the secular conquest of melancholy.

Either is made up of a number of seemingly separate essays, reviews, psychological excursions, aphorisms and fictions, varying greatly in length and style. This deliberate fragmentation, however (the entire work is subtitled 'A Fragment of Life'), does not obscure its central themes. From the isolated 'Diapsalmata' with which it opens, to the concluding (and immediately sensationalized) 'A Seducer's Diary', the interplay of melancholy and erotic love is plainly visible.

The opening aphorisms to *Either*, indeed, could almost be read as a brief and modernized 'anatomy' of melancholy. They convey a complete detachment from, and indifference to, the world. Momentarily interested in the inexplicable succession of his own inner states, he discovers a universal apathy in respect of them all.

> I don't feel like doing anything. I don't feel like riding – the
> motion is too powerful; I don't feel like walking – it is too tiring.
> I don't feel like lying down, for either I would have to stay down,
> and I don't feel like doing that, or I would have to get up again,
> and I don't feel like doing that, either. *Summa Summarum*: I don't
> feel like doing anything.
>
> (*Either*, p. 20)

Overcome by 'a strange, sad mood', he is at once indifferent to
everything and tormented by restlessness: 'How sterile my soul and
my mind are, and yet constantly tormented by empty voluptuous
and excruciating labor pains!' For him 'time stands still', and his
entire existence is a twilight state between sleeping and dreaming.
He is self-absorbed: 'My soul is so heavy that no thought can carry it
any longer', yet at the same time he feels his life, and himself, to be
'empty and meaningless'. Everything is 'dreadfully boring'; nothing
makes a difference. He is bound by a 'chain formed of gloomy
fancies, of alarming dreams, of troubled thoughts, of fearful
presentiments, of inexplicable anxieties', a chain that is 'soft as silk'.

The 'Fragment of Life' begins in the most fragmentary of ways,
with the simple juxtaposition of melancholic observations. Yet this
is not a Romantic work in the style of Friedrich Schlegel. Here the
'fragment' does not contain, either as a miniature copy or as a
condensed symbol, the entirety of the work.[6] The fragmentariness
of *Either*, and the particular arrangements of its parts, become more
comprehensible in the light of the long essay 'The Immediate
Stages of the Erotic or the Musical Erotic' which immediately
follows the melancholic 'Diapsalmata'. In a coherently argued and
systematically ordered argument the young man claims (in spite of
the admission, 'I am well aware that I do not understand music')[7] a
natural affinity between music and the sensuous-erotic. He insists,
in fact, that 'sensuousness in its elemental originality is the absolute
theme of music'.[8] This, given the author's romantic credentials,
might be seen as an extension of Lessing's aesthetics.[9] Mozart's *Don
Giovanni* he thinks, therefore, the most perfect of musical
compositions just because its content and form are perfectly suited
to each other: it is the immediate expression of sensuousness.
Through it sensuousness is, so to speak, directly communicated,
and in it music is revealed as sensuousness. Of course many other
things can be communicated musically, but the sensuous-erotic is
here revealed to be its 'absolute theme'.[10]

The young man's text, the book called *Either*, cannot aspire to this perfection, but it can imitate it, by adopting an analogically musical form of composition. The 'Diapsalmata' constitute a kind of overture to the main theme which is developed in his essay on Mozart, and transformed in a series of virtuoso variations before receiving its climactic restatement as 'A Seducer's Diary'. The separate fragments are thus linked without forming a whole, or developing towards any sense of completeness or totality. Of course it might well be argued that Mozart's musical structures are aesthetically valuable just because they do express such a totality. The central issue, however, is not Mozart's music, or even the reasonableness of the young man's aesthetic theory of Mozart's music, so much as the relevance of the latter to a reading of the 'young man's' text.[11] And the fragmented text is the appropriate form through which to represent an aesthetic existence; it aspires to a consistency of view and, to that extent, avoids the arbitrariness and merely fortuitous combination of elements we might imagine typical of an unreflective consciousness of the Present Age; at the same time it eschews the systematic interconnection of its parts according to some logical rule or principle.

The sensuous appears first as a 'still quiescence', marked 'not by delight and joy but by deep melancholy'.[12] And adopting at least the mask of the Romanticism the young man develops an appropriately idealist psychology of desire through which to describe the immanent development of sensuousness. In this initial stage desire is 'only a presentiment of itself', it lacks an object, or rather the relation between object and longing subject that is felt as desire has not yet been formed.[13] Desire is contained here in 'a quiet ever-present longing, absorbed in contemplation'.[14] It is just this contradiction that we feel as melancholy, as aimless and objectless longing, a self-absorbed restlessness. The young man is the very archetype of the Romantic youth, a second Werther.[15] But a second stage supervenes, apparently by some inner developmental necessity. Desire is then 'torn out of its substantial repose in itself', and loses itself in multiplicity. The second stage of the sensuous-erotic is thus seeking rather than dreaming, and is overtaken by a fully developed third stage of desiring proper, in which a specific object of longing is defined and possessed.

The elaboration of this trinity with its advanced Hegelian terminology is liable to mislead readers, who, forgetting the 'Diapsalmata', might think they have stumbled upon a psychological treatise. This is not, however, an abstract philosophical system, but, rather, an original application of Romantic psychological assumptions to an individual drawn with novelistic persuasiveness. The entire armoury of post-Kantian terms, therefore, must first be transferred back to the real world (from which they originated) if its limitations and deficiencies are to be revealed. And in the real world things never go smoothly. The dialectic is no sooner under way, therefore, than it is interrupted by extraneous and fortuitous lines of thought. The reader is, thus, abruptly thrust into a new chapter, a consideration of the tragic which is characteristically viewed from the vantage point of the young man's own melancholic isolation. Melancholy emerges, in fact, as a variety of suffering that lies between fate (ancient tragedy) and guilt (modern tragedy).

In retrospect it becomes clear that Don Juan, in fact, is no seducer. There is no element here, as there is so prominently in, for example, the fictions of Richardson or Laclos, of craftiness and unscrupulous planning.[16] His endless conquests are the effortless result of the primal force of which he is possessed: 'that by which he deceives is the sensuous in its elemental originality, of which he is, as it were, the incarnation'.[17] His spirit has not liberated itself, and he remains bound to the 'pure' spiritless sensuousness which is 'the most abstract idea conceivable'.[18] He remains, in being possessed by an uncontrollable 'frenzy', melancholic in the original Platonic sense. But, added to this, and fundamentally redefining its entire nature, is a new Christian determination of sensuousness and, therefore, of melancholy. It is in Christianity, according to the author, that sensuousness is first posited as a principle and, thus, brought to awareness as 'a specific realm of being'. He claims, paradoxically, that 'Christianity brought sensuality into the world', and at the same time it is Christianity that has 'driven sensuality out of the world'. By distinguishing spirit as a 'higher' mode of being, 'sensuality was placed under the qualification of spirit first by Christianity'.[19]

There is no suggestion here that Christianity is a universal 'cure' for melancholy. The young man of *Either* is a decidedly 'spiritual', if not a decisively Christian, being. He is no Don Juan, his melancholy is not the insistent tug of an unconscious creaturely instinct, but is itself 'qualified' as spirit. He is seduced by his own sorrow, and comes to love solitude. He speculates, for example, that:

Perhaps nothing ennobles a person so much as keeping a secret. It gives a person's whole life a significance, which it has, of course, only for himself; it saves a person from all futile consideration of the surrounding world.[20]

(*Either*, p. 157)

The connection between erotic love and the 'reflective sorrow' which is 'unceasingly reserved, silent, solitary, and seeks to return into itself' is taken up in the following section 'Silhouettes' which, reverting to a fragmented style, is described as a 'Psychological Diversion'. Here the young man uses his sorrow to illuminate 'the subtle interior picture' of 'unhappy love' which never shows itself directly on the faces of deceived lovers.[21] In Marie Beaumarchais, a character from a story of a broken engagement by Goethe, deception turns the 'incorruptible essence of a quiet spirit' into the 'barren busyness of a restless spirit'.[22] This is the reflective sorrow of inverted eroticism, an inner restlessness which is never betrayed in expressive movements but remains perpetually 'enclosed' and melancholic. The world, for her, becomes meaningless, remote, indifferent. Donna Elvira, one of Don Giovanni's innumerable conquests, is thrown by deception into an 'endless introspection' over his love. And Margaret, seduced by Faust, leaves us wondering if her secret sorrow might not be the instigator of a real deepening of her personality and inwardness. Faust (possibly) deceives her out of her bourgeois complacency. It is her innocence and childlike transparency that are irresistible to Faust, the master-doubter who has seen through existence to its very depths. His striving can rest momentarily in the erotic: 'what he is seeking, therefore, is not only the pleasure of the sensuous, but the immediacy of the spirit . . . whereby he will be rejuvenated and strengthened'.[23]

These ingenious, and insightful, psychological considerations might be regarded as an investigation into the aesthetics of deception, even as an aesthetic defence of deception. The root of Kierkegaard's own melancholy in 'dreaming sensuousness' and its possible consequences (for both Regine and himself of the deception through which he broke their engagement) lie fairly close to the surface of the text. The result, however, is inconclusive, less because Kierkegaard is unclear in his own mind (he had already formulated a more convincing defence of deception as the 'maieutic art'), than because the actual author, the young man, lives exclusively within aesthetic determinants.

Melancholy is a kind of inwardness, and can impart through its indifference to the world something that might be mistaken for a spiritual glow. What is in reality a reflective sorrow which, like a toothache, he cannot let alone seems to him more immediate than the entire world of actuality that stands opposed to it. He is consumed by his own melancholy, which colours his every relation. He remains 'locked up' within himself, an object of his own psychological curiosity. It is without self-pity, therefore, that he can discuss the 'Unhappiest One', which (writing as the young man) is a kind of self-portrait. 'The unhappy one is the person who is always absent from himself, never present to himself ', he writes, fascinated by his own fugitive nature.[24] If he is not present to himself where is he? How does he live? His own answer is that he exists either for the future, as hope, or for the past, as recollection. His relation to the normal 'flow' of events has been disturbed. He hopes (hopelessly) for what should be recollected, that is he imagines the past to be changed even when he knows this to be impossible; or he recollects what should really be hoped for. He 'lives', that is to say, either in the past or in the future, and finds in the present only boredom.

This analysis is continued in an essay on 'The Rotation of Crops' which represents a new level of aesthetic self-awareness and a fresh effort to throw off melancholy. The present is oddly elusive. Immediacy, which seemed the least demanding of realities, has somehow slipped through his fingers. Immediacy, in reality, is nothing but boredom, that is to say nothing at all. 'Boredom is the demonic pantheism', he proclaims and falls into the trap of arguing that 'it is annulled by amusing oneself '.[25] But the error is quickly rectified: 'amusement' is only another form of boredom in a world of hectic and meaningless activity: 'a mistaken, generally eccentric diversion has boredom within itself '.[26] He regards boredom, as had Pascal, as neither inactivity nor repetition of the same task, but meaninglessness. On this point it is worth quoting the young man's insight into his own condition at greater length:

> Boredom rests upon nothing that interlaces existence; its dizziness is infinite, like that which comes from looking down into a bottomless abyss. That the eccentric diversion sounds without resonance, simply because in nothing there is not even enough to make an echo possible.
>
> (*Either*, p. 291)

The vulgar notion of wrecking boredom 'upon the boundless infinity of change', where change is understood extensively as alterations in the external environment, is abandoned in favour of an aesthetic conception of variety, as a continuous internal modulation of the soul. This openness to variety depends upon mastering the art of forgetting, literally of forgetting who one is. One must 'continually vary oneself '.[27] He therefore advises against friendship, marriage and opening official post. And he is at least half-serious in doing so (as an aesthetic individual he resists becoming wholly serious). 'Arbitrariness is the whole secret', he says finally. In living aesthetically 'one enjoys something totally accidental'.[28] In this way 'everything in life is regarded as a wager'.[29] The young man holds himself in a continuous state of expectation, ready 'if something should come up'.

It is in this spirit of arbitrariness, and from a readiness (which in no way annuls his deep and secret melancholy) to utilize whatever 'turns up' in the quest to experience diverse moods, that he interrupts what might otherwise develop into a dangerously systematic psychology of sorrow with a review of *The First Love*, a play by Augustin Scribe. Though he devotes considerable space to a description of the comic character of this work, which in one sense balances and completes his essay on modern tragedy, its fortuitous inclusion in *Either* is emphasized by the excessively elaborate reconstruction of the 'occasion' of its writing which precedes the review proper. The young man makes of the occasion an opportunity to analyse the 'occasional' as such.[30] In addition to inspiration, he argues, the production of a work of art requires quite specific circumstances which are not artistically reflected in the work itself, but remain external and accidental to it. Every work of art represents in this sense a paradox in that 'the accidental is absolutely just as necessary as the necessary'.[31] Without the occasion inspiration remains a movement of the imagination alone: 'the occasion is the final category, the essential category of transition from the sphere of the idea to actuality'.[32]

An aesthetic conception of erotic love (and properly understood there can be no other valid conception of erotic love) accentuates the arbitrary, occasional and accidental. 'The Seducer's Diary' provides a 'running commentary' on a love affair conceived in just this fashion.[33] The fundamental preoccupation of the seducer is to realize his love as an 'interesting' moment. Victor Eremita, as the editor of these papers, understands this very well and alerts the reader to it in an introduction to the 'Diary'. This is neither a Don Juan nor a Faust, but a peculiarly modern seducer, for whom 'individuals were merely for stimulation'.[34] He grasps the specific nature of the aesthete:

> His life has been an attempt to accomplish the task of living poetically. With a sharply developed organ for discovering the interesting in life, he has known how to find it and after having found it has continually reproduced his experiences half poetically.
>
> (*Either*, p. 304)

Actuality is reflected in him poetically, so that he is never really present to the immediacy he had consecrated as his goal: 'he continually ran lightly over it, but even when he abandoned himself to it, he was beyond it'.[35] Conscience, which was only a kind of 'sterile restlessness' within him, was no obstacle to his quest for interesting love.

Yet it is love and not sensuous gratification which is his aim. And the search for love begins in the street, in chance encounters, in the anonymous mass of the public. His falling in love is an accidental occurrence, he simply waits for the 'sensuous jolt' to announce its decision. Thereafter he pursues the loved one with the utmost care and circumspection. He finds a way of being introduced, and approaches her with the greatest restraint, as an interesting companion, thus 'neutralizing her womanhood'. He encourages the infatuation of a younger admirer and, while her feelings are aroused and confused, engineers an engagement. This is, in terms of the constraints of bourgeois civility, an essential prelude to the seduction. There is, additionally, an aesthetic piquancy to an engagement which, for a time, he relishes:

> Under the aesthetic sky, everything is buoyant, beautiful, transient; when ethics arrives on the scene, everything becomes harsh, angular, infinitely *langweiligt* (boring). But in the strictest sense an engagement does not have ethical validity (*Realitet*) such as marriage has.
>
> (*Either*, p. 367)

His well-practised deception (he hints at previous affairs) is full of artful half-truths. He does, after all, love her, at least 'in the aesthetic sense, and surely this should mean something'.[36] Indeed he thinks he can succeed only because his love is real: 'She will believe me, partly because I rely on artistry, and partly because at the bottom of what I am doing there is truth.'[37]

The incommensurability of love and deception – which may have been at the heart of Kierkegaard's own failure to marry – is of no consequence to the genuine aestheticist. 'I am not afraid of contradicting myself ', he boasts 'if only she does not detect it and I achieve what I wish. Let it be the ambition of learned doctoral candidates to avoid every contradiction.' He is more realistic than the philosopher: 'a young girl's life is too abundant to have no contradictions and consequently makes contradictions inevitable.'[38]

In the 'Diapsalmata' which introduce *Either*, the author had boasted: 'My life is utterly meaningless'.[39] He wishes only to give way to his wishes, to live playfully, absorbed by the most insignificant as well as the most sublime life-elements, each 'to an equally high degree the momentary passion of the soul'.[40] But remaining melancholic, rather than being absorbed by nothing, nothing absorbs him. There is an internal development within *Either*, however, a movement expressed in the two Danish terms normally translated by the English term melancholy. The Diapsalmata and the initial 'dreaming' stage of the musical-erotic are filled with *Melancholi*, the obscure 'blackness' of the Greek medical and philosophical traditions, while the later stages, and more particularly the 'Diary of a Seducer', give way to the lucidity of *Tungsind*, the transparent 'heaviness' typical of modern life.[41]

THE ETHICAL

Or, which is apparently the work of an older friend of the young man, Judge William, consists of three letters written in response to *Either*. Two are extremely long and, their author admits, would amount to treatises if it were not for the more 'admonishing and urgent tone appropriate to the epistolary form' in which they are deliberately written. This formal stylistic matter is of some importance. The 'ethical' is described in response to the 'aesthetic', and as a complaint against it. The two halves of the argument (if argument it is) are not strictly equivalent. While the young man describes 'aesthetic' existence by acting as a kind of searchlight for its evanescent forms, catching first one and then another of its changing moods in the reflective brilliance of his own experience, Judge William does not similarly act as a sounding board of the 'ethical'. Judge William's own experience of life is relevant primarily as a point of reference, which is for the most part discreetly hidden from the reader, and from which he offers a comprehensive critique of *Either*.

Kierkegaard's mastery of these stylistic shifts allows the various 'collisions' within and between 'existence-spheres' to be explored with great sensitivity and depth. Judge William does not exist 'immediately' but within the universal categories of good and evil. And what is offered in *Or* is ostensibly an 'ethical' conception of the 'aesthetic' to place alongside the 'aesthetic' conception of itself.

Thus, although Judge William can understand in an intellectual sense the subject matter of *Either*, he cannot immediately enter into its content and he describes the young man's life, in fact, at the cost of transforming it. The assumption of a new point of view lends an entirely different colour to the 'young man's' aesthetic experiments. The aspiration towards playful innocence has gone. 'You love the accidental', he writes, quite accurately, but his words are an accusation, not an affirmation. He goes on at once to accuse his young friend of 'aimless fantasy' and 'a hypochondriacal inquisitiveness'.[42] He is intellectually 'loose jointed', a person whose 'life disintegrates into nothing but interesting details'.[43] This collector of beautiful moments is the 'epitome of every possibility'.[44] What is at issue here is clearly not a simple misunderstanding, but the incompatibility of two entirely different conceptions of life's central value. When Judge William describes the life-technique of *Either* as 'atomistically losing oneself in life's social hordes', the young man would no doubt applaud his critical acumen and, at the same time, lament the stuffiness of his implied criticism.[45]

Judge William, to show that the pleasure in love which the young man has so ardently, and vainly, sought within immediacy is only attainable when the immediate is itself ethically transformed, undertakes to demonstrate the 'aesthetic validity' of marriage. According to his older friend, the young man has refused, through his attachment to a wholly fantastic vision of romantic love, 'to let love transfigure itself in a higher sphere'.[46] And what makes his conception of romantic love so fantastical is its isolation from the ethical seriousness of life.

This does not mean, of course, that Judge William is defending a calculating or utilitarian conception of marriage, in which there has to be some 'reason' for marriage other than love itself. Far from it, his argument is just that marriage is a means of preserving the love which is its only foundation. 'Marital love' is, in one sense, no different from 'romantic love'; it 'feels' the same. 'In order to be aesthetic and religious', he argues, marriage 'must have no finite "why", but this was precisely the aesthetic in the first love'.[47] The difference is that in existing within ethical determinants, it is protected from the disintegrating moment in which the young man despairingly seeks its consummation. Marriage is an ethical form, the form best adapted, in fact, to the expression and preservation of erotic love. We can see Judge William's argument at this point as an ethical rejoinder to the young man's brilliant analysis of the 'musical erotic'. Just as Mozart's *Don Giovanni* – an opera about erotic love – is held to be an aesthetic triumph just because it perfectly integrates form and content, so marriage is an ethical value of the first order because it is the legitimate form within which eroticism can overcome the endlessly dying moment of its aesthetic existence.

Having asserted that the 'first love' is perpetuated in marriage, Judge William goes on to argue that it is, in fact, only within ethical determinants that the 'poetic' can be realized at all. Romantic love is illusory, it lacks any relation to time. Properly considered, the 'moment' is an endless transition which contains nothing. Thus 'romantic love continually remains abstract in itself . . . its eternity is illusory'.[48] Marital love, on the contrary, gains the solidity of 'an inner history', and in persisting, transforms immediacy into an eternal relation. It is not the institution of marriage which carries within it, so to speak, the scent of eternity; it is rather the spontaneous force of love, expressed in this relation, which transfigures existence in its entirety.

The genuinely aesthetic can only be experienced, therefore, within the ethical sphere, where it persists in a new way. This persistence, which the young man views as the most appalling boredom, is, from the standpoint of ethical existence, a continuing and ever-varied source of pleasure. From the aesthetic standpoint this inner life and variety remain invisible. 'Marital love does not come with external signs', and so, for the person who is 'outside himself', it seems to be a characterless and indifferent state of mutual toleration. And marriage is just one, though in the present context the most decisive, example of the impenetrability of the ethical life for anyone so wholly devoted to a purely aesthetic sensibility: 'You believe that only a restless spirit is alive. For you, a turbulent sea is a symbol of life; for me it is the quiet, deep water.'[49] Judge William would have us believe that while the young man is transparent to him, he, on the contrary, remains opaque to his younger friend.

In his second, even longer, letter, 'On the Balance Between the Aesthetic and the Ethical in the Development of the Personality', Judge William presents a more general analytic account of the difference between himself and the young man.

The protagonist of *Either* had expressed his life-view most generally in the 'Diapsalmata', and Judge William replies directly to the melancholic refrain: 'do it or do not do it, you will regret it'. Such a statement is, for him, so contradictory that he can only interpret it as an affectation. It could not have been intended seriously, because to be serious (by definition) is not to regard existence so lightly. Judge William believes he has outmanoeuvred his opponent, and takes his sardonic remarks as evidence that he does not really want to end 'with the disintegration of your essence in a multiplicity'.[50] There is about his young friend a hidden earnestness which he cannot wholly conceal in melancholy.

The 'young man' had reduced his life to a series of disconnected moments, and each moment appears to be an arbitrary choice from a more or less extended set of possibilities. But none of these choices really matter to him, so that he remains indifferent to the outcome; indeed it is his indifference, and not the specific outcome, which he regrets. 'Your choice is an aesthetic choice', he points out, 'but an aesthetic choice is no choice.'[51] Ethical choice is quite another matter: 'For me, the moment of choosing is very earnest'.[52] In this earnestness the personality becomes more concrete, more fully determined and more sure of itself:

> The choice itself is crucial for the content of the personality: through the choice the personality submerges itself in that which is being chosen, and when it does not choose, it withers away in atrophy.
>
> (*Or*, p. 163)

The young man's personality is thus undeveloped because either he does not choose at all but plunges unreflectively into immediacy, or he chooses only by deliberation, holding each possibility away from himself, reviewing each as if it were an external object of inde-terminate worth, before deciding upon what appears to be the most advantageous. But real choice, ethical choice, 'does not depend so much upon deliberation as on the baptism of the will'.[53]

The fundamental ethical choice is not that of good over evil, but the choice 'by which one chooses good and evil or rules them out'. In linking the notion of personality directly to the act of choosing 'seriously', Judge William makes the personality the first fruit of an ethical life. It is the peculiar nature of this activity which he argues is the foundation of his claim that the ethical 'contains' the aesthetic; indeed that only in relation to the ethical is the aesthetic possible at all. In a somewhat Hegelian formulation he writes:

> In choosing itself, the personality chooses itself ethically and absolutely excludes the aesthetic; but since he nevertheless chooses himself and does not become another being by choosing himself but becomes himself, all the aesthetic returns in its relativity.
>
> (*Or*, p. 177)

This seems to imply that all the particular characteristics that we recognize in ourselves and others as comprising their 'personality' are essentially relative and therefore aesthetic contents. In being internally related as 'personality', however, these characteristics are established through a form which has a universal validity. This is a generalization, in other words, of his argument about marriage. And if the example of marriage lacked persuasiveness, this more general formulation will surely catch the young man's wandering attention.

The melancholy which is such a feature of the young man's experience is now revealed to be a hidden but wilful obstruction to the development of his personality, and is a kind of repressed expression of this personality. Indeed, since he seeks enjoyment in the transitory and makes of his own life nothing more than a series of 'moments', he continually acts against himself: 'hollowing himself out'. Whether he knows it or not, whether he accepts it or not, the young man is in despair, because, quite generally, 'every aesthetic view of life is despair'.[54] Thus, however exalted his intellectual and artistic achievements, he remains undeveloped as a person:

> You continually hover above yourself, but the higher atmosphere, the more refined sublimate, into which you are vaporized, is the nothing of despair, and you see down below you a multiplicity of subjects, insights, studies, and observations that none the less have no reality for you but which you very whimsically utilize and combine to decorate as tastefully as you

can the sumptuous intellectual palace in which you occasionally reside.

(Or, p. 198)

In being occasionally absorbed in trifles he is displaying a genuinely aesthetic disregard for the reality of his personality. It is not that his melancholic mask occasionally slips and his hidden self temporarily makes contact with actual life, it is simply that the occasionally 'interesting' is one possibility among every other and so, from time to time, may be 'chosen'.

Yet this despair is already beyond the purely aesthetic, and is therefore in a sense already beyond despair. It is commonplace to despair over some particular circumstance, but the young man is already deeper in despair than that, and his friend advises him to 'choose despair, then, because despair itself is a choice'.[55] In choosing despair, which is 'an expression of the total personality', he will choose himself as a personality, or at least as a potential personality, 'in its eternal validity'.[56] A profound despair of this kind can become the foundation for an ethical choice of the self, hence of an inner transfiguration of the personality. The young man has advanced to the point where his despair lies wholly within himself, his sorrow no longer depends (as historically it had in paganism) upon external conditions. If he were to become conscious of choosing this despair, of grasping it ethically, then his potential and hidden selfhood would, so to speak, rise to the surface and the rich world of actuality would be restored to him. And rather than existing 'like a ghost, among the ruins of a world that is lost to you anyway', he would become a fully active individual. This choice 'penetrates everything and changes it'.[57] It is, again, not a choice of something in particular, but 'it is the total aesthetic self that is chosen ethically'.[58]

Unlike the Romantic ego, the ethical self is quite specific and individuated. Gaining the universal does not mean a loss of specificity. Once again it is only in the transfiguration of the aesthetic as an ethical choice that the self comes into full possession of its inner qualifications. He becomes conscious 'as this specific individual with these capacities, these inclinations, these drives, these passions, influenced by this specific social milieu, as this specific product of a specific environment'.[59] The choice of the self, that is to say, is not in the least asocial, it does not isolate the personality in some ideal and insubstantial space, but is, rather, the choice of the self in all its complex, immediate relations to the world. 'He chooses himself as a product', and as a product 'he is squeezed into the forms of actuality', but at the same time the choice 'transforms everything exterior into interiority'.[60] The self is chosen, finally, as a task, as a duty, and actuality becomes a goal as well as a condition of life.

The fundamental difference between the aesthetic and the ethical, 'the crux of the matter', he claims: 'is that the ethical individual is transparent to himself '.[61] This assertion, however, is far from convincingly demonstrated in Judge William's text. One of the most striking features of his book-length letters is their 'constant reference' to the religious. Nowhere does the ethical stand on its own. Every attempt to establish the universal character of the ethical – marriage, personality, connection with the social world – leads him directly to the religious as an ultimate source of authority for the categories of good and evil. It is clear that he conceives of an unbroken continuity here, an 'ethico-religious' rather than a wholly autonomous ethical sphere. His favourite expression for the despairing choice of the self – to repent the self – in fact takes a religious form.

We might well imagine the young man's reaction to his friend's heartfelt advice (we are told he did not reply in writing or verbally). That as the ethical cannot stand on its own but is only a kind of civic arm of the religious, it cannot, in fact, be the universal. Nor, of course, can it be interesting, so he will happily ignore all these lengthy remarks. He might even argue that as Judge William depends for everything upon the religious, then his supposedly more mature conception of reality must be equally as fantastic as the aesthetic.

It must, in fact, be borne in mind that while *Or* represents a direct communication between Judge William and the young man, it is something rather different in terms of the relation of the reader to either the imagined editor, Victor Eremita, or the actual but hidden author, Søren Kierkegaard. However much *Or* appears to be an ethical view of the relation between the aesthetic and the ethical, it remains, from another perspective (if we keep Kierkegaard's distant personality in mind), an aesthetic presentation of this same relation. The literary fiction of the pseudonym transposes this internal division into a differentiation within the 'aesthetic' sphere. Kierkegaard, in other words, does not claim the advantage of occupying some 'neutral' place somehow outside the 'aesthetic' or the 'ethical' from which vantage point he can 'objectively' describe and compare the characteristic experience of life within each.[62] Rather, by adopting two pseudonyms, he presents both a view of the aesthetic, and of the difference between the aesthetic and the ethical, but does so 'aesthetically'. The 'ethical' as an independent category does not really exist within *Either/Or*, and though an initial reading might suggest Judge William's views are supposed to take precedence over the young man's, the elaborate staging of the encounter, in the end, guarantees that 'the last word' lies with the aesthetic.[63]

EXCEPTIONAL INDIVIDUALS

In May of 1843 Kierkegaard left Copenhagen for Berlin. It was his second visit there; the first had been in October 1841, when he had stayed for several months to attend Schelling's lectures, and had written the bulk of *Either/Or*. The 'repetition' of this visit coincided with the possibility of an emotional 'repetition' of his relation with Regine (one day she had nodded affectionately towards him in church, indicating, he believed, a wish for reconciliation). Kierkegaard, again taking literary advantage of the occasion, thus bestowed upon another of his 'marionette theatre' of pseudonyms, Constantin Constantius, the task of illuminating the psychology of repetition.[64]

The existing form of *Either/Or* lent itself to this purpose. This time a young man, poetically charged with unhappy love, is the letter writer, and Constantin provides a narrative context and analytic framework for their reading. The reader is this time provided, at the outset, with the ethical life-view towards which he had struggled in the reading of *Either/Or*. And whereas that earlier work had tried to define as clearly as possible two mutually exclusive 'spheres' of existence, *Repetition* is focused on the transition between them.

Constantius begins with the claim that '*repetition* is a crucial expression for what "recollection" was to the Greeks'.[65] Thus, just as Plato had taught that all knowing is a recollecting of ideal forms, modern philosophy will teach that all life is a 'repetition'.[66] The possibility of experience had emerged in modern philosophy, particularly in Hume's scepticism and in Kant's reaction to it, as directly linked to the coherence and continuity of the 'self' as a perceiving and active subject. But this continuity itself remained mysterious and 'baseless'. The unity of perception seemed to depend on a kind of spiritual buoyancy which miraculously kept the 'self' afloat, as it were, on the stream of time. This hidden act of self-assertion is continually threatened, however, by processes of 'atomization' which break up and fragment all forms of continuity.[67] In the Present Age these processes have reached into the innermost aspects of human individuality and threaten to break time itself into atomistically conceived 'moments' between which the 'self' might simply 'fall' into an abyss of nothingness. The possibility of experience depends, then, upon a continually renewed 'leap' from moment to moment; balancing, as it were, on the stepping-stones of existence. The 'self' is, thus, a continuous and inexplicable 'repetition' of itself. This conception of the continuity of life in its actuality as a 'repetition' is directly and polemically linked to the fashionable nihilism of the modern age. 'What would life be if there were no repetition?' asks Constantin, and answers with a rhetorical flourish: 'Who could want to be susceptible to every fleeting thing, the novel, which always enervatingly diverts the soul anew?'[68] The reader of *Either/Or*, of course, is only too well aware that this is no rhetorical figure, but the real question mark hanging over modern existence. There is nothing 'necessary' in repetition; it is not a 'natural' but a 'spiritual' category and it is perfectly conceivable, therefore, that human existence might dissolve into nothing. 'Aesthetic' immediacy must, at some level, and in spite of its infatuation with the fragmented appearance of modern life, undergo its own unconscious form of repetition.

The universal, but inexplicable, process of repetition offers, for the pseudonymous aesthete, a model for the possibility of more strenuous and radical 'leaps' of 'self-development'. Aesthetic immediacy, that is to say, contrary to Judge William's ill-considered strictures, does possess its own thoughtless form of inner continuity. And, therefore, without departing from the aesthetic sphere the individual personality might be able to generate a series of less mundane repetitions through which he is brought into contact with 'higher' forms of life. This is the foundation for Constantin's 'poetic' vocation. Like Novalis he views poetry as a form of spiritual 'heightening', with which to counteract the 'levelling' tendencies of modern culture.[69]

The narrative content of *Repetition* is an imaginative reworking of Kierkegaard's engagement story, designed in part perhaps to offer

Regine an alternative 'confession' of his behaviour. In some sense he wanted to undo the deception of 'The Seducer's Diary' which had seemingly confirmed him in the persona of unscrupulous deceiver, and offer a new 'either/or': either the aesthetic 'exception' of *Repetition* or the ethical 'exception' of *Fear and Trembling*.

Constantin befriends another young man who, having fallen passionately in love, becomes engaged, and then, almost at once, as a result of his 'melancholic absorption' realizes that he cannot commit himself to marriage. Constantin advises him to break with his fiancée by the subterfuge which Kierkegaard had himself adopted. The parallel, however, as always, is inexact. Constantin understands that (contrary to Kierkegaard's case) 'the young girl was not his beloved: she was the occasion that awakened the poetic in him and made him a poet'.[70] And the young man, realizing the real truth of their relationship, cannot go through with the ingenious scheme of deception; his soul 'lacked the elasticity of irony' required of such deception.[71]

Constantin was convinced by this case that repetition was not possible, that every effort to grasp reality, in drawing out new aspects of ourselves, changes us, cancels our original intentions, and that, consequently, all existence is really a form of despairing recollection. As if to 'prove' his conviction he departs for Berlin in replication of a previous visit. He stays in the same lodgings, goes to the same restaurant, and has an evening out at the theatre to see again a farce which had greatly amused him on his previous visit. But he found that 'the only repetition was the impossibility of a repetition.'[72] Everything disappoints him; his recollection cannot be relived.

This is, of course, an aesthetically false conception of repetition, and we are not meant to be persuaded by Constantin's comic narrative. It is just in providing such an obviously fallacious view of his own doctrine that the reader is led to formulate, on his own behalf, a more persuasive conception. There is, in fact, nothing didactic in *Repetition*, which is one of Kierkegaard's most alluring maieutic works. The reader cannot be a neutral observer, simply eavesdropping on the exchanges between Constantin and the young man. It is the reader who constitutes, in his or her own reaction to the work, the ethical counterpoint to the aesthetics of repetition. Neither Constantin nor the young man has the inner strength to make a repetition, to confront actuality in terms of ethical categories, and by doing so regain the 'lost time' of immediacy: 'I can circumnavigate myself', proclaims Constantin, 'but I cannot rise above myself. I cannot find the Archimedean point.'[73]

The young man, plunged into unhappy love, becomes a poet, and from one point of view this is certainly a decisive change. It is not, however, a change of the type advocated by Judge William. It is experienced as an affliction and not as a self-generated transformation. 'Has something happened to me, is not all this something that has befallen me?' he asks in bewilderment. 'Could I anticipate that my whole being would undergo a change, that I would become another person?'[74] And the feeling of guilt which the incident engenders in him seems more connected with his own self-doubt than with any sense of responsibility for the consequences of his actions. The poet represents, therefore, a break within, rather than with, the aesthetic. The poetic is just another melancholic disguise that in the end fails to disguise melancholy, and what is reinforced for the reader is the conviction that this starting point, though not arbitrary, is certainly not typical, and that 'beneath' the poetic a whole series of simpler, less reflective and less imaginatively taxing aesthetic forms characterizes modern life. What is also reinforced is the inconclusive nature of the exchange in *Either/Or*. Whatever the reader is meant to think, the argument between the young man and Judge William has not been settled. This young man answers back:

> Eventually one grows weary of the incessant chatter about the universal and the universal repeated to the point of the most boring insipidity. There are exceptions. If they cannot be explained, then the universal cannot be explained either. Generally, the difficulty is not noticed because one thinks the universal not with passion but with a comfortable superficiality.
>
> (*Repetition*, p. 227)

Kierkegaard had planned a different ending to *Repetition*. In his poetic despair at being unable to marry, the young man commits suicide. But then he received news of Regine's marriage to Johan Schlegel, and allowed the young man, if not himself, to declare 'I am myself again'. But he is restored to himself fortuitously, a kind of accidental salvation, the only kind to which the aesthetic individual, who lives at the mercy of chance, leaves himself open.

The reader is left, not to draw a conclusion, but to sense the power of repetition within himself or herself. More than Constantin or the young man, the reader occupies a position of continuity and stability. And it is the reader, thus, who is the real focal point of this eccentric literary work. Only the reader can grasp 'actuality and the earnestness of existence' as a repetition, as a continuous process in which they are vitally implicated.[75] He suggests, in fact, that 'repetition proper is what has mistakenly been called mediation'.[76] Repetition is a 'category' of existence, not of thought alone, and although existence does not form itself into a neatly self-enclosed system of categories, it does possess a glue-like continuity which, when it becomes part of our own experience, he terms repetition. The notion of repetition, at once more philosophical and less moralistic than the central ethical category of 'choice' which had been Judge William's only dialectical weapon, presents a somewhat different view of the boundaries of the aesthetic. The possibility of a 'leap' from the aesthetic to the religious, by implication at least, is considered. Constantin's love affair would not have turned out differently had he summoned the will to live earnestly and accepted universal categories. Rather, in being transformed into a poet, the possibility of another, saving, transformation beyond that (independently of all ethical 'development') is tentatively raised: 'If he had had a deeper religious background, he would not have become a poet', Constantin assures us; 'then everything would have gained a religious meaning'.[77] But such a possibility seems, for the time being, to be closed off. Even as it is, however, the poet represents an 'exception', not simply as a type within the aesthetic sphere, but, more significantly, as an exception to the ethical sphere.

While *Repetition* deals with the 'exception' from an aesthetic standpoint, the idea of an exception viewed ethically is the central theme of *Fear and Trembling*, which was published simultaneously with *Repetition*.

The central issue of this work is the possibility of a 'teleological suspension of the ethical'. Can there be, beyond the ethical, a new and higher immediacy? The ethical is viewed by Judge William as the human universal, a social morality. And Johannes de Silentio, the author of *Fear and Trembling*, agrees with him in accepting that, in relation to the aesthetic, the task of the individual is to annul his or her private and personal wishes, and realize themselves more fully within universal categories. However, if there were nothing 'higher' than this social morality, then all spiritual categories would be included in or deducible from Greek philosophy. But if

Christianity has introduced something of real spiritual worth into the world, then it cannot be expressed in terms of this merely social morality. Nor can it be comprehended in terms of universal, rational concepts.[78]

Johannes de Silentio illustrates his central idea by an extended discussion of the story of Abraham. His willingness to sacrifice his son is a terrifying example of faith. 'I cannot think myself into Abraham', declares the author.[79] There is something incommensurable between such a faith and any humanly rational or moral concept. From a human point of view Abraham's action, or rather the preparation for his action, is wholly unjustifiable. The incomprehensibility of Abraham brings the reader 'to an awareness of the dialectical struggle of faith and its gigantic passion'.[80] Abraham's faith saves him; through it he regains his original world, but in order to have his son restored to him he has to be willing to lose him, willing himself to kill him. This destroys any cosy image of religious faith as a consoling and comfortable companion to life's smaller problems. And the author, though capable of the 'infinite resignation' which precedes it, admits that, personally, he cannot 'make the movement of faith', he cannot 'shut my eyes and plunge confidently into the absurd'.[81] Faith is no 'aesthetic emotion', it is not 'the spontaneous inclination of the heart but the paradox of existence'.[82]

We cannot learn from Abraham's example, we can only be bewildered, and it would be foolish to attempt to 'suck worldly wisdom out of the paradox'.[83] The understanding is helpless just because, properly speaking, it belongs to the ethical sphere. It is a human universal, and cannot make sense of the exception. Yet the 'knight of faith' does not strike anyone as a peculiar, or eccentric individual, in the way in which they might be struck by an aesthetically exceptional individual. The knight of faith, in regaining immediacy in the higher form of faith, 'enjoys everything he sees', and everything he does is 'with the assiduousness that marks the worldly man who is attached to such things'.[84]

The ethical is the universal, but faith is the paradox 'that the single individual is higher than the universal'.[85] Abraham acts 'by virtue of the absurd', and neither from calculation nor in conformity with a universally binding norm. It is not that he claims a 'higher' ethical duty, and legitimates his action, or intention, by reference to this secret obligation. Abraham himself recognizes that his action puts him outside the universal and ethical, and places him in a position of terrifying solitariness. We should not be misled by the outcome of the story: that Isaac was restored to him does not draw him back, so to speak, into the ethical. For Johannes de Silentio the central point of the story is the anxiety, the suffering, the terrible isolation, of Abraham's faith. There is no one to advise him, and 'no one understands him'.

Fear and Trembling is, thus, a compelling rejection of the basic tendency of modern ethical thought from Kant to Hegel. The progressive absorption of the notion of human obligation within a universal moral order destroys the specific character of religious life as faith. In this sense the young man of *Either* is a spiritually more lively figure than Judge William of *Or*. The latter is so stuck in a rational social ethics that, finding it is not a self-supporting edifice, he draws religion into its mundane qualification rather than drawing himself out into faith.

Johannes de Silentio advances an important distinction between the universal and the absolute. While in faith there is an absolute duty to the absolute, in the ethical there is an absolute duty to the universal. The first wholly involves the person's specificity as an individual, the latter involves the person's universal aspect as a human being. This is a distinction which his religiously more mature pseudonymous colleagues were to develop at some length. Yet however different *Repetition* and *Fear and Trembling* appear to be, they share a common aesthetic form, and remain essentially 'aesthetic' works. Just as, for the aesthetic, the ethical can have no real existence, so for both Constantin Constantius and Johannes de Silentio religion is represented aesthetically, and appears fantastic.

THE SPHERES OF EXISTENCE

The interrelated elements of the pseudonymous works can be more clearly grasped by going forward to the comprehensive (but still highly allusive) work, *Stages on Life's Way*.

This collection of 'Studies by Various Persons' is an even more fragmented work than *Either/Or*. Kierkegaard contrives to introduce additional pseudonymous authors, and varies the method of 'psychological construction' (experimenting) with more conventional ethical discourses and narrative sections, interrupting both with digressive commentaries attributed to yet other writers. In form at least it is wholly an aesthetic work, modelled in part on Plato's *Symposium*. But just as, in some respects, *Repetition* can be seen as the young man's response to *Or*, so the *Stages* develops in a different way and to a dizzying point of refinement, a series of 'replies' to Constantin Constantius's 'new category' of repetition.

The problem with living aesthetically has by this point resolved itself into the impossibility of gaining a repetition. To live immediately is, in fact, to thrust immediacy into the inaccessible regions of recollection. The continuity of actuality is fragmented and arbitrarily restructured according to a whim, only to break down and reform itself according to a succeeding whim. The narrator of the first major section of *Stages*, William Afham, is not convinced by this. He remains a staunch defender of 'recollection', which is, he claims, a kind of spiritual power that has very little to do with the functionally operating memory. The memory merely preserves events so that they might 'receive the consecration of recollection'.[86] Recollection, far more significantly, preserves the sense of unity which is fundamental to personal experience. For him the idea of repetition is unconvincing just because this unity cannot find itself in the immediate unfolding of events, but must be retrospectively constructed: 'Recollection wants to maintain for a person the eternal continuity in life and assure him that his earthly existence maintains *uno tenore* (uninterrupted), one breath, and expressible in one breath.'[87] Thus, while memory is accidental, 'only the essential can be recollected', and the essential is the hidden inwardness of personality, the conditions for which ethical writers had wrongly believed to be their unique discovery.[88]

This is an altogether more highly 'developed' form of the aesthetic. By making recollection, rather than immediacy, its essential category Afham hopes to reclaim personal existence for the aesthetic, and rescue it from the priggishness of Judge William. His task is not to grasp the present in its immediacy, but, in order to become 'contemporaneous' with its actuality, to 'conjure away the present'.[89] To demonstrate his thesis, that actuality can be aesthetically preserved (and only aesthetically preserved), he organizes a banquet, which he afterwards recollects and reports to his readers.

What he recollects, however, is a caricature, or a series of caricatures, ostensibly offered by each of his guests in turn as they are asked to talk on the nature of erotic love. Each chooses an aesthetic category through which to represent woman. For the young man (presumably the author of *Either*) it is contradiction, the incommensurable antithesis between reflective thought and the irrational 'choice' of love. The choice of love is genuinely incomprehensible, and from this he claims that 'love is just an imaginary construction'.[90] Worse, it is 'essentially nothing at all, for not a single antecedent criterion can be stated'.[91] And as, for him, thought is everything, he falls into the self-delusion of believing he can simply renounce love. Constantin, having abandoned the quest for repetition, regards woman under the category of jest, which he claims to be an 'embryonic ethical category'.[92] Pretending to ethical earnestness he argues that as man exists 'absolutely' and to express the 'absolute', while woman exists in finite and changing forms, there is no possibility of a genuine relation between them. Woman is an incomplete man to whom man ties himself; and in subordinating himself to her whims, denies his own nature. Victor Eremita, the editor of *Either/Or*, describes woman as a mixed and 'fantastic' creature, as 'giddiness'. She is, like the age in which she lives, 'an abstraction that means everything', in relation to which he prefers to be a 'concretion that means something'.[93] These previously encountered aesthetic authors are joined by a Fashion Designer, who confirms the contemporary relevance of women to the aesthetic sphere of existence, and seeks to exploit it: 'if woman has reduced everything to fashion, then I will use fashion to prostitute her as she deserves'.[94] The final speaker is Johannes the Seducer who claims that 'trying to conceive the idea of woman is like gazing into a sea of misty shapes continually forming and reforming . . . only a workshop of possibilities'.[95] But, of course, 'for the devotee of erotic love this possibility is the eternal source of infatuation'.[96]

These terse and varied aesthetic exaggerations, a kind of misogynistic embodiment, each more perfect than the last, of all the reflective tendencies of the Present Age, create a somewhat different effect to the literary fireworks of *Either*. Not only are a variety of aesthetic views exemplified (rather than one aesthetic view exemplified by variety), but, as if anticipating the ethical rebuttal, each portrays 'woman' and the possibilities of romantic love inherent in relation to her, as a self-created image. Immediacy begins to take on the character of a previously chosen 'self'; and the aesthetic sphere, rather than existing only as the mirror to fortuitous and changing circumstances, is posited as a freely chosen possibility expressive, in some sense, of a consistent inner selfhood.

The rebuttal, by 'A Married Man', however, does not simply repeat Judge William's aesthetic defence of marriage. That earlier argument is included here, but is superseded by a rather different and a more general position.

Just as the exponents of the aesthetic, in conformity with the tendencies of the age, have developed a progressively more 'inward' view of themselves, so the 'Married Man' transfers the external and institutional aspects of Judge William's defence into the subjectivity of 'resolution'. Marriage, thus, takes up the erotic and preserves its immediacy in the decisive resoluteness of a new relation: 'the most immediate of all immediacies must also be the fiercest resolution'.[97] And resolution is not simply a consequence or an aspect of erotic love, but must be formed simultaneously with love's proper development. Marriage, thus, is 'a synthesis of love and resolution'.[98]

The intense resoluteness that is required to hold on to erotic love and thereby gain the 'immediacy that carries a person through life' is not the same as ethical earnestness. Resolution is itself a synthesis, a synthesis of reflection and passion: 'without passion one never arrives at any resolution'.[99] And it is passion which grasps and preserves immediacy. Where Judge William had been obliged to call upon the authority of the religious to support the universality of his ethical categories, the 'Married Man' acknowledges that the fundamental truth of marriage is that it is an expression of passion, which is in itself a 'higher' form of immediacy. In this perspective religion becomes a 'new immediacy', rather than a continuation or development of an ethical life-view. And marriage becomes just one form in which it may be expressed. The ethical, thus, becomes a kind of intermediary, within which forms of life are ideally organized according to a rational and universal order, and receive their life-giving energy from both the aesthetic sphere 'beneath' it and the religious sphere 'above' it. Kierkegaard, still writing within an essentially aesthetic (pseudonymous) mode, allows the Married Man to speculate that marriage may not be, after all, the highest form of life. Following the aesthetic theory outlined in relation to Mozart's *Don Giovanni*, he points out that 'to find the true concretion for the religious is not easy'.[100] Could there be a form of life, in other words, which as perfectly expresses the higher immediacy of the religious as Mozart's opera captures everything that is essential to music? Whatever the answer might be, and the issue is left for the moment unresolved, the weakness of a purely ethical view has been admitted. All fundamental issues seem to amount to a conflict between an aesthetic and a religious view of life.

This opens the way for yet another reworking of the broken engagement theme. In another manuscript 'discovered' by Frater Taciturnus a third young man ponders the causes of his unhappy love. And while he titles his reflections 'Guilty'/'Not Guilty', this is clearly not an ethical discourse. 'I was no fantasizer', he tells us, distinguishing himself from the young man of *Either*. He could not believe that his life depended upon her becoming his: 'I had too many religious presuppositions for that.' He states his dilemma with the brevity of the 'Diapsalmata': 'I marry her, or I do not marry at all.'[101]

The obstacle to marriage, shorn of all aesthetic self-deception, turns upon his own 'primordial depression'. Melancholy has made him deceptive, and he can say in all truthfulness: 'I am never entirely who I am'. He is capable of astonishing feats of self-concealment: 'My cunning is that I am able to hide my depression; my deception is just as cunning as my depression is deep.'[102] There is, he acknowledges, a certain pride in this 'deep and secret sorrow', but as he is unable to overcome this pride, and free himself of it, he cannot 'destroy by initiating her into my sufferings'.[103]

This story of 'quiet despair' is perhaps the most perfect expression Kierkegaard was able to give to his own 'inclosing reserve'. It is a despair he now recognizes to be an inextricable element of his relationship to his father. This unhappy love could not have been resolved by a more determined effort of the will, as it might have been for the first young man. He is convinced he could not have acted differently, for everything had flowed from 'the interior truth of my passion'.[104] The failed love, in this instance, precipitates a profound 'collision' with the religious sphere. A year after the engagement he writes: 'I do not recognise myself . . . it is not with Eros that I must struggle. It is religious crises that are gathering over me.'[105]

The religious stands before him as a possibility. But while his loved one can, with unaffected simplicity, effortlessly grasp the religious he is plagued by a truly Faustian gift for reflectiveness. Truly an 'epigram of the age', in him reflection 'is utterly inexhaustible', and the unquenched longing of thought continually rises as a barrier between himself and the faith within which the terrible contradictions of his existence could be borne. He is forced to admit that 'I am really no religious individuality; I am just a regular and perfectly constructed possibility of such a person'.[106] He cannot emulate either her naive religiosity or the exceptional faith of Abraham:

As possibility, I am all right, but when at the turning point I want to appropriate the religious prototype (*Fforbilleder*), I encounter a philosophical doubt that I would not express to one single person . . . I cannot understand the paradigm at all.

(*Stages*, p. 258)

Yet he will not console himself with the thought that his inability to marry is connected with some reckless and radical impulse infecting his mind.

This psychological impasse is finally broken by his devaluation of his loved one: 'the trouble is that she has no religious presuppositions at all'.[107] She is 'absorbed in her illusion' and, therefore, unreachable. He conceives of her, instead, as a kind of spiritual trial essential to his own inner development. He argues that 'when God speaks he uses the person to whom he is speaking, he speaks to the person through the person himself'.[108] The extremity of the aesthetic is finally reached in this purely aesthetic conception of the religious, in which all self-awareness becomes a secret conversation with God, and all external relations are reduced to being the medium of this empty dialogue: 'God uses the very dialectical power of the person involved precisely against this person himself.'[109]

From this lofty aestheticism he can declare with perfect equanimity that 'the world wants to be deceived'.[110] He has reached the conclusion that 'I benefit a person most by deceiving him'.[111] Yet, just as he cannot pierce the veil of his own dialectical skill and gain the religious, he cannot sustain the isolation of this radical aestheticism. 'I have become a prisoner in the appearance I wanted to conjure up', he complains, admitting his continuing need for others: 'whatever I do – I cannot make myself comprehensible to any human being'.[112] Rather than make the 'progression' from the aesthetic to the ethical and thence to the religious, he has never really left the aesthetic and as a result has become more and more detached from actuality:

My idea was to structure my life ethically in my innermost being and to conceal this inwardness in the form of deception. Now I am forced even further back into myself; my life is religiously structured and is so far back in inwardness that I have difficulty in making my way to actuality.

(*Stages*, p. 351)

Frater Taciturnus in his 'Letter to the Reader' comments on the young man's manuscript rather as Judge William had on *Either*. This serves to reinforce the doctrine of despair. But this obstacle to happiness, when rightly grasped, becomes the unique opportunity to gain happiness. His 'inclosing reserve', therefore, 'is neither more nor less than the condensed anticipation of the religious subjectivity'. If, that is to say, melancholy is 'uncaused sorrow', can it not be transformed inwardly into 'senseless happiness'?

Taciturnus provides a clear summary statement, not simply of the variety of the *Stages on Life's Way*, but of the entire structure of the aesthetic writings:

> There are three existence-spheres: the aesthetic, the ethical, the religious. The metaphysical is abstraction, and there is no human being who exists metaphysically. The metaphysical, the ontological, is (*er*), but it does not exist (*er ikke till*), for when it exists it does so in the aesthetic, in the ethical, in the religious, and when it is, it is the abstraction from or a *prius* (something prior) to the aesthetic, the ethical, the religious. The ethical sphere is only a transition sphere, and therefore its highest expression is repentance as a negative action. The aesthetic sphere is the sphere of immediacy, the ethical the sphere of requirement (and this requirement is so infinite that the individual always goes bankrupt), the religious the sphere of fulfilment, but, please note, not a fulfilment such as when one fills an alms box or a sack with gold, for repentance has specifically created a boundless space, and as a consequence the religious contradiction: simultaneously to be out on 70,000 fathoms of water and yet be joyful.
>
> (*Stages*, pp. 350–1)

If the 'theory of the stages' is identified as 'Kierkegaard's thought', rather than the complex of relations generated within the aesthetic, then it is difficult to avoid turning Kierkegaard into a Hegelian. The 'spheres' then become ordered according to a developmental scheme, driven by a process of *aufheben*, in which the lower is preserved in being elevated into a new higher relation. Then, however much the irreducible freedom of the 'leap' is stressed, the pseudonymous writings, on this view, appear to be a psychological recasting of Hegel's *Phenomenology of Spirit*.[113] But, if their pseudonymity is seen as central to their meaning, then these same works can be read as demonstrating the modern tendency towards the progressive 'aestheticization' of experience. It is aesthetic immediacy, undergoing a series of self-generated internal transformations, which creates the mere illusion of 'movement' into 'higher' and more developed stages.[114] But all stages, in reality, remain aesthetic stages, and the aesthetic pseudonyms become trapped in a process of 'experimenting' in which they are in fact drawn farther and farther away from 'actuality'.

Chapter 5

Between existence and non-existence: an anthropological digression

The method of beginning with doubt in order to philosophize seems as appropriate as having a soldier slouch in order to get him to stand erect.
Søren Kierkegaard, *Journals*, 1: 775

As a new expression, *anxiety* is to designate basically the *discrimen* (ambiguity) of soft subjectivity.
Søren Kierkegaard, *Journals*, 1: 98

The aesthetic works presented a formidable diversity of character types, who, in terms of the inner consistency of their respective life-views, communicated the distinctive features of the possible 'existence-spheres' open to the citizen of the Present Age. The 'aesthetic', conceiving of life as nothing other than a pursuit of pleasure, and the 'ethical', which subordinates all immediacy to pursuit of the good, seemed to be profoundly different, and even incompatible forms of personal existence. But neither position is stable, and neither includes within itself a self-propelling means of transcending its own limitations. Every aesthetic possibility quickly loses its tension and returns the young men who are its exponents to a state of boredom; and equally, each ethical endeavour ends in the consciousness of failure and guilt.

From outside itself each 'sphere' might appear to be filled with an alluring plenitude of human potentiality. The 'ethical' may seem to be a lofty and ideal existence for the despairing but sensitive aesthete, and for the genuinely ethical individual, the aesthetic beckons as a world of limitless, satisfying possibilities. Curiously, it is when viewed exclusively within the perspective of their own spheres that each in turn is rendered unreal, insubstantial and evanescent. The aesthetic moment vanishes before the hand that reaches out to grasp the pleasure it seemed to promise, and the ideal, in the act of self-realization, loses itself in the vagueness of undefined religious categories or falls back into just another arbitrary, and thus aesthetic, choice.

Beyond this *Either/Or* the presence of a 'religious' sphere makes itself known, firstly as a somewhat vague intuition that the renounced aesthetic might be recovered in a 'higher immediacy', and then as 'the absolute' which lies at the heart of any real ethical decision. But there is no 'short cut' out of melancholy; we cannot move directly into the religious sphere. Indeed it is the persistence of melancholy which is the most convincing sign that we have not yet left the 'aesthetic'. The 'leap' into the ethical discloses only another version of the aesthetic. Subordination of life under ethical categories is just one of the possibilities contained within the aesthetic. If the 'religious' sphere were to be elaborated by the pseudonyms simply by extension, by a 'repetition' of a qualitatively similar 'leap' to that bridging the aesthetic and the ethical, we would, once again, fall back into the aesthetic. The 'religious sphere' must be approached from a different perspective. The religious is nothing other than a transition itself, so that it cannot be surmounted in a single, if endlessly repeated, 'leap', but consists in the interstitial 'non-moment' of repetition itself. The transition becomes, as it were, a 'stage' or 'sphere' of existence in its own right. It does not, therefore, have the finished appearance of the aesthetic or the ethical spheres, but remains a continuously undisclosed striving.

DIMENSIONS OF ACTUALITY

In order to grasp, both reflectively and practically, the actuality of this transition personal existence must be viewed as a simultaneous movement along two separate dimensions. The aesthetic works, and their ethical after-image, describe the possibilities of movement along what might be termed the 'horizontal' axis of existence; they are concerned with the progressive discovery of differences inherent in the fragmented and illusory character of the Present Age. But as the aesthetic takes the Present Age as 'given' it generates an illusory sequence of unreal changes rather than a development within actuality itself. Even where it appears to 'escape' the restrictive 'bourgeois-philistinism' of everyday conventions, it constructs for itself a variety of unreal self-possibilities which are, in fact, so many fantastic 'potentiations' of that very same 'bourgeois-philistinism'. To grasp actuality, the actual must in fact be transformed. And to establish the 'self' depends upon 'departing' from the given elements of immediacy in such a way that, in returning to them, they become reconstructed, illuminating previously obscured possibilities. To grasp actuality is, simultaneously, to undergo a 'repetition' in which the 'inner world' of the self and the 'outer world' of the Present Age become mutually developed. However, in the context of the Present Age all 'departures' from the surface of modern life must be in one of two directions: 'outwards' towards the infinite world of 'objects', or 'inwards' towards the inexhaustibly replenished interior of the human 'subject'. Thus, in spite of its 'levelling', an adequate understanding of modern life requires a consideration of the 'vertical' as well as the 'horizontal' dimensions of experience.

This consideration further complicates the theory of the 'stages'. Thus, quite apart from the independent validity or otherwise of the 'ethical' and the 'religious', some of the pseudonyms disclose different 'levels' of reality which accompany and surround each stage with a ghostly shadow. This penumbra of existence, though falling outside the sphere of actuality, is perfectly real and qualifies every available possibility of selfhood.

The 'aesthetic' writers conflate these 'non-existence' spheres with actuality itself. This is, in fact, typical of the Present Age, which is both 'reflective' and Romantic. An insufficiently critical position in relation to the contemporary world, that is to say, leads to the 'aesthetic' illusions typical of the first pseudonymous phase of the authorship. In some respects these young men seem to be characteristic of either Romanticism or Hegelianism. But both Romantics and Hegelians, in different ways, sought to unite 'object' and 'subject' in an infinitude or in an absolute that lay, by definition, wholly outside actuality. They sought, that is, to escape the 'shallowness' of modernity by acts of self-elevation. But the pseudonyms, though rejecting the 'bourgeois-philistinism' of the crowd, sought, above all, to preserve actuality in all its immediate relations. Yet, in attempting to 'purify' their aesthetic visions they inadvertently 'escaped' the determinateness of any 'existence-sphere'. In place of the deceptive imagery of 'object' and 'subject' a number of pseudonyms introduced a modern version of traditional Christian anthropology in which actuality appears as the middle term between what are in effect two 'non-existence spheres'. Thus 'hovering' above actuality is a realm of 'pure' thought, and 'sunk' beneath it a domain of 'pure' sensuousness.

In order to follow the development of the 'non-existence' spheres in the pseudonyms it is helpful to draw on one of the later formulations of actuality as 'selfhood', that provided by Anti-Climacus in *The Sickness Unto Death*. This author describes the self as a synthesis: a synthesis of time and eternity, finite and infinite, necessity and possibility. Those disparate terms taken together define two 'non-existence' spheres which might be spatially represented as a vertical structure extending both 'above' and 'below' the synthesized elements which make up the content of immediate experience. Anti-Climacus has, in effect, rejected all forms of dualism, in which 'mind' and 'body' must remain hermetically sealed off from each other, in favour of a more flexible, and realistic 'body-soul-spirit' schema.

The infinite/eternal/possible is the sphere of 'pure' thought, and more particularly, for the pseudonyms it is represented by the philosophical system of Hegel. Speculative metaphysics, which is itself the culmination of a long tradition of western thought which began with the misrepresentation of Socratic irony as a form of abstraction, appears to have 'escaped' from the constraints of actuality, and to have been liberated into an ethereal realm in which it can freely and indefinitely expand in conformity with an autonomous inner principle of its own. The content of this realm is made up entirely of abstract concepts and pure relations detached as it were from empirical contingencies. Each term becomes defined, then, in terms of its position within a system of similar, and similarly abstract, concepts or 'categories'. The 'system' once complete is self-perpetuating and internally self-referential. Its inner principle is 'mediation'. That is to say there are no discrete breaks or 'gaps' in its internal relations. From any arbitrarily chosen starting point the mind can be led to any other concept within the system through the repeated application of a limited number of simple rules. There is in principle no 'other' category within the system, no alien 'substance' lurking, so to speak, in an out-of-the-way corner closed off from immediate inspection. If the aim of philosophy is the construction of such a system of pure categories, then for the pseudonyms this has been Hegel's great achievement.[1]

'Beneath' actuality there lies another 'non-existence' sphere constituted by the finite/necessary/temporal. This might be termed the realm of 'pure' sensuousness. At first sight this seems to play a far less prominent role in the thought of the pseudonymous writings. Compared to the extensive writings of both Johannes Climacus and his philosophical twin Anti-Climacus which bear directly on the domain of abstraction, only one work, *The Concept of Anxiety* is related directly to the domain of pure sensuousness. However, just as throughout the aesthetic and ethical writings abstraction is continually present as a limiting condition of actuality, so sensuousness makes its brooding presence felt as a perpetual undertow to the entire pseudonymous production.

The sensuous, like abstraction, is continuous and undivided. It is a world of material forms continually flowing into and out of each other. Its inner principle is, ultimately, death, the monistic *telos* of all organic transformation. But, immediately, it is vibrant with metamorphoses, and with appetite. The continuous restless movement of the sensuous is a sign of its inner incompleteness, its perpetual want, continually renewed, which flows through the entire diversity of its forms. Sensuousness is perpetual and aimless movement, its inner divisions meaningless transformations of the same underlying insufficiency of substance.

Johannes might be seen as reworking the traditionally conceived Christian tripartite division of soul, flesh (body) and spirit, in an effort to combat modern philosophical trends which seek to dissolve reality into the abstraction of pure thought, or the equally abstract non-existence of 'matter' or 'substance'. Of course anthropological assumptions had been central to the development of the Christian tradition without there emerging any very clear consensus as to the meaning and proper usage of its basic terms. And within the pseudonymous works themselves, the usage of these terms, as with all others, varies with the 'point of view of the author'. In particular, from an aesthetic standpoint, both the ideality of pure thought, and the 'romance' of sensuousness are ennobled to a greater 'reality' than existence itself. Furthermore, a specifically Christian anthropology had from the beginning interacted with Aristotelian, Platonic and Judaic variants of each of its main components. However, although no orthodoxy had been established, a broad distinction between religious/theological tripartite and secular/philosophical 'dualistic' anthropological assumptions can be made. The fundamental difference, for the philosophically most sophisticated of the pseudonyms, Anti-Climacus, between the two traditions lies in the fact that for the tripartite theory human existence is not simply a relation between two fundamentally different kinds of reality (mind and body, or soul and body), but is a 'relation that relates itself to itself'.[2] And this 'third term' constitutes a fundamentally new reality whose characteristics cannot simply be deduced from the nature of elements brought together in the initial synthesis.

In this view, in particular, the Cartesian distinction of mind and body is not a sufficient foundation for the description of any meaningful human experience.[3] In fact Descartes's project of 'pure thought' turned modern philosophers away from that portion of reality which comes to life in the actuality of a living person. All modern metaphysical systems, and more generally all modern secular thought which embodies within it the conceit of reason, is not so much mistaken as, by virtue of suppressing all personal qualifications of thought, simply uninteresting. Descartes, thus, reports in the 'first meditation' that he only began to philosophize when he could withdraw himself from the normal cares of life.[4] Reason, in the sense of a system of concepts which serves as a medium for reflection, can be perfectly harmonious, non-contradictory, and exhaustive of itself; but it can be so only by the pretence of deserting its 'natural' home, by ignoring the limitations and contradictions of the actuality which makes up all human existence, including itself. Similarly all modern materialism, though Johannes Climacus seems to think this hardly worth discussing, falls beneath the interesting and is a kind of perverse representation of sensuousness as an ideal and universal system of causes. Spinoza, rather than Hobbes, might be taken in this context as the exemplary exponent of a strict monism of substance. The variety of inner forms is reduced to being aspects of a single substance, which can be mirrored in thought as a simple category from which all others can be generated at will (or rather generate themselves however much we might wish to put a stop to them).[5]

Idea and substance mirror each other in their perfection, their purity and in their non-involvement with the humanly interesting realm of actuality. We cannot experience 'pure ideality' or 'pure sensuousness'. The 'young man' of *Either* admitted as much in viewing music as the only immediately available form of the 'sensuous-erotic'. Both ideality and sensuousness are wholly 'abstract', and the process of 'departing' from actuality is referred to by the pseudonyms as a process of abstraction. It is commonplace to view thought as a process of 'abstraction', but pure sensuousness, it is important to note, is just as far removed from the possibility of immediate experience. In a text neglected by the pseudonyms (they are frequently too polemical to give their opponents a fair hearing) Hegel also draws attention to this; for him also sensuousness only has human significance when it is formed and penetrated by spirit. Art, thus, 'by means of its representations, while remaining within the sensuous sphere, liberates man at the same time from the power of sensuousness'.[6] And what is required for artistic representation is, for the pseudonyms, required for actuality in general, a 'sensuous presence which indeed should remain sensuous, but liberated from the scaffolding of its purely material nature'.[7]

Yet actual human existence is composed of nothing but such abstractions, qualified and synthesized as 'spirit'. For Johannes Climacus, then, the specific character of actuality is its mode of integration of idea and substance, which otherwise fall apart into diverse and opposed realms. 'Spirit' combines ideas and substance in particular ways, and holds them together to form that particular segment of being we call personal experience.

To find more specific ways of relating forms of 'non-existence' to the sphere of actuality is the particular concern of Johannes Climacus and Vigilius Haufniensis. Once again, however, the way is barred, or at least forces the reader through numerous diversions. Neither 'pure' thought nor 'pure' sensuousness is of interest to Johannes Climacus or his colleagues. The authorship, on this at least, is united. The many polemical remarks aimed at Hegel's philosophy, and more especially at its Danish theological practitioners, should not mislead the reader into believing that the *Philosophical Fragments* or the *Concluding Unscientific Postscript* are philosophical works, if by philosophy is meant any general system of concepts through which reality, in its entirety, might be represented. We are presented, rather, with a highly self-conscious criticism of such philosophical ambitions. And while most philosophers begin by denouncing the entire western tradition of philosophy only to reconstruct it in their own terms, Climacus has no ambition to incorporate or assimilate previous philosophical endeavours to his own point of view. In fact his point of view does not depend upon arriving at speculative or logical 'conclusions'. He renounces metaphysics, therefore, not as a preparatory device or piece of self-aggrandisement, but as part of a serious effort to recover from philosophy what rightly belongs to life.

He begins with *doubt,* therefore, not in the Cartesian sense, or in the sense in which Descartes most frequently interpreted it, as the beginning of a speculative dialectic, but as an active and practical reflection upon experience. He cannot renounce thought, but neither should thought renounce experience. In doubt, he sees actual thought rather than empty abstraction. Doubt refers to a kind of indeterminate, intermediary 'zone', between a determinate state of actuality and the absolute freedom of abstraction. In doubt there is a kind of continuous oscillation into and out of actuality. It has an elastic quality of resistance, and a lack of transparency which is quite unlike the perfect fluidity of pure thought. Doubt departs from actuality only to return to it, enriching it with fresh qualifications.

Similarly, beneath actuality, sensuousness transforms itself in mute incomprehensible self-absorption. We cannot directly experience 'sensuousness' any more than we can directly experience any other pure category. That is why it cannot be readily represented, and why the pure ideality of thought and the pure materiality of sensuousness, though absolutely distinct, can frequently 'stand for' one another. Where experience is orientated towards the sensuous (rather than the ideal), dipping into the sensuous and returning to itself, we experience anxiety (as distinct from doubt), or as an earlier translation of Vigilius Haufniensis's work expressed it, *dread.*

Doubt and dread are the penumbra of existence, the soft and muffled intermediary zones between existence and non-existence. The vertical division of reality is thus marked by a distinctive 'logic' of its own. There is, even more clearly than in the divisions into horizontal 'spheres', no hierarchical ordering involved here. The norm of existence is, so to speak, the middle term rather than the extremes which depart from it in either direction. Even more significantly, the boundaries along this dimension are much less precise. There is no void or abyss dividing them. The blurring and merging of boundaries (so unexpected in the light of everything that is well known of Kierkegaard) denotes a continuous interchange, a perpetual traffic from one zone to another. Yet the task of existence is to set and maintain distinctions, and to reject as invalid incursions into the sphere of actuality. Actuality, that is to say, in becoming itself, in establishing itself as actual, draws into itself the elements of non-existence which lie on either side of its specific 'range', while simultaneously resisting the temptation to empty itself into either of its component elements. And the task of existence is to develop, through the continuous assimilation of what lies beyond it, the specific characteristics of individuality. The discontinuous leaps of the personality, the real growth of individuality, expands the sphere of actuality by successively incorporating more and more of non-existence into itself. The 'aesthetic' individual is, thus, an insubstantial creature in whom doubt and dread touch and intermingle as melancholy. The ethical individual succeeds in distinguishing and pushing apart these dangerously entangled elements, opening up a larger and more expansive area of inner freedom. Where Hegel had seen this entirely in terms of an immanent dialectic of selfhood, the pseudonymous writers bring into the sharpest possible focus the discontinuities in this process, and point to the incomprehensible breaks which make it possible. The aim of individuality – the conquest of despair which becomes identical with the task of becoming a Christian – involves a fuller expansion of the sphere of existence, pushing doubt and despair ever further apart by transforming and incorporating into experience the alien pure forms which lie beyond its boundary zone.

Turning to *Either/Or* in the light of the specific nature of the vertical divisions of existence (which is fully elaborated only much later in *Sickness Unto Death*), a new and rich content of reflection is revealed. There is not simply a movement between pleasure and unpleasure, the despair of boredom and the melancholic eroticism of the moment, but all these characteristic expressions become so many evanescent attempts to establish a space, to prise apart and open up the dimensionality of the actual, and thus prevent doubt and despair touching and entangling the person in an impenetrable psychic fog. In *Either/Or*, the starting point is the impoverished inwardness of melancholy, the 'quiet despair' in which sensuousness and abstraction meet without penetrating each other. And the twin *motifs* of, on the one hand, Romantic enthusiasm for ideality, and on the other, the continuously inventive presence of the erotic, become more significant. The 'young man' is not only in danger of 'volatilizing' himself out of existence, he is equally at risk of sinking into a state of turbid eroticism. He is not only 'infinitized' in the direction of pure ideas, an abstraction of his real self, he is also 'finitized' in the direction of pure sensuousness, and composed in equal measure of dread and doubt.

The interaction between these two fundamental dimensions of existence, their separate logics, different boundary conditions and transitional forms, gives rise to an extremely intricate and realistic dynamic psychology. And as many of the pseudonyms remain ignorant of the work of their colleagues, the reader is forced to make a long journey through the entire range of modern forms of selfhood.

DOUBT

Johannes Climacus, the personification of 'Kierkegaardian' doubt, makes his appearance in the authorship at an early date. During the latter part of 1842 and early 1843 Kierkegaard began, but did not complete, a work entitled 'Johannes Climacus, or De Omnibus Dubitandum Est'. Significantly it was designated a 'Narrative', emphasizing that the personal element was to remain at the centre of the most sophisticated of reflections. Johannes, another in the retinue of 'young men', is its hero rather than its author.[8]

Its author, indeed, is quick to draw attention to his departure from modern conventions of philosophical discourse. Academic philosophers, he admits, will 'think it strange, affected, and scandalous that I choose the narrative form'.[9] But he is equally quick to defend himself; the narrative form places a specific person, Johannes Climacus, at the centre of the work, and makes his existence the central focus of everything that is to follow. It is by this means that he seeks 'to counteract the detestable untruth that characterizes recent philosophy', which, he declares, 'has never been so eccentric as now, never so confused'.[10]

Johannes, more markedly than any of his pseudonymous colleagues, is in love with thinking. For him, sensuousness has lost any relation to existence, and, however romanticized and idealized it might become, he remains untouched by the erotic. His is an ideal nature, and even his body, 'delicate and ethereal, almost transparent', seems designed for reflection.[11] He is, for all that, another in the series of 'enclosed natures' who knows melancholy too well; but rather than hope to be drawn out from the narrow focus of his inner preoccupations by erotic attraction, he turns at once to the promise of the immense, the infinite, liberation of pure thought.

He is a 'stranger in the world', for the world itself is not composed of thought, nor does it, as it had for the medieval philosopher, exist as part, or symbol, of a fixed cosmological structure.[12] Yet an echo of that older cosmological picture persists in Johannes's hierarchical conception of the realm of pure thought as a *scala paradisi*: 'it was his delight to begin with a single thought', we are told, and 'by way of coherent thinking, to climb step by step to a higher one . . . when he arrived at the higher thought, it was an indescribable joy'.[13] The original of the pseudonym, John Scholasticus, a monk living around the turn of the seventh century, wrote an influential devotional handbook, *The Ladder of Divine Ascent*, that was noted for its psychological insight and aphoristic style.[14] For the pseudonym, however, there is no graded sequence of spiritual exercises bridging the gulf between the human and the divine. The modern *scala paradisi* is a purely conceptual realm which, conceiving itself to be independent of all actuality, represents, for the thinker caught up in its interconnections, both a domain of absolute freedom and a 'model' of reality as a whole.[15] The thought of Johannes Climacus is driven by admiration for the completeness of purely internal connections among thoughts themselves, an admiration mixed with a pronounced erotic satisfaction sublimated into this 'higher' realm. The pleasure he takes in thought is a purely personal pleasure, a kind of passive excitement at being carried off into the furthest realms of abstraction, helpless before the continuous unfolding of ideal inner connections. It was, thus, an equally 'passionate pleasure, for him to plunge headfirst down', back to his arbitrary starting point.[16] He is an essentially 'aesthetic' thinker, for whom 'this up-and-down and down-and-up of thought was an unparalleled joy'.[17] He delights in the spectacle of thought itself: 'the result was not important – only the process interested him', and he longs, not so much for the attainment of the 'highest' thought, as for the image of a completed sequence of reflections.[18] He thus becomes troubled by the prospect of incomplete or interrupted thoughts, and worries over the stability of the entire ideal edifice. He is 'anxious lest one single coherent thought slip out, for then the whole thing would collapse'.[19]

Thus, although the development of his mind 'deprived him of a sense of empirical actuality', it did not leave him untroubled. His nervousness over the fate of systematic thought, that, like an insecure house of cards, might at any moment topple to the ground, betrays the fact that he has not after all wholly deserted the sphere of actuality. This nervousness he interprets as an intuitive doubt, and takes comfort from the discovery that doubt has indeed become the starting point of modern philosophy. After all the fundamental thesis of modern philosophy is simply that everything must be doubted except the existence of the thinker, which, as it lies outside the sphere of pure thought, is of no philosophical interest. This raises in Johannes's mind a number of related questions, centred on the problem of defining a new beginning for philosophy. If philosophy deals with eternal and universal truths how can it have a new starting point? And why should its old starting point be abandoned? Has philosophy in some way changed its nature, in spite of being essentially related to the eternal? These questions are raised rather than answered – the work was never completed – but in the course of elaborating their meaning 'doubt' takes on a rather different significance.

For the Cartesian (and Johannes is writing against contemporary Cartesians but in support of what he takes to be the original spirit of Descartes), doubt is a stimulus to thought. Doubt once admitted as a starting point is taken into the sphere of thought itself and extends itself to infinity. Doubt is the inner principle of movement of thought; it is doubt which forces the thinker from one thought to the next in a connected sequence. Doubt, thus, does not undermine thought; in fact it propels the thinker into the midst of systematic reflection. But Johannes's doubt is of a rather different sort. He does not doubt the truth, or the reality, of thought. His doubt is really the tension of a nervous spectator, in trepidation that the incomparable image unfolding before his eyes might never reach completion or end in something ugly and ill formed. This doubt is not only, or even primarily, an intellectual mechanism – a principle of 'mediation' or 'transformation' – so much as a recalcitrant hanging on to the incompleteness and messiness of actuality itself. A lumpy piece of existence is taken up, so to speak, into the realm of thought and thought cannot dissolve it; if it could Johannes would no longer be a spectator because there would be no 'place' from which to spectate. He would cease to exist and become part of the abstract system which – just because he cannot become part of it – he enjoys so much. Indeed, it is this longing to be absorbed in thought that Johannes claims to be characteristic of modern philosophy. But doubt, for Johannes, is a continuous reminder of his non-ideal existence:

> so long as he could not question, thought twined itself alarmingly around him, but as soon as he began to question, he was happy and extricated himself from thought inasmuch as thought developed for him in dialogue.
>
> (*Climacus*, p. 147)

Johannes, therefore, draws an important distinction between reflection, or reflective doubt, which is a disinterested and abstract relation within thought itself, and doubt proper, which is always an interested and, therefore, always a mixed relation. Schematically, it might be said that reflection is the movement from actuality into thought, while doubt is the movement back from thought into actuality.

When Johannes begins to think on his own behalf, therefore, he asks what it is about existence that makes doubt (rather than reflection) possible. He fixes on doubt as a means of anchoring thought in existence rather than – as among the Cartesians and even more strikingly among the Hegelians – as a means of giving wings to thought so that it becomes wholly liberated from the constraints of existence.

It might be argued that Johannes is still too philosophical for his own good. He has discovered existential doubt before he has accumulated the wealth of immediate experience upon which it might work to enrich his personality and give it depth. His existence is too thin – he is almost 'transparent' – for doubt to work positively. In this respect he is a shadow, or rather a 'silhouette', of Kierkegaard's original plan to write on the much more substantial and complex Faust figure as the prototype of existential doubt. Johannes is not just a simplification, he is a one-sided simplification of that original plan. Faust is composed of both doubt and dread. His is a genuinely demonic personality, driven by insatiable desire for knowledge of the secrets of nature, a desire 'desublimated' into erotic longing for Margaret. The sensuous and the ideal are inextricably bound together in his personality. One reason, perhaps, why his plan was never brought to fruition is just because of the internal complexity in such a personality. And just as irony had proved to be a false starting point because it contained too much, coalescing and compounding the distinctions the pseudonymous authors were to establish in their exploration of existence, so Faust, as an intermingling of doubt and dread, could not serve the analytic purpose to which Kierkegaard put Johannes Climacus.

It is worth noting at this point that, by way of his pseudonyms, Kierkegaard is indeed engaged in a process of careful analysis. His strictures against the 'system', the project of 'pure thought' and 'mediation' should not be taken as a wholesale denial of the significance of any form of analytic thinking whatever.[20] Johannes is a thinker, but in doubting he is drawn more closely into the web of existence, and brings his thoughts with him, adding fresh qualifications to the relations of actuality.

Doubt in the sense of systematic doubt – reflection – is a specifically modern phenomenon. Ancient philosophy had begun with wonder, which is a form of immediacy. Doubt, however, introduces a fundamental dichotomy into existence, and creates a distance between the person and his thought world. The peculiarity of Johannes is that he maintains an immediate relation to doubt, that he can use it as a support for, rather than the subversion of, actuality. Doubt, for Johannes, is always something interesting.

The possibility of both reflective doubt and doubt proper can be traced to the condition of modernity which has fostered the emergence of new forms of individualism. The specifically modern form of individualism had, in turn, encouraged a false conception of universality as a directly inaccessible realm of abstraction to which thought was joined as a kind of bridge. In this context reflective doubt was a way of 'negating' the specific and particular qualification of the individual that tied him or her to a specific situation and a particular thought. Johannes, alternatively, practices a kind of interested doubt which seeks to idealize, rather than to abolish, the moment. He moves abruptly between a contingent and particular starting point to a conceptual universal. Doubt carries him 'up', and elevates him into a sphere of non-existence, only to drag him back again, and almost at once, to an existence he cannot forget, and which can never wholly be mastered conceptually.

The 'aesthetic' young men lived in recollection, concentrating their energies in an attempt to rehearse experience, and thus to preserve and magnify the moment. Johannes, equally reluctant to 'forget himself' in pure thought, discovers in the immediacy of doubt a means of self-elevation, a way, so to speak, of carrying himself over the threshold into the infinite freedom of thought.

ANXIETY

Doubt, for Johannes, is not a purely intellectual process; indeed its possibility is rooted in the fact that he cannot wholly rid himself of the encumbrance of actuality. Doubt might be viewed as the unintegrated presence of actuality within the ideal, while the 'interesting' is the equally unrelated presence of ideality within the sphere of existence. This double 'misrelation' marks the fuzzy boundary between actuality and abstract thought, an imprecise demarcation zone between existence and non-existence. And because this is an intermediary zone doubt can be both 'felt' as dizziness, and 'thought' as incredulity.

A symmetrical boundary zone between actuality and sensuousness is productive of a different set of 'qualifications' of existence. The tendency of actuality to 'slip beneath' existence is, of course, a staple of the tradition of Christian anthropology, and a continuous refrain within the homiletic literature. The primary spiritual danger, in almost all the ages of the Christian tradition, has been seen as the temptation of sensuousness. Certainly, from time to time, Christian leaders and reformers have warned against the mortification of the flesh, excessive penitential asceticism, or any attempt to deny the creaturely nature of human beings, but more frequently, and with greater insistence, they have warned against insufficient effort of self-mastery over the promptings of a merely instinctual life.[21]

Another pseudonymous author, Vigilius Haufniensis, refers to this continuous undertow of sensuousness as *dread*, or, as it is now more commonly translated, *anxiety*. As erotic melancholy, however, it had already made its appearance in the opening pages of *Either/Or*, and played an unanalysed but significant part in the entire aesthetic production. Beginning from the 'aesthetic sphere', that mode of existence in which actuality is most 'compressed' between doubt and anxiety, there are two symmetrical sets of relations between existence and non-existence. Doubt and interest are reciprocal relations between actuality and ideality, while anxiety and the erotic are reciprocal relations between actuality and sensuousness. Thus, for all his distrust of the 'system', Kierkegaard, through the interconnected pseudonymous works, develops, so far as is possible, an orderly and coherent account of existence; and while he resists the temptation of solipsistic reflexivity and refuses to close his categories back upon themselves, it is clear that the distinctions he draws and develops are conditioned not only by the demands of existence itself, but simultaneously by an 'aesthetic' requirement for symmetry. Then, as if reluctant to draw attention to such formalism, this symmetry is concealed, firstly by the disproportionate space allotted to the discussion of certain specific relations, and secondly by the multiplication of pseudonymous authors and forms of presentation through which they are 'analysed'. The formal aspects of his account become more apparent, however, when the notion of anxiety is examined in relation to the existing, but at the time unpublished, discussion of doubt.

Like a later work, *The Sickness Unto Death*, to which it is closely related in terms of content, *The Concept of Anxiety* is didactic rather than narrative in form. This is not because Kierkegaard believes he can approach the issues he raises here in a clearer or a more 'logical' fashion than was the case with the major 'aesthetic' works. It is, more significantly, because he is beginning here with sensuousness rather than with actuality. Subsequently, when he dealt with the relation between existence and ideality from the side, so to speak, of ideality, he again adopted a more conventional philosophical form of discourse. The realm of actuality, as he never tires of demonstrating, is the sphere of individuation, and must always be represented through the medium of a personality. Sensuousness, however, which is just another form of abstraction, is a domain of depersonalized relations and can therefore be discussed systematically.

It is also a domain which is peculiarly recalcitrant of representation. It is, to put it simply, difficult to talk about; as soon as it is 'expressed' in words it loses its real quality of sensuousness and all too easily 'disappears' into some other abstract form.[22] This difficulty, however, is not fundamentally different from that embedded in any discourse about something 'other' than the rules of discourse itself. Words are equally removed from all the 'ideal forms' which the philosopher seeks to represent through them, they are only signs of another reality from which they remain forever divorced. Words are part of our experience, and cling to actuality by their very nature. We have come to imagine, however, that, as used by the philosopher at least, they do not simply represent, but actually are, eternal and abstract forms of reason. Kierkegaard is well aware of the difficulty and his mode of presentation, always sensitive to the inner character of the world he hopes to represent, becomes compressed, dense and obscure (where in his more philosophical works he becomes expansive, aerial and lucid, and in his descriptions of existence, personal, ambiguous and contradictory).

Anxiety is, then, first of all, a weighty presentiment. As early as 1839 Kierkegaard had confided to his *Journal* that 'all existence makes me anxious'.[23] And an even earlier entry talks, as had Pascal, of the 'anxiety over the possibility of being alone in the world, forgotten by God'.[24] But while such feelings of isolation and inner loneliness are, doubtless, commonplace, and have a special significance for the experience of modern life which is predicated on an 'anticosmic' infinitization of space and time, Haufniensis, when he came to write *The Concept of Anxiety*, saw in the phenomenon of 'groundless fear' something universally and inescapably present in human experience.

Anxiety, as a relation to sensuousness, is not only the presentiment of 'otherness' or the fear of undergoing some sort of regression to a wholly undifferentiated mode of being (though it may include such fears) so much as the form through which sensuousness can, so to speak, represent itself within human life as an independent and autonomous 'spirit'. The 'otherness' of nature, as the 'otherness' of abstract thought, does not really belong to existence and cannot ever become actual. Sensuousness can enter into the personal dimension of actuality, therefore, only in disguise, as a 'demonic' force which grips the will and bends it to its own hidden purpose.[25]

Thus, just as doubt represented the uncomfortable 'otherness' of the thought-world, so anxiety, or dread, represents the individual's impotence in the face of the 'force of nature' acting within him. Both abstraction and sensuousness thus have about them a quality of necessity, a compulsive and ineluctable interconnectedness which sweeps people up and, so to speak, carries them away. In this view of sensuousness Haufniensis makes a step away from the Romantic *Naturphilosophie* towards Schopenhauer's pessimism. Even so his conception of sensuousness remains aloof from the tradition of modern materialism and positivism. By sensuousness he refers always to sensuous spirit, to an embodied form of spirit, to which human being might have, indeed must have, some sort of relation.

'Pure sensuousness', like 'pure thought', can never be experienced. It is in a relative form that we conspire with these antithetical forms of nothingness to create within ourselves the double movement of doubt and anxiety, interest and desire. Both anxiety and doubt stem ultimately, that is to say, from undetected tendencies within ourselves, from inner spiritual transformations or a kind of inner splitting, through which we can represent to ourselves the unreachable world of pure forms.[26] The two tendencies away from actuality, a depersonalized abstractedness, and an equally depersonalized concreteness, thus constitute the two fundamental forms of unconscious self-destruction, which, grasped religiously, is sin.

'Anxiety is a sympathetic antipathy and an antipathetic sympathy', writes Haufniensis; it is nothing and the fear of nothing, the fascination of freedom represented to ourselves as its opposite.[27] The experience of anxiety is of a bewildering, indeterminate fear, literally a fear of nothing; it is groundless. We imagine it must be related to something outside ourselves, have some 'objective' point of reference. We do not know what this object is but, as an unknown, it both attracts and repels. Anxiety, a 'heavy spiritedness', is a fascination with an unknown but presumed reality.[28] The author interprets this 'something' to be our own nature, to be the freedom of possibility; but it is a freedom 'entangled in itself'.[29]

There emerges in this discussion two distinct notions of 'nothing'. Firstly anxiety 'contains' nothing in the sense that it is an immediate relation to the sensuousness which, lacking spirit, is, humanly speaking, nothing. More precisely, it is related to the lower form of spirit given in sensuousness. In a passage closely related to both the opening sentences of *The Sickness Unto Death*, and to the first section of the essay on the musical erotic in *Either/Or*, he writes:

> Man is a synthesis of the psychical and the physical; however, a synthesis is unthinkable if the two are not united in a third. This third is spirit. In innocence, man is not merely animal, for if he were at any moment of his life merely animal, he would never become man. So spirit is present, but as immediate, as dreaming. Inasmuch as it is now present, it is in a sense a hostile power, for it constantly disturbs the relation between soul and body.[30]
>
> (*Anxiety*, p. 43)

Secondly, in a formulation more closely related to the writings of Johannes Climacus, anxiety is conceived as a relation to the nothing of possibility: 'In the moment actuality is posited, possibility walks by its side as a nothing that entices every thoughtless man'.[31] In this latter sense it is part of actuality, rather than a relation between existence and non-existence. These two rather different senses of 'anxiety' are distinguished by Vigilius, and it is usually apparent from the context which sense is being used, but he does not feel obliged to designate these two meanings by separate terms. He clearly feels these two senses are so closely related as to be two aspects of a single relation. While the first meaning encompasses all the possibilities of non-existence, the second refers specifically to the possibilities within existence itself; the first is an anxiety implicit in the 'vertical' structure of being, the latter is immanent in its 'horizontal' extension.

DIZZINESS

These spatial metaphors draw upon phenomenological evidence to which Kierkegaard later refers in an important *Journal* entry written in 1848. Both doubt and anxiety can be felt as 'dizziness'. And, though he illustrates this notion primarily in relation to the specific boundary experience of anxiety, it is precisely dizziness which marks the limits of actuality in general:

> The possibility of dizziness lies in the composite of the psychical and the physical, an ambiguous joint boundary between the psychical and the physical. . . . Thus dizziness is an interplay between the psychical and the physical, even where it is easier to decide which is primarily active, although in many cases it is very difficult to decide.
>
> (*Journals*, 1: 749)

Kierkegaard likens despair, which is a 'developed' and 'spiritual' form of melancholy, to this dizziness. But the more 'expanded' and differentiated form of melancholy retains the essential characteristics of the original:

> A person thus afflicted often complains that something has fallen upon him, that it is as if he had a weight to bear etc. This pressure, this weight, is not anything external; it is, as one says of an optical or acoustical delusion, it is an inverse reflection of something external.
>
> (*Journals*, 1: 749)

Doubt and anxiety are specific forms of melancholy in which an individual is seized with an inexplicable 'weight' and disorientation, a fear of falling.

Equally, however, it is a weightless indefiniteness, a fantastic self-expansion into the infinite. Johannes Climacus later associates both the ideal and the sensuous forms of dizziness with the typically modern and fantastic conception of God, which 'as in a dream' combines the infinite with 'the disintegration of a sensual, soft despair'.[32] And in his unpublished study of Adler, Kierkegaard makes much of this 'lack of focus' as it affects the writings of this 'deranged genius'. Adler is completely carried away in dizziness:

> The dizzy is the wide, the endless, the unlimited, the boundless; and dizziness itself is the boundlessness of the senses. The indefinite is the ground of dizziness, but it is also a temptation to abandon oneself to it. . . . The dialectics of dizziness has thus in itself the contradiction of willing what one does not will, what one shudders at, whereas this shudder nevertheless frightens only . . . temptingly.
>
> (*Adler*, p. 128)

The boundlessness of sheer abstraction is dizziness, but this can take an ideal form as in Adler, or, more commonly, it might appear as a kind of sensuous undertow that continually threatens our sense of 'balance'. Indeed, it might be argued that the more usual form of dizziness is more common as a result of the long western prejudice in favour of the 'spiritual' over the 'earthly'; looking 'down' is more likely to make us dizzy than looking 'up'. And it might be argued, elaborating somewhat on the implicit contrast between the doubt of Johannes Climacus and the anxiety of Vigilius Haufniensis, that one of the novel characteristics of melancholy in modern society is that it gives rise to both 'ascending' and 'descending' forms of dizziness. The fact that the pseudonyms do not clearly distinguish these opposing 'directions' has the unexpected benefit of 'equating' the 'sensuous' with the 'ideal' as forms of abstraction, and thereby effecting an overdue revaluation of the sensuous. As the 'ideal' is frequently (if wrongly) viewed as a 'means' to self-development, the sensuous, by analogy, might also provide its own potential for spiritual growth, a supposition other pseudonyms were to take quite seriously.

Anxiety is a state of panic-stricken suspension and inactivity; at once attracted and repelled, the individual is 'frozen', as if on the edge of an abyss, fearful of the next moment, as of the end of time itself.[33] But there is less of the ideal in anxiety which is 'felt' in the stomach, as nausea, an inner emptying, as if the insides of the body were in the process of dissolving. Anxiety is a visceral dizziness, whereas doubt, which is 'located' in the head, is a kind of ideal vertigo. It is a disorientation in, or of, space and time; a feeling of being 'lost' and simultaneously moving in all directions. Both are characteristically modern forms of experience but draw on and adapt much older body-images. Anxiety, as nausea, links the ancient obscurity of 'black bile' with the modern preoccupation with 'heaviness', while doubt, as dizziness, exhibits an element of demonic 'light-headedness', or frenzy, as well as a peculiarly modern transparency.

These bodily metaphors are instructive. The associations to which the authors allude, between bodily states, inner feelings and the ontological structure of existence, are very general features of the western tradition.[34] Their significance here, apart from tying their thought directly to the immediate features of experience, lies in his covert but pronounced revaluation of anxiety (and therefore of sensuousness) as a positive, or at least potentially positive, aspect of that experience. The implicit linking of doubt and anxiety as dizziness follows from viewing both as the fluid boundaries between actuality and 'abstraction'. It is important to note that these boundaries are fluid, and that the pseudonyms do not claim that actuality can be preserved undialectically, as it were, by simply avoiding these vague states. The individual cannot help but become 'entangled' in abstraction: to withdraw into the 'safe' centre ground of the actual is merely to 'shrink' the sphere of personal existence. The individual would find only the refuge of melancholy, in which doubt and anxiety touch and intermingle. We have no option but to live 'on the edge' of existence.

In addition to anxiety over 'falling' into abstraction (what lies 'above' or 'below' actuality) Haufniensis introduces a consideration of a somewhat different kind: anxiety over the future (what is not yet actual). The peculiarly intimate connection between anxiety and the formation of a new selfhood is taken up by Anti-Climacus in *Practice in Christianity* and *Sickness Unto Death*, and became one of the most characteristic themes of the last of the pseudonymous authors.

It is in discussing the intricacies of anxiety that Vigilius completes the formal presentation of the structure of selfhood that was to be contained in *The Sickness Unto Death*. The 'misrelation' of finite and infinite, necessity and possibility, are dealt with there in some detail, but it is in *The Concept of Anxiety* that the relation of time and eternity within the structure of the self is more fully considered. This synthesis cannot be understood in terms of the aesthetic conception of time as infinitely divisible succession. In a brief but precise analysis Vigilius argues that any such conception annuls the present and relies on the purely metaphorical suggestiveness of a spatial image of past and future. Time for the existing self, however, must be actual. Actuality, in this context, can be conceived of as annulled succession – the present – and in this sense is the presence of the eternal. The actual present thus becomes the synthesis of the self, of the temporal and the eternal; and 'thus understood, the moment is not properly an atom of time but an atom of eternity'.[35] There is a fundamental difference between this 'first attempt, as it were, at stopping time' and the aesthetic pursuit of the vanishing moment.[36] The former introduces a new form of existence, it is the positing of spirit as spirit, and begins the development of religious subjectivity. Significantly, in the Christian tradition, 'the fullness of time' describes the inner transformation of a religious subjectivity, it is 'the moment as the eternal'. The eternal touches the self, and flows, as it were, into actuality. The duration of the self, the earnest self-determination of the ethicist, is once again revealed as a 'stage' rather than a completed unity. However extended and enduring, it cannot place itself beyond the relentless subversion of succession.

Thus, just as the development of the ideal, through doubt, returns the subject to actuality at a 'higher' point than the point of departure from it, so anxiety contains within itself the potential for spiritual development. The development through doubt is a kind of unlooked-for consolation that comes after the apparent failure of thought to reach its goal in the ideal; sinking back into actuality it finds itself again in an altered and enriched form. Development through anxiety is equally an unconscious process, which seems, in fact, to run counter to the consciousness of the subject. Anxiety brings the subject into a much more intimate relation to sin, an intimacy from which faith might be born.

PARADOX

Johannes's doubt is a barrier to the self-affirmation in absolute freedom for which he might have wished, but at the same time it betrays a love of truth essential to any genuinely thoughtful existence. In fact he is drawn apart equally by the claims of actuality and the claims of pure thought. He can neither integrate and harmonize these demands nor forget either one of them. He could not abandon his thesis – universal doubt – and 'it seemed as if a mysterious power held him to it'.[37] He has neither mastered doubt nor has he actualized himself in an 'existence-sphere'. The limbo of doubt is mirrored in the purgatory of anxiety in which the person is held motionless before the dual possibility of either realizing the self in a more developed actuality or of falling into the sensuous as an independent and immanent power (the demonic). The careful separation of these symmetrical relations can be seen as an essential part of the pseudonyms' elaboration of a Christian anthropology in place of an exclusive reliance on Socratic self-knowledge. Socrates had been unable to separate doubt from anxiety, so that his intellectual questioning was eroticized and his sensuousness intellectualized, both held together in a captivating immediacy. The Socratic entanglement is only another form, in fact, of the false 'projection' of the ideal and the sensuous, their expulsion from actuality into fantastic self-determining domains of their own. From the Socratic viewpoint, either immediacy is everything, or part of the immediate must be broken off and represented as something other than itself. In neither case can actuality itself be conceived as 'containing' its own possibilities of inner development and transcendence:

> In the Socratic view, every human being is himself the midpoint, and the whole world focuses only on him because his self-knowledge is God-knowledge.
>
> (*Fragments*, p. 11)

Four days before the publication of *The Concept of Anxiety*, Kierkegaard, under the name of Johannes Climacus, published *Philosophical Fragments*, which might have been termed 'the concept of actuality'. In this work, Johannes develops the theme of doubt to its furthest extremity in order to return it, so to speak, to the world of existence. In its monumental *Postscript* Johannes comments that the *Fragments* 'took its point of departure in paganism in order by imaginatively constructing to discover an understanding of existence that truly could be said to go beyond paganism'.[38]

Johannes has moved beyond his initial doubt and seeks in this work 'of almost bottomless dialectical complexity' to circumscribe existence philosophically.[39] He insists it is a 'fragment' and is to remain a fragment. There is no ambition to provide the point of departure for some new metaphysical 'system'. The aim is neither to 'purify' thought of the corruption of actuality, nor to set out some logically binding *a priori* categories of experience, but, in returning thought to the domain of actuality, to find ways of describing more precisely the peculiar character of existence itself. To this end his return to Socrates is not historical but what he terms 'algebraic': an effort to clarify at least one form of actuality.

In the *Fragments* Johannes Climacus finally asks aloud a question which has implicitly connected the pseudonyms whose works he himself comments upon: 'What is the change of coming into existence?'[40] Johannes Climacus and Vigilius Haufniensis had answered that question with respect to the coming into existence of the self as a synthesis that 'relates itself to itself ', a synthesis of soul and body through the 'medium' of spirit. Further, body has been identified as sensuousness, with the finite, temporal and necessary, while the soul has been defined as the mind's abstraction, as the infinite, eternal and free. Actuality, therefore, is at once a compound and a derived category, 'temporal and spatial being'.[41] Now 'coming into existence' is a change in being, not in essence, and while all existence is being, all being is not existence. In particular necessary being, or necessity, cannot come into existence:

> Precisely by coming into existence, everything that comes into existence demonstrates that it is not necessary, for the only thing that cannot come into existence is the necessary, because the necessary *is*.
>
> (*Fragments*, p. 74)

Hence, 'necessity stands all by itself ' and is immune to the changing qualification of existence. 'Nothing whatever comes into existence by way of necessity', he asserts with some vehemence, 'no more than necessity comes into existence or anything in coming into existence becomes the necessary'. And, conversely, 'all coming into existence occurs in freedom'.[42] And although he is particularly interested in the manner in which human being comes into existence, these remarks apply in principle to the whole realm of nature, whose sequence of efficient causes can be followed back to a freely acting cause. In the realm of human history, however, there is a 'redoubling' of this freedom in that its sequence of efficient causes is itself composed of freely acting agents. The historical thus has in itself 'the illusiveness of coming into existence'.[43]

The change of 'coming into existence' is the realization of a possibility, not the determination of necessity. It is a movement from the possible to the actual, in which necessity plays no part whatever. This argument has important and wide-ranging consequences, indeed it takes Johannes Climacus and Anti-Climacus an imposing volume each to set out the major philosophical and religious implications of this insight.

It is sufficient at this point to note the historical context of such an argument, which is apparently directed against the whole tendency of modern thought towards a conception of truth as, on the one hand, nature, viewed as a self-moving mechanism of efficient causes, or, on the other, as a realm of freely constructed concepts, unified as a network of 'necessary' logical relations. In particular Leibniz's version of ideal rationalism had been interpreted by some of his eighteenth-century followers, most notably Lessing, as a 'model' for Christian truth. The inner spiritual coherence of religious truth, that is to say, was conceived as analogous to (if not identical with) the consistency and systematic completeness of a perfected system of rational concepts. It is Leibniz indeed, rather than Hegel, who might be seen as the main target of Johannes's polemic.[44]

The Enlightenment understanding of belief as 'knowledge' and doubt as 'scepticism', even if they are adequate in relation to a 'system' of natural or of ideal categories, cannot in Johannes's view, be directly applied to any human reality. The difficulty arises from a failure to separate the 'vertical' from the 'horizontal' dimensions of existence. In terms of actuality, which is a continuous 'coming into existence', for example, doubt and belief are opposites, but not by virtue of their relation to an objective fact or truth:

> Belief and doubt are not two kinds of knowledge that can be defined in continuity with each other, for neither of them is a cognitive act, and they are opposite passions. Belief is a sense for coming into existence, and doubt is a protest against any conclusion that wants to go beyond immediate sensation and immediate knowledge.
>
> (*Fragments*, p. 84)

Doubt and belief as relations within existence are opposing dispositions to possibilities which have yet to come into existence. The difference is a distinction within the sphere of actuality rather than between existence and non-existence. The movement from doubt to belief, therefore, even if it were a matter of some limited empirical 'coming into existence', could not be effected by the demonstrative power of a train of reason.

Inasmuch as both doubt and belief encourage 'thought', it is thought permeated by existence, and both tend ultimately towards the affirmation – the most stringent criticism is also an affirmation – of this existence. Both are opposed, then, to the certainty which expresses itself in the abstraction of 'pure' thought. Uncertain thoughts – doubt and belief – remain embedded in existence and for this reason cannot perfect themselves as holistic images. The thought of actuality, and actual thought, do not lead to certainty but to the paradox. In a characteristically vivid and complex passage Johannes describes the paradox:

> But one must not think ill of the paradox, for the paradox is the passion of thought, and the thinker without the paradox is like the lover without passion: a mediocre fellow. But the ultimate potentiation of every passion is always to will its own downfall, and so it is also the ultimate passion of the understanding (*Forstand*) to will the collision, although in one way or another the collision must become its downfall. This, then, is the ultimate paradox of thought: to want to discover something that thought cannot think. This passion of thought is fundamentally present everywhere in thought, also in the single individual's thought insofar as he, thinking, is not merely himself.
>
> (*Fragments*, p. 37)

A self-willed destructiveness is given to thought by passion, by its resolute clinging to existence. And it can be observed wherever passion is evident:

> It is the same with the paradox of erotic love. A person lives undisturbed in himself, and then awakens the paradox of self-love as love for another, for one missing. . . . Just as the lover is changed by this paradox of love so that he almost does not recognize himself any more . . . so also that intimated paradox of the understanding reacts upon a person and upon his self-knowledge in such a way that he who believed that he knew himself now no longer is sure whether he perhaps is a more curiously complex animal.
>
> (*Fragments*, p. 39)

Passion is an expansive movement of existence, which is continually colliding with an unknown, and the paradox is the perpetually renewed encounter with this unknown:

> What, then, is the unknown? It is the frontier that is continually arrived at, and therefore when the category of motion is replaced by the category of rest it is the different, the absolutely different.
>
> (*Fragments*, p. 44)

The understanding, however, can grasp only those differences which are contained within it, and the paradox 'is the absolutely different in which there is no distinguishing mark'.[45] The paradox cannot be thought at all, it is a limit to thought, not a category within it: 'Defined as the absolutely different, it seems to be at the point of being disclosed, but not so, because the understanding cannot even think the absolutely different.'[46] This being the case, the 'absolutely different' is often assimilated to other forms of difference, and represented, or rather misrepresented, as the 'fantastic', the 'prodigious', the 'ridiculous' and so on.

The boundary, or 'frontier' as Johannes terms their point of contact, between the understanding and the paradox is unlike all other boundaries which define the pseudonym's topography of existence in all its complexity. The boundary between the 'spheres' of the aesthetic and the ethical (and by implication, in this perspective, between the ethical and the religious) is a spaceless void, while the boundaries between actuality, and both ideality and sensuousness, are regions of fluid ambiguity. The collision of the understanding with the paradox is topologically unique and productive of new and yet more allusive forms of experience.

There is nothing abstract and ideal about the transition of doubt into paradox. It must be conceived, rather, as another aspect of the transitions of despair, the melancholic defence against melancholy, which is the emergent structure of personal experience in the Present Age. But it would be quite misleading to imagine Kierkegaard as having little regard for the significance of 'thought' for human self-development. Quite the contrary; doubt impels the subject towards the limits of its existence-sphere, and once this existence is grasped ethically, transforms itself into the paradox from which the understanding shrinks back in bewilderment. While Johannes is firm in his rejection of systematic metaphysics, he none the less presents a view of thought as a privileged relation within actuality. It is in thought that an immanent principle of self-development is planted. And while thought, which for Johannes is never 'pure thought', cannot 'leap' the abyss between one existence-sphere and another, it introduces into actuality a dynamic and independent inner principle of development, or, more circumspectly, it might be said that such an inner principle manifests itself more clearly in the aspect of thought than in any other actual relation.

SIN

From the 'inclosed reserve' of melancholy the pseudonyms trace two movements through which the 'self-relating self ' emerges and expands. Each movement carries within it the possibility of a 'misrelation', a one-sided development that leads away from actuality into the non-existence of idealist thought or mute sensuousness. From melancholy springs both doubt and anxiety. The paradox is the potentiation of doubt as it passes through the earnestness of the ethical. It points beyond any aesthetic view of the ethical towards the construction of a religious form of actuality. In a symmetrical development, the demonic is conceived as the freely chosen self-development, or potentiation, of anxiety, and the demonic, as sin, also brings the subject to the boundary of the religious.

Anti-Climacus, in *The Sickness Unto Death*, calls despair a sin, and Vigilius Haufniensis investigated anxiety primarily as an 'orienting deliberation' on the problem of sin. The movement towards the religious, therefore, is not straightforward; it may involve a confrontation with sin rather than, or as well as, an encounter with the paradox. The aesthetic works had exposed any 'direct' seizure of the religious as a self-delusion. From the starting point of melancholy, it seems, the extremities of the paradox and of sin have to be intimately 'worked through' if the individual is to be liberated from the fragmentation of modern life. In another sense, these extremities condition every life-possibility, and play a hidden part, therefore, in the development of the least troubled of individuals. Anti-Climacus himself points out that the vast majority of people go through life unaware of such dialectical difficulties:

> Most men are characterized by a dialectic of indifference and live a life so far removed from the good (faith) that it is almost too spiritless to be called sin – indeed almost too spiritless to be called despair.
>
> (*Sickness*, p. 101)

There is a 'dialectical frontier' between despair and sin which is revealed in the most developed form of aesthetic 'poet-existence'. A poetic longing for God itself becomes an element in despair, and, therefore, an attractive illusion obscuring the genuinely religious. Such a poetic individual 'loves God above all, God who is his only consolation in his secret anguish, and yet he loves the anguish and will not give it up'.[47] Despair is transformed into sin when the despairing self is defined in relation to a self-generated, sentimental, illusion of God. The ideal and the sensuous in this self-deception are, once again, closely related:

> He becomes a poet of the religious as one who became a poet through an unhappy love affair and blissfully celebrates the happiness of erotic love. . . . Yet this poet's description of the religious – just like that other poet's description of erotic love – has a charm, a lyrical verve that no married man's and no His Reverence's presentations have.
>
> (*Sickness*, p. 78)

Sin is a new 'qualification' of despair, and not simply the intensification of a previous state or condition. It is a genuine transition. Now while Anti-Climacus admits that 'there is nothing meritorious in being in despair to a higher degree' and, from an ethical standpoint, 'the more intensive form of despair is further from salvation than the lesser form', it is difficult to escape the impression that (spiritually) he considers the extremity of sin to be a *religiously* terrifying (and, therefore, a religiously valuable) position.[48] As Johannes de Silentio had illustrated, religious categories (including sin) cannot be comprehended within universal moral rules. Such rules are ultimately conventions of human behaviour, and the difference between sin and despair is precisely that it is a movement beyond ethical categories towards the intuition of a religious truth. Sin also is a leap, an unprecedented form of existence which unpredictably breaks free of despair just at the point where it seems to have become despair's most profound possibility.

The contradiction which is at the root of sin is to will not to be the self. In one sense this is a general formula of despair, as the 'expanded form' of melancholy, but in sin the will has developed through the existence-sphere to a point where, implicitly, it recognizes its own inner freedom and yet negates it. The remote Augustinian tone of Johannes's discourse – the conception of will as implying spirit, the insistence on the freedom of the will, and the notion of despair as primarily a weakness of the will – is given a darker and more distinctly modern tone in the idea of a demonic and self-destructively defiant subjectivity as an alluring spiritual possibility.[49]

How can such a possibility be understood? Certainly it cannot be grasped intellectually, as a pure thought, or as part of a system of dogmatic categories. It must be accepted as an aspect of the paradox, as a boundary against which existence continually pushes and continually falls back. None the less Vigilius Haufniensis attempts to clarify the psychological presuppositions of such a view. Anxiety, properly understood, then becomes a psychical 'representative' of sin's possibility.

Anxiety is the intuition of sin, but sin breaks free of anxiety by a leap. Sin, that is to say, has a quality of its own, a quality which is not contained within any aesthetically constituted sphere of existence. The dogmatic problem of original sin, thus, cannot be understood as if it were the natural consequence of a human act of misdirected will. The 'first sin' was sin in the sense that it opened up an entirely new world: 'The new quality appears with the first, with the leap, with the suddenness of the enigmatic.'[50] Thus, 'through the first sin, sin came into the world', and nothing 'caused' this first sin, so we can only say that 'sin came into the world by a sin'.[51] Rather than say that Adam's action, however motivated, brought sin into the world – which is really a failed attempt to 'explain' sin – we should say that 'by the first sin, sinfulness came into Adam'.[52] And, notes Kierkegaard, 'the sexual is not sin; when I first posit sin, I also posit the sexual as sinfulness'.[53] The Fall is a continually original qualitative leap. This remains true for every subsequent sin, which is free of the determination of both logical necessity and efficient causality: 'sinfulness is not an epidemic that spreads like cowpox', Vigilius acutely remarks.[54] Nor is sin a one-sided temptation to evil. This is a confusion of religious and 'ethical' forms of being. Just as faith cannot be assimilated to the good, sin is not the same as evil. Indeed, there is a powerful temptation to the good, which, as much as the tendency to evil, proves to be an obstacle to the religious life. Inner spiritual freedom, that is to say, may be subordinated under some falsely projected ethical norm: 'The bondage of sin is an unfree relation to the evil, but the demonic is an unfree relation to the good.'[55] Sin, if not a religious category in its own right, thus refers to transitional forms through which actuality is transformed.

The religious 'sphere' is also an existence-sphere; it is the most determinate of actualities, but it is determined 'before God', rather than in terms of finite human values and relations. Sin is a religious category in just this sense; it exists not in the nature of a specific act, but in the qualification of the individual's inner personality as formed 'absolutely', that is 'before God'. The discovery of sin is at once a realization of this absolute inwardness and the consciousness of the absolute difference between man and God:

> Sin is the one and only predication about a human being that in no way, either *via negationis* (by denial) or *via eminentiae* (by idealization), can be stated of God.... As sinner man is separated from God by the most chasmal qualitative abyss.
>
> (*Sickness*, p. 122)

Sin discloses, in relation to the Absolute Paradox, the purely human character of the human. That sin is a qualification of the personality, rather than an intellectual construct or a form of self-understanding, is shown in its bewildering possibility as both the consciousness of sin, and the sin which is the absence of the consciousness of sin.

The mysterious relation between anxiety and sin raises, in a different way, a problem central to the thought of Johannes Climacus. What is the relation of individual experience given in its 'topological structure', on the one hand, and the history of human experience, on the other? The issue had been raised initially by the claim that philosophy now begins with doubt rather than in wonder. Philosophy, which deals with the universal, seems to have changed, implying that human being has, in some profound way, also changed. The problem is not resolved at that point by Johannes, who subsequently raises it in a yet more acute form, in the claim that the possibility of the religious is inherent in the structure of our experience. In a similar fashion Vigilius insists that 'every human life is religiously designed', that actuality discloses to us the possibility of the religious, even if it cannot open a way for its immediate occupation.[56] Both faith and sin, however, seem to have some specific historical point of origin in the history of the world.

By two distinct routes, then, the reader has been brought back to actuality; to a new existence charged with the possibilities of religious transformation. The oscillations of doubt and dread, whether or not they are taken to the extremities of the paradox and the consciousness of sin, more certainly than any aesthetic 'leap' gather together and coalesce the elements of experience and form them into a developing selfhood. The 'self ' emerges in this process as a kind of spatial extension of actuality, and casts the originally intermixed elements of melancholy into two distinct realms of non-existence. Sensuousness, thus, takes up the singular 'heaviness' of melancholy, and represents its lethargic and undignified immobility as sunk 'beneath' existence, while abstraction projects its dislocated 'dizziness' into a domain that hovers 'above' actuality. The ethical dissolves under the impact of a double oscillation. Its movement into abstraction collapses on contact with the paradox; and its movement into sensuousness is repelled by the discovery of sin. By neither route, however, is the self wholly freed from the guilt-consciousness which is the common legacy of the ethical 'stage', and both bring the individual to a second and more fearful abyss.

These issues are dealt with by Johannes Climacus and Anti-Climacus in, respectively, *Concluding Unscientific Postscript* and *Practice in Christianity*. And they are addressed in a somewhat changed context. Where *Sickness Unto Death* and *The Concept of Anxiety* deal with the 'negative' side of human existence (and do not wholly escape a certain aesthetic fascination with their extremities) and *Philosophical Fragments* advertises the dangers of thought (without even disguising the author's infatuation with the dialectic), these two major works approach the central questions of existence in a more positive light. The focus is shifted away from the universal 'misrelations', in the synthesis of the self (despair) towards the real possibilities (passion) inherent in actuality. Despair is the disintegrative process of modernity at work in the individual personality; passion, though it is all but absent from the Present Age, remains its positive counterpart.

Chapter 6

The religion of inwardness: an offensive philosophy

Faith is not a work of reason and therefore cannot succumb to any attack by reason, because believing happens as little by means of reason as tasting and seeing.

J.G. Hamann, *Socratic Memorabilia*

Conflict and distress, sin and death, the devil and hell make up the reality of religion. So far from releasing man from guilt and destiny, it brings man under their sway. Religion possesses no solution of the problem of life, rather it makes of the problem a wholly insoluble enigma.

Karl Barth, *The Epistle to the Romans*

The transition to the religious, unlike the transitions within the aesthetic, is filled with innumerable intermediate forms; and from the viewpoint of philosophy the religious is this transition. Johannes Climacus, in *Philosophical Fragments*, undermined the foundations of the conventional, ethical view of religion. In doing so, he had not claimed any special intimacy with the religious. He had not claimed to be an 'exceptional individual' who, by virtue of a personal command, freed himself from the constraints of ethical demands. Neither did he pose as an 'ordinary' religious individual, naively questioning the tenets of his own faith. His distinctively philosophical approach towards the religious, like Vigilius Haufniensis's parallel approach through sin, leads to the disclosure of new and extreme forms of individuation, but does not yet bestow upon him the prize of religious subjectivity. He can clearly visualize the possibility of the religious, but it remains, for him, a frustrating truth outside himself and to which (in spite of his strictures against the system) he can relate himself only through the mediation of dialectical reflection. The religious seems to retreat before this dual approach, and, like a mountaineer exhausted by effort and disappointment as each new peak is scaled only to reveal the final goal to be a yet more distant and inaccessible pinnacle, the reader begins to wonder at the resilience and folly of those who persevere in an apparently fruitless task.

Throughout the pseudonymous work each new position is not simply a discrete objective possibility for existence, but an entire subjective world placed within existence and related to, but not coincidental with, any other position. To represent the transition to the religious, therefore, demands a further prodigious creative effort on Kierkegaard's part. Climacus, in taking up the challenge of describing the transition, produces a far bulkier work than the *Fragments* which had established its possibility. In the *Postscript* the religious is not a contentless leap from which the subject awakens, so to speak, as a new person in the midst of a transformed world. The transformation begins, certainly, in a series of discontinuous and unheralded categories, but these have to be interrelated and synthesized within the individual. The religious transition does not simply 'happen'. Anti-Climacus traces the same ground as Johannes, and describes the same transition but, so to speak, from the other side, from a position secured within religious categories themselves. Climacus looks forward to the religious, constantly turning towards it as the *telos* of all his reflections, while Anti-Climacus, looking back from the religious, redefines these transitional forms from his new point of view. Anti-Climacus is 'prior to' or 'before' Johannes Climacus, and less in a temporal or a logical so much as in an ontological sense.[1]

The movement out of and back into the ethical, by way of either doubt or anxiety, reveals the possibility of a religious subjectivity which this same movement puts beyond the reach of actuality. Both excursions return the subject to actuality, but to an actuality of a new sort. The elements of subjectivity, disunited by the departure from existence, cannot come together again in immediacy. This further potentiation of despair both authors call *offence*. From the perspective of doubt it is a token of the 'unhappy encounter' between the paradox and the understanding: 'If the encounter is not in mutual understanding, then the relation is unhappy, and the understanding's unhappy love, if I dare call it that . . . we could more specifically term *offence*'.[2] And from the direction of anxiety 'the sin of despairing of the forgiveness of sins is *offence*'.[3] In both cases, although the subject has a powerful intuition of a new religious existence, he or she clings to some conception of the ethical, to the humanly universal demand for reason and goodness.

The 'natural person' (in the sense of the modern secular individual rather than the 'primitive') is bound to be offended, intellectually and morally, by the claim that were the individual freely to trust in a being whose very possibility (given his definitional attributes) is contrary to reason, then his or her sins would be forgiven.

Johannes Climacus sets out to resolve this difficulty, or at least to set out what would be required for its resolution, in *Concluding Unscientific Postscript to Philosophical Fragments*, published in February 1846. He describes this work as 'a renewed attempt in the same vein as the pamphlet, a new approach to the issue of the *Fragments*'.[4] It is not initially altogether clear that the *Fragments*, which raises a host of philosophical and psychological issues, is in fact organized around a single problem. The relation between the two works might be expressed, however, by saying that the issue of the relationship of individual existence to the truth – or what is truth for an individual – is so many-sided that it can be treated only in a fragmentary fashion. But once the issue has been clearly raised, in a series of partially connected discourses, it can be given a more fundamental and connected treatment. This treatment is possible only because the reader has been advanced to a new position from which the underlying connectedness of the *Fragments* can be glimpsed. The issue of what is truth for an individual only comes fully to light, that is to say, when the existence of the individual itself nears the point of religious realization. The *Postscript*, it must be remembered, is still not a direct work, it conceals its actual author in a characterization, and it cannot be read, therefore, as a straightforward philosophical treatise. It is abundantly clear from the *Fragments*, in fact, that neither it nor its *Postscript* is to be mistaken for any systematic metaphysics. Its dialectic is the dialectic of existence. So the truth which is contained in the writings of Johannes Climacus has to be stored up, as it were, and held in abeyance until the reader has reached that stage of preparatory exhaustion in which it can be received. The *Fragments* appears to be the final anticipatory exercise to which the *Postscript* releases, as a kind of extended exhalation, the entire pent-up energy of the pseudonymous authorship.

HISTORY

The aesthetic pseudonyms might be viewed as so many failed attempts to provide a practical answer to the question: 'How, in the context of the Present Age, am I to become an "I"?' In Kantian terms, what are the preconditions for the emergence of individuality? Some of the pseudonyms had, implicitly, asked: 'How might I become an "authentic I"?' In the *Fragments* the problem of the individual's relation to truth was taken up: 'How am I to become "an eternal I"?' But this was in a purely Socratic fashion. The *Postscript* now addresses the question in terms of Christianity; in the context of the Present Age, 'How am I to become a Christian?' The concluding pages of the *Fragments* had already raised this question in the form in which it was first to appear in the *Postscript.* Alluding to Lessing's discussion of Reimarus, Johannes remarks that

> Christianity is the only historical phenomenon that despite the historical – indeed, precisely by means of the historical – has wanted to be the single individual's point of departure for his eternal consciousness, has wanted to base his happiness on his relation to something historical.
>
> (*Fragments*, p. 109)

Johannes subjects to detailed scrutiny Lessing's views about the relation between the historical 'evidence' for Christianity and the character of contemporary 'belief '. In fact, he develops Lessing's criticism in a rigorous fashion, and regards Lessing as fully justified in his assertion that the 'accidental truths of history can never become the proof of necessary truths of reason'. But where Lessing makes an exception for the immediate followers of Christ, who had enjoyed the privilege of direct eye-witness 'evidence' of the miracles, Johannes takes the view that no empirical events whatever can, or could, provide such an evidential basis for Christianity.[5] Johannes goes back, through Lessing, to the argument of Reimarus that in the sayings of Jesus 'there were no exalted mysteries or points of doctrine which he explains, proves, and proclaims'.[6] And though he agrees both that the 'inner truth' of Christianity is something independent of its actual history (and not simply of the contingencies of its recorded history), he does not view, as they had, this 'inner truth' as either a philosophical statement or a moral code.

Empirical evidence is always doubtful, and the process of history itself a series of contingencies:

> with regard to the historical the greatest certainty is only an *approximation*, and an approximation is too little to build his

> happiness upon and is so unlike an eternal happiness that no
> result can ensue.
>
> (*Postscript*, p. 23)

In spite of the enormous wealth of scholarly effort 'a little dialectical doubt' will always remain. Indeed, the scholar, in investing so much time and labour in trying to 'establish' the foundational 'facts' of Christianity, runs the risk of becoming 'stuck in the parenthesis of his labor'.[7] The error is to look for certainty where, in principle, none could exist. Scholarly endeavour does not lead to faith because 'faith does not result from a straightforward scholarly deliberation; nor does it come directly'.[8]

More than this, if objective certainty in the matter of the origins of Christianity could be reached, it would be destructive of genuine faith. 'Existing uncertainty' Johannes claims to be a 'profitable schoolmaster'. Faith exists for an individual in the form of a 'passionate interest' in his or her own happiness, and 'if passion is taken away, faith no longer exists'.[9]

Conversely, the critical understanding of scripture can do nothing to undermine faith. Schleiermacher's *Speeches* had made similar arguments well known, and had already freed critical historical scholarship from the demands of faith. Johannes, however, wants to go much further. These arguments are merely the prelude to an assault on the central problem of the relation between faith and history. As a conclusion that springs directly from his conception of Christianity, the 'objective' route to faith is dismissed:

> Christianity is spirit; spirit is inwardness; inwardness is
> subjectivity; subjectivity is essentially passion, and at its maximum
> an infinite, personally interested interest for one's eternal
> happiness.
>
> (*Postscript*, p. 33)

Christianity is not an 'objective' doctrine or 'sum of propositions' whose credibility depends on the likelihood that specific historical events have been accurately recorded. Nor, equally, is it 'proved' by the mere persistence of a community of believers.[10] And it is just this apparent lack of historical foundation that has made a speculative viewpoint appealing to modern 'enlightened' individuals. The problem of the truth of Christianity has, thus, been wrenched from any historical context and turned into a contemporary metaphysical encounter:

The question of its truth therefore becomes a matter of permeating it with thought in such a way that finally Christianity itself is the eternal thought.

(Postscript, p. 50)

The speculative approach, however, is equally objective in its method. Christianity is defined through it as a reality external to the observing subject. But Johannes wonders, rhetorically, if such a method can penetrate Christianity at all, or whether it is rather a way of concealing its reality in thoughtful illusions: 'what if objective indifference cannot come to know anything whatever?' he asks; or, indeed, whether 'like is understood only by the like', and 'Christianity is indeed subjectivity, is inward deepening'. Then any objective method, historical or speculative, will succeed only in misrepresenting its truth, and diverting attention towards religiously irrelevant philosophical problems.[11]

The thinker who wishes to grasp Christianity – that is to say, wishes to relate intellectually rather than religiously to Christianity – must, in fact, be genuinely 'interested' in its inwardness. The originality of Johannes's claim, therefore, is not so much that Christianity, as an authentic religion, can exist only in a specific form of inwardness, but that a proper understanding of this depends upon the philosopher's direct experience of this form. There can be no such thing as 'objective knowledge' of Christianity:

> In all knowing in which it holds true that the object of cognition is the inwardness of the subjective individual himself, it holds true that the knower must be in that state. But the expression for the utmost exertion of subjectivity is the infinitely passionate interest in its eternal happiness.
>
> *(Postscript,* p. 53)

The philosopher who claims to be a believer becomes comic when he makes his eternal happiness hinge on the outcome of his speculation; he both religiously and philosophically misconstrues the issue of the truth of Christianity. This truth lies in the 'recessive self-feeling of the subject', so that the philosophical task of elucidating Christianity (which is an essential task for some people only) must begin with the subject.

It is just in this context that Johannes praises Lessing, whose real significance, he claims, lies in the dynamic and plastic character of his thought. In Lessing thought is always an aspect of existence, to which, as a process of becoming, it is continually adapted, so that 'his thought must correspond to the form of existence'.[12] And as an 'existing thinker' or an 'existence-thinker' Lessing must resort to forms of 'indirect communication'. The more his thought grasps and penetrates existence, the more it becomes absorbed in existence, the less it can take on the role of a medium of communication. And in existing in his thought, 'he becomes more and more subjectively isolated'.[13] And 'while the elusiveness of existence isolates me whenever I apprehend it', the need for self-expression is forced into indirect paths.

While finding a justification for the method of indirect communication in Lessing, Johannes fails to find a satisfactory resolution of the difficulty of relating the inner truth of Christianity to history. Lessing's error, he argues, lies in his residual hope that historical certainty about the origins of Christianity might, at some future date, be achieved and, with it, the elucidation of the necessity of Christian truth. Johannes, however, has rejected such a possibility, and with it any route to Christianity other than the self-confirming leap.

According to Johannes, however, this does not mean that Christianity has been freed from any relation to its own history or to the history of the societies within which it has developed. This is just another instance of the fundamental character of Christian truth as paradox: 'the basis of the paradox of Christianity is that it continually uses time and the historical in relation to the eternal'.[14] Incomprehensibly Christianity requires a historical point of departure, and must maintain, throughout its development, a constant relation to the historical. This, indeed, is one of the central arguments of Johannes's complex book, and can best be understood as an aspect of his most fundamental contention – that Christianity, because it is a form of actuality, rather than an idea or a sensuous form, has within it all the characteristics of existence, namely becoming, subjectivity and passion. Christianity does not, therefore, unite history and belief in some exalted ideal state of mind; rather it holds them apart, generating through the tension of their difference the very passion in which they are none the less bound together.

THE SUBJECTIVE THINKER

Johannes concludes that while a logical system is possible, an existential system is an impossible contradiction. Hegel is charged, consequently, not so much with departing from actuality into speculation, but with attempting to carry actuality up into the ether of pure thought. His fundamental error (and at the same time his fundamental insight into the true character of contemporaneous existence) lies in his effort to introduce motion into logic. But a logical system must exclude all existential 'qualifications', and movement (in the sense of purpose or intention) belongs uniquely to the spirit of actuality.[15] Hegel, furthermore, begins not with immediacy, as he claims, but with reflection through which he tries (and fails) to reach the immediate.[16]

System and existence cannot be merged: 'system and conclusiveness correspond to each other, but existence is the very opposite. . . . Existence is the spacing that holds apart; the systematic is the conclusiveness that combines.'[17] The incompleteness of existence cannot be properly represented, far less explained, as a 'category' within any system. The modern idea of reason has traversed an enormous distance from Descartes to Hegel, yet the speculative system is immanent in its birth as a project of 'pure' thought. The ideal of detachment, objectivity and logical coherence ends in a formalism which cannot even mirror the world from which it has detached itself. Even so, non-existent illusion that it is, the system has come to disguise and dominate people's conceptions of themselves, unnecessarily constraining the possibilities of actuality left open to them. Johannes draws attention to this false idealism which the Enlightenment has bequeathed to the contemporary world:

> To be a human being has been abolished, and every speculative thinker confuses himself with humankind, whereby he becomes something infinitely great and nothing at all.
>
> (*Postscript*, p. 124)

If Christianity is made an 'object of knowledge' and part, therefore, of an 'external' reality, it is destroyed. And to approach it 'religiously' in this light is even more fundamentally mistaken: 'an objective acceptance of Christianity (*sit venia verbo*) is paganism or thoughtlessness'.[18] Christianity is not an 'object' which, external to the subject, can be known in its detachment, it is not a 'thing' which can be understood in that way at all:

Christianity, therefore, protests against all objectivity; it wants the subject to be infinitely concerned about himself. What it asks about is the subjectivity; the truth of Christianity, if it is at all, is only in this; objectively, it is not at all.

(*Postscript*, p. 130)

Christianity is wholly inward; all its apparently outward forms are no more than attempts at indirect communication – attempts which have themselves been absorbed into a historical process through which they become misrepresented as authoritative statements.

The theory of the spheres, when combined with the anthropology of doubt and anxiety, provides a precise means of charting the possibilities of subjectivity within modern life. The aesthetic is an initial form of subjectivity, but one shrunken and crushed by melancholy. What the pseudonymous authors describe is a series of developments of subjectivity itself. Inwardness is expanded, becomes more highly differentiated and complex, and contains a wider variety of content. This process, though at points discontinuous, seems to chart the underlying development towards a 'natural religion'. But it does not 'unfold' as a consequence of rational thought and reflection, or of the slow and unconscious evolution of nature itself; its possibilities are given – in relation to the conditions of modern life – and have the appearance, at least, of an immanent structure. There is, that is to say, nothing necessary in this 'structure', which is nothing more than the arrangement of the pseudonyms into a 'developmental' sequence. The reader is free to accept or reject any position. These 'natural' positions, however, do not exhaust the possibilities of subjectivity. Johannes assures us that 'faith is indeed the highest passion of subjectivity'.[19] And faith lies outside the realm of 'natural' possibilities, in the passionate embrace of the paradox.

Christianity is the highest form of subjectivity; it is pure inwardness, rather than pure thought. Johannes, as a 'subjective thinker', tries to grasp the character of Christianity by developing the contrast between an objective and a subjective thinker. The importance of his effort lies not simply in demonstrating (if such a demonstration were really required) that, his polemical stance in relation to the philosophy of his own day notwithstanding, thought which is tied to existence is fundamental to the proper understanding of life, but, more importantly, that such thought is a crucial lever upon existence itself, and a way through which the subject may develop in inwardness.

His famous dictum, therefore, that 'truth is subjectivity' does not mean that 'knowledge of the world' is a matter of subjective whim, nor does it mean that subjectivity is always valid 'in itself '. He is referring exclusively to his own approach to Christianity. The truth of Christianity is subjectivity, and this is not to be confused with the many 'objective truths' in relation to the external world of nature and history which Johannes is perfectly willing to concede exist (though they cannot be known with certainty). And, as the other pseudonyms had amply demonstrated the possibility of the personality losing itself in provisional, undeveloped, illusory and false self-images, it is clear that not all forms of subjectivity are truthful.

In relation to the exclusive focus on the truth of Christianity, Johannes feels let down by current metaphysical orthodoxies. Empiricism declares that an underlying conformity of thought and being guarantees our knowledge of the world, while idealism maintains that a conformity of being with thought defines the world. But if being is understood as empirical being then:

> truth itself is transformed into a *desideratum*, and everything is placed in the process of becoming (*Vorden*), because the empirical object is not finished, and the existing knowing spirit is itself in the process of becoming. Thus truth is an approximating whose beginning cannot be established absolutely, because there is no conclusion that has retroactive power.
>
> (*Postscript*, p. 189)

'Knowledge' is not to be confused with 'truth', and it is only the latter which interests Johannes. And efforts to conflate the two, as in Fichte's influential Romanticism of the ego, are wholly misguided. The 'I-am-I' is sheer fantasy, and is reached only by a process of abstraction in which every statement is emptied of any actual content. The conformity of thought and being is realized uniquely in God: 'but it is not that way for any existing spirit, because this spirit, itself existing, is in the process of becoming'.[20] Thus, for any existing individual, thought and being are kept apart, and truth must be quite distinct from a relation of identity. In this context Johannes distinguishes two forms of truth for the existing individual:

To objective reflection, truth becomes something objective, an

> object, and the point is to disregard the subject. To subjective reflection, truth becomes appropriation, inwardness, subjectivity, and the point is to immerse oneself, existing in subjectivity.
>
> (*Postscript*, p. 192)

Objective reflection, it is again worth emphasizing, is not regarded by Johannes, or any other of the pseudonyms, as false. Rather, its validity is held to be limited to specific circumstances. It leads to mathematical or logical truth which is wholly independent of the subject, and of value for precisely that reason. Thus,

> the way to the objective truth goes away from the subject, and while the subject and subjectivity become indifferent (*ligegyldig*), the truth also becomes indifferent, and that is precisely its objective validity.
>
> (*Postscript*, p. 193)

Equally, subjectivity is no guarantee of truth, for we have in the beautiful example of Don Quixote 'the prototype of the subjective lunacy in which the passion of inwardness grasps a particular fixed finite idea'.[21] Finite things must be understood objectively, but infinite things must be understood subjectively, that is to say they cannot be understood through abstraction. To confuse the two is characteristic of the modern age:

> Of what help is it to explain how the eternal truth is to be understood eternally when the one to use the explanation is prevented from understanding it in this way because he is existing and is merely a fantast if he fancies himself to be *sub specie aeterni*.
>
> (*Postscript*, p. 192)

Rather, it is the case that,

> he must avail himself precisely of the explanation of how the eternal truth is to be understood in the category of time by someone who by existing is himself in time, something the honoured professor himself admits, if not always, then every three months when he draws his salary.
>
> (*Postscript*, p. 192)

The philosophical demand for unity, for the identity of subject and object, cannot be the basis of actual life. To become aware of the truth means to exist inwardly and, therefore, to be conscious of the self a process of becoming which is unrealizable as an '*I-I*'.

Yet from time to time, 'this instant is the moment of passion'. The modern philosopher, therefore, is wrong to condemn passion, which, far from obscuring truth, 'for the existing person is existence at its very highest'. Johannes pleads eloquently on behalf of passion, in which 'the existing subject is infinitized in the eternity of imagination and yet is also most definitely himself'.[22] A critical reader might think him too eloquent, and ask if there is any difference between the passionate 'eternity of imagination' and an 'abstraction' of the mind? But this unsystematic unity is just the paradox that sets his reflection apart from Hegel's:

> The fantastical *I-I* is not infinitude and finitude in identity, since neither the one nor the other is actual; it is a fantastical union with a cloud, an unfruitful embrace, and the relation of the individual *I* to this mirage is never stated.
>
> (*Postscript*, p. 197)

The essential relation in the knowledge which interests Johannes is not that between subject and object, but that between knowledge and the knower.[23] 'All ethical and ethico-religious knowledge', he writes, 'has an essential relationship to the existence of the knower'. Thus, Socrates (unlike Hegel), for all his profession of ignorance, is essentially related to the truth. His ignorance (which is a species of knowledge) is held with 'infinite inward passion'.[24]

From his beginning with the burden of doubt, and the obstacle of uncertainty, Johannes moves relentlessly towards a new point of view from which 'objective uncertainty' becomes a precondition for the existing individual's appropriation of Christian truth. Truth is '*an objective uncertainty held fast, through appropriation with the most passionate inwardness*'. It is precisely 'the daring venture of choosing the objective uncertainty with the passion of the infinite'. And it is just this uncertainty which 'intensifies the infinite passion of inwardness'.[25]

This conception of truth is 'an equivalent expression of faith', and Johannes, thus, takes the view that faith is essentially linked to uncertainty. Doubt, therefore, is a fundamental element of faith, and without it faith is accepted naively as an objective doctrine. 'Without risk there is no faith', he concludes pointedly, and in a passage resonant of Pascal writes:

I observe nature in order to find God, and I do indeed see omnipotence and wisdom, but I also see much that troubles and disturbs. The *summa summarum* of this is an objective uncertainty, but the inwardness is so very great, precisely because it grasps this objective uncertainty with all the passion of the infinite.

(*Postscript*, p. 204)

Faith is a contradiction, rather than a mediation: 'the contradiction between the infinite passion of inwardness and the objective uncertainty'.[26] It is not necessarily the case that the 'eternal essential truth' is in itself a paradox, but in relationship to an existing individual it must appear so. For Socrates this relationship was incompletely interiorized as 'ignorance', which is a kind of 'analogue of faith' which maintains, so to speak, one foot in objective reflection. The more developed Christian form is the 'absurd', which, having no natural or objective equivalent, rests entirely within the subject.

Not only, therefore, is uncertainty a precondition of faith, it must be continually present within it:

Faith has, namely, two tasks: to watch for and at every moment to make the discovery of improbability, the paradox, in order then to hold it fast with the passion of inwardness.

(*Postscript*, p. 233)

The temptation to construe God's necessity from the 'evidence' of nature ought, therefore, to be resisted. Any view which proclaims a direct and immediate relation to God is viewed by Johannes as paganism, for while 'nature is certainly the work of God, only the work is directly present, not God'.[27] And Johannes derives from the anticosmological vision of the *deus absconditus* his most powerful argument in favour of the indirect communication of Christian truth:

No anonymous author can more slyly hide himself, and no maieutic can more carefully recede from a direct relation than God can.

(*Postscript*, p. 243)

In concluding that 'every direct communication with regard to truth as inwardness is a misunderstanding', Johannes is drawn towards the 'contemporary effort in Danish literature', which most conspicuously adopts an indirect approach.[28] He discusses the previously published pseudonymous works, placing them in the context of his now clearly defined philosophical question: what does it mean for an existing individual to be a Christian? The earlier pseudonyms had, in fact, already asked the question in a less philosophical fashion: what does it mean for an individual to exist in the modern world? Johannes claims that neither question can be answered by 'objective reflection', and that adopting the method of 'subjective reflection' already contains an implicit answer to both:

> My main thought was that, because of the copiousness of knowledge, people in our day have forgotten what it means *to exist*, and what *inwardness* is, and that the misunderstanding between speculative thought and Christianity could be explained by that.
>
> (*Postscript*, p, 249)

EXISTENCE

Christian truth is the truth of existence; a truth which, in contrast to the tempting certainties of idealism and materialism, can be realized in actuality, and only in actuality. Johannes never tires of making this point. Abstract speculation serves only to 'elevate' the whole of existence into a tensionless void of non-existence. It grants a kind of salvation 'by killing me as a particular existing individual and then making me immortal'.[29] But this 'facile deification of pure thought' cannot even succeed in its own terms. As the abstract thinker remains an existing individual, 'in one way or another he must be absentminded'.[30] The speculative philosopher cannot cease being an existing individual, even in the moment of his most rarefied thought, and is thus drawn into a contradiction. And as this contradiction is itself a sign of existence there is a sense in which the speculative system, for all its distortions, none the less grasps an element of truth.[31]

Compared to the thin and distorted vision of existence offered by philosophy Christianity grasps and holds on to the full meaning of actuality. Johannes exemplifies the existential concern of Christianity first of all by elaborating a point that, implicit in the earlier aesthetic production (particularly in *Repetition*), was raised explicitly in the *Fragments*. Existence is not a changeless state but a continuous 'coming into existence', so that actuality is always moving forward, always disclosing itself in new forms of being, and this fundamental condition is reflected in Christianity:

> when I join eternity and becoming, I do not gain rest but the future. Certainly this is why Christianity has proclaimed the eternal as the future, because it was proclaimed to existing persons, and this is why it also assumes an absolute *aut/aut*.
>
> (*Postscript*, p. 307)

Existence is full of contradictions, it is incomplete and unfinished. It appears so 'thoughtless' as to resist conceptualization. Yet thought is, and remains, part of existence, penetrating its particularity with reflective categories:

> Existence, like motion, is a very difficult matter to handle. If I think it, I cancel it, and then I do not think it. It would seem correct to say that there is something that cannot be thought – namely, existing. But again there is the difficulty that existence puts it together in this way: the one who is thinking is existing.
>
> (*Postscript*, pp. 308–9)

This remains a fundamental problem of representation; existence in its entirety can be represented only by part of itself, and we always run the risk of mistaking the internal relations of the system of representation for the entirety of what it represents. Johannes's complaint is not that 'thought' is in some sense unreal, but that it cannot replicate all the characteristics of the reality we have to think about. The difficulty is made worse when, in an effort to clarify the 'rules of the system', we ignore existence altogether:

> Now, whereas pure thinking summarily cancels all motion, or meaninglessly introduces it into logic, the difficulty for the existing person is to give existence the continuity without which everything just disappears.
>
> (*Postscript*, p. 312)

It is precisely this difficulty which is addressed by Christianity, whose subjective truth perpetuates itself in the passion of 'momentary certainty'. In Christian truth thought interpenetrates and qualifies existence. This is felt as passion, which is an intellectual and an emotional category. Passion is a primordial awareness of existence such that 'for an existing person it is impossible to think about existence without becoming passionate'.[32] Indeed, 'all existence-issues are passionate, because existence, if one becomes conscious of it, involves passion'.[33]

The central problem of the aesthetic writings is now placed in a deeper and more systematic context. The problem of 'despair', of 'becoming oneself', becomes identical with a proper understanding of the problem of appropriating Christian truth: 'except that this *self* has received much richer and much more profound qualifications'.[34] Johannes has no time for the 'dizzy pantheistic haze' of philosophical piety. Christian truth, subjective thought and personal identity, for him, come together in the clarification of existence as a process of self-actualization. And this process of becoming a Christian, which 'really is the most difficult of all human tasks', is made more difficult rather than less so by Johannes's subjective reflection. He warns that

> The introduction that I take upon myself consists, by repelling, in making it difficult to become a Christian and understands Christianity not as a doctrine but as an existence-contradiction and existence-communication.
>
> (*Postscript*, p. 383)

It is at least equally difficult for all, since 'when faith requires that he relinquish his understanding, then to have faith becomes just as difficult for the most intelligent person as it is for the person with the most limited intelligence', and, thus, the task 'varies in relation to the capabilities of the respective individuals'.[35]

PATHOS

The task of the individual is to deepen and expand the actuality of existence, to fill it out with his or her own 'self'. This, ultimately, is the task of becoming a Christian, in the sense of relating the self to the truth of Christianity, of inwardly appropriating this truth as a living force. Once this task is seen in the context of the subjective thinker, however, the individual is seen as oddly powerless to accomplish it. The 'leap' from the aesthetic to the ethical can be seen, from one perspective at least, as a willed movement; but between the ethical and the religious lies a gulf too deep for the will. In the consciousness of sin, and in the face of the paradox, the individual cannot will a transcending leap to a sphere 'beyond' their aggravating limitations and particularities. The task becomes, rather, one of acceptance and of resignation. 'In relation to an eternal happiness as the absolute good', Johannes points out, 'pathos does not mean words but that this idea transforms the whole existence of the existing person'.[36]

The 'absolute good' must be willed unconditionally and for its own sake, but no act of will can grasp the religious as a positive value. Thus, for Johannes and in sharp contrast to the earlier aesthetic pseudonyms, the ethical has a central place in the formation of a new religious possibility. The religious emerges firstly as the ethical chosen absolutely, as opposed to the acceptance of an ethical determination as a matter of social convenience, moral training or rational reflection. This is, in fact, a consequence of Johannes's insight into the religious as the paradox which, as it is inconceivable, must remain outside the determination of the will.

The pathos of the religious is an incommunicable otherness, which inwardly transforms existence. Thus, while the task of existence is that of self-actualization, its highest development, as the religious form of Christian self-appropriation, so transforms the inner world of experience, that the self seems no longer itself. This is the happy dialectic of religious inwardness. Where objective thinking takes the thinker 'out of himself' in a 'sceptical freedom from affections', the subjective thinker, in passion, is reunited with existence. Passion annihilates the particular and momentary elements of experience, but it does not launch the individual into a void, for 'it is in the very moment of passion that he gains the momentum to exist.'[37]

Johannes's use of the term 'pathos' here is significant, and alludes to an earlier discussion of passion in the *Fragments*. There, in opposition to all rationalistic modern psychologies, Johannes had maintained that passion is essentially a passive affliction, a form of suffering.[38] The passionate shock of erotic love, for example, even if its force of attraction is 'explained' by an ingenious observer, is felt inwardly as if it were something imposed from without. The subtle dialectic of willing and suffering is all the more evident in the pathos of the religious transition, where the self is related absolutely to an absolute good, rather than relatively to a relative good.

The 'essential expression' of the existential pathos of religion, therefore, is suffering, and Johannes does not hesitate to maintain that 'the distinguishing mark of religious action is suffering'. Action, in the aesthetic sphere, leaves the individual untransformed, while within the ethical it develops the self through a relation of striving towards a goal. Religious action uniquely and paradoxically transforms the self through resignation. The aesthetic individual regards suffering as a contingent misfortune, but religiously speaking it is essential to existence. The religious individual 'wants suffering in the same sense as the immediate person wants good fortune, and wants and has suffering even if the misfortune is not present externally'.[39]

The pathos of the religious integrates suffering into existence and makes it essential to it. Johannes argues that humour, which similarly recognizes suffering as essential to existence, lies on the boundary of the religious. But where religion lies, pathetically, in acceptance of this suffering, humour is an effort to annul it. A religious discourse does not avoid existence with a jest, but reconciles the individual to suffering, and in so doing triumphs over it. This calm acceptance is quite distinct, Johannes claims, from the perverse excitement of aestheticized suffering; it is, rather, an indirect joy at grasping, in and through pathos, an absolute relationship to the absolute.

In a more general sense suffering 'is the expression for the relationship with God'.[40] This relationship, viewed from the limited and constraining side of the human, is bound to appear as the intuition of something unconditional and absolute, and at the same time as a separation from, and loss of, this absolute. The God relationship, arrived at in the philosophical fashion of the subjective thinker, that is, accentuates the wretchedness of human existence. Religious suffering, Johannes affirms with Pascalian rigour, is the highest form of human misery to which we are condemned by existence. But suffering is the hope of the subjective thinker, who

> in his joy over the significance of this suffering as relationship, cannot be beyond the suffering, because the suffering pertains specifically to his being separated from the joy, but also indicates the relationship, so that to be without suffering indicates that one is not religious.
>
> (*Postscript*, p. 453)

Religion is the ultimate confirmation of human actuality, but does not confer complacent satisfaction upon the existing individual. Johannes goes further: in a yet darker moment he claims that 'poetry is illusion before understanding, religiousness illusion after understanding', and 'between poetry and religiousness, worldly wisdom about life performs its vaudeville'.[41]

Are we to understand from this that there can be no transition 'into' the religious sphere, as if the religious were simply a 'higher' form of existence to be placed in a developmental sequence after the aesthetic and the ethical? The impenetrable 'otherness' of God places the religious sphere beyond all dialectical cunning. The religious consists, therefore, in a continuous transition, and inasmuch as this transition is then represented in specific social and cultural forms as if it were completed, it is an illusion.

The authorial ambiguity of indirect communication, in this context, is given further justification simply as a consequence of the real relationship of the existing individual to the absolute. And

> right there is the deep suffering of true religiousness, the deepest imaginable: to relate oneself to God absolutely decisively and to be unable to have any decisive outward expression for it.
>
> (*Postscript*, p. 492)

The Christian truth discovered by the subjective thinker is a religion of 'hidden inwardness', and Johannes aspires, therefore, to the 'incognito' of ordinariness. In spite of his complaint that modern life lacks passion, the passion of religion cannot show itself in the world, and the religious rejection of modern secular life has in fact the appearance of its tolerant acceptance. The subjective thinker embodies an odd contradiction that 'with all this inwardness hidden within him, with this pregnancy of suffering and benediction in his inner being, [he] looks just like the others'.[42]

Towards the end of the *Postscript* Johannes admits that 'my intention is to make it difficult to become a Christian'.[43] Inasmuch as he has made the religion of inwardness 'the passionate qualification of the incomprehensible', and forced it deep into 'the vanishing point' of subjectivity, it might well be argued that he has surpassed his ambition and made it impossible.[44] As a final dialectical flourish, Johannes distinguishes a religion of immanence, Religion A, which has been the main subject matter of the *Postscript*, from a religion of transcendence, Religion B, which was the implicit subject matter of the *Fragments*, and the *telos* towards which *The Sickness Unto Death* and *The Concept of Anxiety* were turned. Religion A is a 'natural religion' in the sense that a 'subjective thinker' may arrive at the paradox through a sustained and passionate encounter with existence, whereas Religion B develops in response to a special revelation of God's divine presence. Johannes had just argued, however, that God's presence was incommunicable, so that the notion of revelation is a further 'logical absurdity' in the schema of faith.

What Johannes has tried to demonstrate is not so much a

'Postscript' to the outline of Religion B offered in the *Fragments* as a 'Preface' to its possibility. It is not the dialectically 'offensive' character of transcendence which makes Religion B the more difficult to attain. It is rather the impossibility, even when wholly tied to the 'straitjacket of existence', of the dialectic ever surmounting the Absolute Paradox which is Religion A which makes Religion B the only hope of ridding actuality of its melancholy.

It has to be borne in mind that Johannes's magnificent writings are no more Kierkegaard's than are the productions of the other pseudonyms. The reader becomes so entangled in the elaborate joke that the whole production is seen and talked about as if it were completely 'serious'. Johannes Climacus has become invisibly merged with the historical image of Søren Kierkegaard. The attack on the System, the characterization of the 'subjective thinker', the defence of passion, have subsequently, and doubtless with some justification, been seen as typically 'Kierkegaardian' positions. Yet, for all that, the *Postscript* gives expression to a point of view which Kierkegaard himself claims to have struggled against. It defines a problem, how to exist in the modern world, and claims there is an answer, to become a Christian; then annuls the answer by demonstrating that it cannot be reached, and substitutes for it a secret religion of passionate inwardness. Johannes seems to trap himself into a kind of inversion of the ontological argument. Because God cannot be thought, He (though supremely real) does not exist and religion, as the hidden inwardness of a God-relation, cannot be expressed and cannot find its way into actuality. This supreme effort to outwit melancholy ends by once again confirming its presence; the only presence is the presence of nothing.

But this is just the prelude. In comparison to the dialectical difficulty of 'natural religion', the religion of transcendence, which begins with an unprovoked 'leap' into history, appears surrealistically logical. Johannes, however, cannot make this leap and continually falls back into the same existence from which he sprang with such passionate hope. He falls back into guilt, rather than stumbling forward into sin. To make a superficially ethical paradox, he is too good for religion, his heart is too pure, his spirit, untouched by anxiety, is too light. Like Kierkegaard, he is sufficiently melancholic to break free of the superficial ways in which melancholy is present in the Present Age; but unlike Kierkegaard (perhaps), he is insufficiently melancholic to invest contemporary existence with that sorrow through which existence itself is transformed and melancholy dispelled. The highest potentiation of doubt excludes him from all conventionally acceptable forms of the natural religion of immanence, and protects him, also, from the consciousness of sin, in which the real possibility of the religion of transcendence is announced.

OFFENCE

Johannes Climacus attempted to become a Christian through subjective reflection. And even though he was conscious of the dangers of objective thought, the temptation of the System and the risk of abstraction, all of which he scrupulously avoided, he could not succeed. He penetrated his own existence with thought, with universal categories that left him clinging to an essentially ethical view of life. In fact his life exemplifies the ethical in its fullest and most complete development. Thus, although 'the essential consciousness of guilt is the greatest possible immersion in existence' it cannot, by its own self-determination, move itself beyond guilt-consciousness.[45] The category of 'self-determination' belongs to the ethical, the 'will' is and remains an ethical category. Thus, just as the aesthetic personality cannot 'lift' itself into the ethical by the use of an aesthetic determinant (pleasure, excitement, 'the moment') but requires the aid of the ethical itself (will), so the ethical individual cannot break free of the ethical by an act of will alone, but requires the aid of an essentially religious category. Johannes cannot accept such 'external' assistance. His quest is bound up with a purely ethical self-preoccupation. Consequently, as 'the guilt-consciousness that still lies essentially in immanence is different from the consciousness of sin', he remains guilty.[46]

There is no philosophical bridge between the ethical and the religious. Johannes has deepened and enriched the ethical with the astonishing range of his insight, stretched thought to its breaking point, and, in the end, failed to become a Christian. He has failed where his literary double, Anti-Climacus, has succeeded in making the inner movement of faith. Anti-Climacus therefore describes the same transitional phenomena as Johannes, but from a wholly new perspective.

Kierkegaard wrote two books attributed to Anti-Climacus during 1848, the year he described as 'beyond all comparison the richest

and most fruitful I have experienced as an author'.[47] But neither
The Sickness Unto Death nor *Practice in Christianity* was published
immediately. After the *Postscript*, which he had intended to be
genuinely *Concluding* (though not, of course, conclusive),
Kierkegaard toyed with the idea of becoming a country minister.
The matter (like much else) caused him considerable anguish
before he finally decided against the plan, but it was during this
period of intensified inner struggle that he composed the works of
Anti-Climacus. Unlike the earlier pseudonymous works, which were
conceived and written from points of view that, without ever
identifying himself wholly with them, he understood and had in the
past partially shared, these new works were written under the direct
inspiration of an inner vision of life he felt to be entirely his own. It
was only later, as they were about to be published, that he once
again drew back from any open declaration or commitment. The
new pseudonym he declares to be 'above' the others, 'is higher than
I am myself '.[48] This new authorial position is not only productive
of a fresh set of existential categories, it creates new interpretative
difficulties for the reader.

The aesthetic works can be regarded as works of recollection,
expressing forms of inwardness with which Kierkegaard was actually
acquainted. The novelistic realism of his characterization derives, in
some measure, from his own experience, or the imaginative
construction of experiences formally similar to his own. The
writings of Johannes Climacus, similarly, are eccentrically autobiographical and express Kierkegaard's more mature position on
many central philosophical and existential questions. But if
Anti-Climacus represents a more advanced position than
Kierkegaard's own, how could his books have come to be written?
Johannes Climacus had already demonstrated the impotence of
reflection, even properly subjective reflection, to penetrate the
religious sphere. For Johannes, therefore, religion is only an ideal
possibility, or rather an ideal impossibility. The imagination, that is
to say, can only construct alternative characterizations of life at the
same 'level' as the author's own direct experience. The fact that
Kierkegaard was able to write *Practice in Christianity*, which he found
to be 'the most perfect and the truest thing I have written', implies
that, while writing it at least, he was able, in *actuality*, to live as
Anti-Climacus.[49] It was only in its aftermath that he felt equivocal,
and found it necessary to provide himself once again with an
aesthetic disguise.

Clearly Johannes Climacus and Anti-Climacus are closely related. Anti-Climacus comes after, as well as standing 'before', Johannes and differs from his philosophical twin in two important respects. Firstly, having direct experience of the religious he can actually name the relations with which Johannes had to deal in circumlocutions. The paradox is Christ, an 'infinite interest in one's eternal happiness' is salvation, and so on. And secondly, although dialectically gifted, Anti-Climacus approaches the religious primarily in terms of offence, rather than in terms of intellectual passion. Johannes Climacus, it is true, had already introduced the notion of offence in the *Fragments*, but there had defined it intellectually as the 'misrelation' between the paradox and the understanding. This remains important for Anti-Climacus, but he broadens the category considerably, and, as he has access to a direct experience of Christianity, can express this inclusive meaning more directly.

Offence is, first of all, 'That an individual human being is God, that is, claims to be God'; this quite simply 'conflicts with all (human) reason'.[50] Anti-Climacus, as perceptively as Johannes, but in confidence rather than bewilderment, points out that 'He has no doctrine, no system: basically he knows nothing'.[51] And, equally, 'we can learn nothing from history about him inasmuch as there is nothing at all that can be "known" about him'.[52] The stress, however, now lies on the personal nature of the paradox: 'He is the paradox that history can never digest or convert into an ordinary syllogism'.[53]

There is something more deeply unsettling than logical contradiction in the paradox. It is the absolute, and in relation to it all human judgement and valuation falter. In relation to human sympathy, for example, divine compassion is offensive:

> Divine compassion, however, the unlimited *recklessness* in concerning oneself only with the suffering, not in the least with oneself, and of unconditionally recklessly concerning oneself with *each* sufferer – people can interpret this only as a kind of madness over which we are not sure whether we should laugh or cry.
>
> (*Practice*, p. 58)

Then, even worse, to abolish all distinction between himself and the suffering people, to identify completely with suffering, and still to be completely free of all feelings of human superiority, gratitude or sentimental generosity, is 'too much' for people:

Humanly speaking it is something downright cruel ... something shocking, something over which one could become so embittered that one could have the urge to kill the man – to invite the poor and sick and suffering to come – and then to be able to do nothing for them, but instead of that promise them the forgiveness of sins.

(*Practice*, p. 61)

Anti-Climacus is uncompromising in his insistence that the paradox cannot be assimilated to human feelings any more than it can be harmonized with human thought. It remains utterly alien to our immediate sympathies: 'Christianity', he declares, 'did not come into the world as a showpiece of gentle comfort ... but as the *absolute*'.[54] And it is just this uncompromising absoluteness that has been eroded by modern life: 'all the vitality and energy was distilled out of Christianity; the paradox was slackened, one became a Christian without noticing it and without detecting the slightest possibility of offence'.[55] So that, for the modern age, 'the sign of offence and the object of faith has become the most fabulous of all fabulous characters, a divine Mr. Goodman'.[56]

The task of becoming a Christian has now become that of 'introducing Christianity into Christendom'. And this cannot be done speculatively or dogmatically, but only paradoxically, by being 'contemporary with Christ'. That is to say, Christ must be an actual person, with whom the individual must become 'contemporary', rather than being a historical or mythological character. The paradox which appears in the work of Johannes Climacus – that the possibility of eternal happiness rests on a fact which is both historical and certain – is given a fresh definition in terms of 'being contemporary with Christ'. The absolute cannot become part of history, even if it is revealed at some point in the historical process. The appropriation of religious truth ought not to be conceived as some enormous effort of 'going beyond' ordinary relations, but, rather, as an encounter with the absolute as if it were an ordinary relation. It is just this ordinariness in relation to the absolute which is offensive and terrifying. God has willed 'not to be transformed by human beings into a cozy – a human God; he wills to transform human beings, and he wills it out of love'.[57] He does not need to do anything to effect such a transformation; it is quite sufficient to reveal himself as the absolute. This is by no means a charitable act of enlightenment:

> There is an infinite chasmic difference between God and man, and therefore it became clear in the situation of contemporaneity that to become Christian (to be transformed into likeness with God) is, humanly speaking, an even greater torment and misery and pain than the greatest human torment, and in addition a crime in the eyes of one's contemporaries.
>
> (*Practice*, p. 63)

And if to be a Christian 'is something so terrifying and appalling', it is hardly surprising that Anti-Climacus is forced to wonder 'how in the world can anyone think of accepting Christianity?' It is, he argues, only the consciousness of sin which 'can force one . . . into this horror'. But at the 'very same moment the essentially Christian transforms itself into and is sheer leniency, grace, love, mercy'. Considered in any other way, apart from the consciousness of sin, 'Christianity is and must be a kind of madness or the greatest horror'.[58] In the light of the essentially religious character of offence and of its centrality to any religious psychology of modern life, Anti-Climacus reflects on the significance of Christ's words: 'Blessed is he who is not offended at me'.[59]

Offence stems from the incomprehensible unity in Christ of God and man. The 'infinite chasmic difference' between God and man is somehow held together in the unity of Christ. And it follows from this that there can be two basic forms of offence: an offence of loftiness, at the outrageous presumption that an individual speaks or acts as if he were God; and an offence of lowliness, at God's astonishing self-abasement in accepting the limitations of an individual existence.

In early Christianity the offence was subverted by the suppression of one or other side of this unity. Christ was 'conceptualized' as a being of pure divinity or of pure humanity.[60] The modern confusion, which has succeeded in 'going beyond' these historic errors, consists in propounding a fabulous speculative unity between the two, or an absorption of both into a notion of pure being. Most generally of all, Christ is simply ignored in favour of his 'teaching', and Christianity is reduced to an inoffensive form of direct communication.

But in Christianity, Anti-Climacus insists, 'Christ is infinitely more important than his teaching'.[61] Christianity, that is to say, is a form of indirect communication, in which Christ acts exclusively as a sign. Indeed, the God-man is a 'sign of contradiction' in that, as a man, not only is He not immediately what he appears to be, but he appears to be wholly other than He is. This 'infinitely qualitative contradiction' between being God and man imposes upon Christ the 'impenetrable unrecognizability' of the 'most profound incognito'.[62] Christ, for Anti-Climacus as for Kierkegaard, is the prototype of non-melancholic inwardness.

Christ's perfect inwardness is, from a human viewpoint, offensive because it conceals even those human qualities which would make Him admirable. It is to make Himself only an object of faith that he must avoid arousing human admiration:

> He is love, and yet at every moment he exists he must crucify, so to speak, all human compassion and solicitude – for he can become only the object of faith. But everything called purely human compassion is related to direct recognizability.
>
> (*Practice*, p. 137)

The modern age, however, has forgotten the 'infinite qualitative difference between man and God' and has, in consequence, reduced faith in Christ to purely human compassion: 'it has been made into a pleasant, a sentimental paganism.'[63]

THE ABSOLUTE

'What is Christianity, then, and what is it good for?' asks Anti-Climacus in all seriousness.[64] If Johannes Climacus had made Christianity difficult, or indeed impossible, Anti-Climacus now reveals it to be something profoundly disagreeable. Not only is Christianity, in his eyes, wholly incomprehensible, but the wish to become a Christian appears foolish. The premise of the argument in both the *Postscript* and in *Practice in Christianity* appears somewhat different at the end from at the beginning of those works. At first both seem to take the desire to become a Christian for granted and place in its path, so to speak, the formidable obstacle of living in Christendom. In uncovering a more profound meaning for Christianity, however, they place a question mark over the initial ambition itself. Why should anyone entertain the hope of becoming a Christian when it brings nothing but suffering?[65] The question is a perfectly real one, and Anti-Climacus goes to considerable lengths to define more precisely the nature of this suffering:

To suffer in a way akin to Christ's suffering is not to put up patiently with the inescapable, but it is to suffer evil at the hands of people because as a Christian or in being a Christian one wills and endeavours to do the good.

(*Practice*, p. 173)

And not the good defined in terms of relative human values, but as defined absolutely in terms of an absolute value. It is this absolute relation which is incomprehensible, cannot be communicated, and generates a unique form of suffering which is quite distinct from secular tribulations.

But to ask of the absolute 'what good is it?' makes no sense, and the question can only be rhetorical and contradictory. The pseudo-nyms strive towards Christianity because they are bound to do so, because such a striving is inherent in the reality of human existence. Becoming a Christian, that is to say, is another term for the urge towards self-actualization. And self-actualization means 'synthes-izing' the elements of experience and bringing them into relation with the absolute. But the 'self' is not wholly self-moving. Any conception of a purely immanent process of self-development ends in aestheticism, which is, in fact, the common form of self-denial or despair. The root of melancholy lies in the denial of reality to anything lying 'beyond' the 'surface' of the self, a denial which, through its characteristic wretchedness, simultaneously expresses a perverse conviction that reality can never be wholly superficial. The genuine self can generate itself only through contact with what lies outside it, as absolutely free and independent being. This contact is expressed religiously, in Christianity, as contemporaneity with the Christ-man.

To move beyond despair the self must transform itself in relation to the absolute; it is 'drawn' towards the absolute. Anti-Climacus here insists on the biblical expression that 'From on high He will draw all to Himself '.[66] This is a corollary to both Christ's absolute being and to the method of indirect communication implicit in His 'hidden inwardness'. There can be no deception or seduction in Christ's practice of the maieutic art. To be 'drawn' into selfhood is to be drawn towards something more elevated than the self which is yet still only the self, and nothing fantastically 'beyond' the self: 'to draw to itself means first to help it truly to become itself in order then to draw it to itself, or it means in and through drawing it to itself to help it become itself '.[67]

This process of being 'drawn' into selfhood is akin to subjective thinking, but does not use reflection as the single medium of 'reduplication':

> The being of truth is not the direct redoubling of being in relation to thinking, which gives only thought-being. . . . No, the being of truth is the redoubling of truth within yourself.
>
> (*Practice*, p. 205)

The self's encounter with the absolute is a process of existential reflection, rather than thought reflection. But reflection requires a mirror, a reflecting surface upon which the subject can focus the self. This is, from a psychological viewpoint, just the meaning of the 'sign of contradiction'. A contradiction 'attracts attention' to itself:

> There is a something that makes it impossible not to look – and look, as one is looking one sees as in a mirror, one comes to see oneself. . . . A contradiction placed squarely in front of a person . . . is a mirror.
>
> (*Practice*, pp. 126–7)

The metaphor of the mirror is both instructive and potentially misleading. In medieval theology the metaphor of the mirror had stood for the central location of man in the divine cosmological plan. In the human soul was a model of the entire cosmic structure which man, as a microcosm, reflected internally. But Anti-Climacus has a very different notion of 'reflection' here. His is a religion of 'hidden inwardness' in a cosmos from which the human subject has become detached. There is no longer any separation between the mirror, the observer and the reflection. The peculiar uniformity and dullness of the modern world is here given a specifically religious development; the 'compressed' subjectivity of melancholy is rediscovered in the most 'advanced' of the pseudonyms. Anti-Climacus expresses the notion in the language of *Either*: 'The contradiction confronts him with a choice, and as he is choosing, together with what he chooses, he himself is disclosed.'[68]

The absolute, that is to say, does not need to do anything in order to 'draw' the self towards itself. The transformative power of the absolute lies simply in its being absolute, and this is the fundamental reason for Christianity's paucity of positive doctrine. The absolute defines the boundary of existence, which is simultaneously a boundary within existence, a mirror. The relation of selfhood, which is the paradoxical 'containment' of the absolute within the self and simultaneously the annihilation of the self in the absolute, is quite distinct from any self-generating psyche. The self does not 'posit' the absolute as the 'other' and then relate itself to this projective image of itself, nor does it simply define itself as self-identity. The absolute may be discovered by the self as a necessary condition of its own existence. And if it is thus discovered it is by way of despair, not by way of speculation or reason. Anti-Climacus in *The Sickness Unto Death* provides a systematic analysis of the forms of despair from a reflective-aesthetic perspective. But this is just a prelude to his defence of despair as sin, and of sin as, ultimately, the only route to religious subjectivity. There is a curious dialectic here. Strictly speaking sin is a rarity; as an essentially Christian category, it plays no part in the pagan world, and in the modern age has been all but abolished along with Christianity itself. The universality of sin is, in fact, a Christian 'idea' the truth of which awaits the development of Christianity itself.

Anti-Climacus claims not to be proposing an elevated spiritual status for sin. His argument is an extension of Judge William's. The majority of people are in despair but remain unconscious of their condition, yet to despair 'seriously', even though it is a prelude to a leap into the ethical, is further from, rather than nearer to, salvation. Similarly,

> Most men are characterized by a dialectic of indifference and live a life so far from the good (faith) that it is almost too spiritless to be called sin – indeed, almost too spiritless to be called despair.
>
> (*Sickness*, p. 101)

Just as evil is opposed to the good, but also to the whole of the aesthetic, so sin is opposed both to faith and the whole of the aesthetic and ethical spheres. It is, therefore, both nearer and further than the ethical from Christianity. The central difference between the consciousness of sin and purely ethical guilt-consciousness is that 'the earnestness of sin is its actuality in the single individual'. Hence the 'dialectic of sin is diametrically contrary to that of speculation', and it is just here that Christianity begins: 'with the teaching about sin, and thereby with the single individual'.[69] And as the consciousness of sin is a direct expression that 'man is separated from God by the most chasmal qualitative abyss', it is simultaneously an expression of offence. An active, voluntaristic element comes to the surface here. Offence is 'taken', it is a qualification of the single individual in which the single individual is aroused against something, and defines itself absolutely against something absolute: 'offense is the most decisive qualification of subjectivity, of the single individual, that is possible.'[70]

THE SELF

The relation between despair and selfhood is given a more open and didactic treatment by Anti-Climacus in *The Sickness Unto Death*, which was published, after a year of prevarication, in July 1849. Its 'dialectical algebra' was published in the context of the appearance of a second edition of *Either/Or* and is, in one sense, a completion of the 'anthropological contemplation' inaugurated by the earlier book. In completing the inner development of the aesthetic pseudonyms Anti-Climacus also links his work to his own earlier productions, and to those of his *alter ego*, Johannes Climacus.

Two important ideas may serve as guides to this challenging text. Firstly he openly declares his opposition to the aesthetic writers' melancholic sentimentality: for him 'despair is interpreted as a sickness, not as a cure'.[71] True, the possibility of despair (which is despair itself) is a mark of humanity and man's advantage over the beasts. But properly understood, this privilege is a miserable condition from which all should seek relief. Secondly, in *The Sickness Unto Death*, the 'true concretion for the religious', the nature of which had baffled the 'Married Man' in *Stages*, is established as the self. Briefly stated, then, the argument of the book is that the religious sphere of existence is the self, and that despair is to be other than the self.

Anti-Climacus accepts the traditional presupposition of any religious anthropology, that 'a human being is spirit'. But his understanding of spirit is distinctively modern: 'spirit is the self '.[72] What, then, is the self? His answer at first appears to be unfortunately opaque:

> The self is a relation that relates itself to itself or is the relation's relating itself to itself in the relation; the self is not the relation but is the relation's relating itself to itself .
>
> (*Sickness*, p. 13)

One thing, at least, is clear from this statement, the self is to be considered as a 'relation' rather than as an 'object'. It does not exist in some sort of primitive unity, but emerges in some way from more basic elements of human nature. This relation, Anti-Climacus goes on at once to inform us, forms (ideally) a rather complex unity: 'a human being is a synthesis of the infinite and finite, of the temporal and eternal, of freedom and necessity'.[73] This synthesis is not, in itself, a self; it is merely the relation between the sensuous and the psychical. The self emerges from this relation, and is a kind of reflection of and upon this relation. The distinction is similar to that which Hegel makes in the *Phenomenology* between consciousness and self-consciousness. Here, however (and the difference is fundamental), the self's 'relating itself to itself' does not mean that the self constitutes a realm of absolute inner freedom. Such a radical, romantic view – as exemplified particularly by Fichte – is rejected by Anti-Climacus on the grounds that if the self were genuinely a groundless self-creation there could be no despair of the form 'in despair to will to be oneself', and this is just the form of which the author has an especially intimate knowledge. The self-relation, therefore, 'has been established by another', and its gradual emergence is in conformity to an absolutely given structure. The self may indeed fail to emerge, or emerge as a 'misrelation' – and this is despair – but in any instance where it does succeed in establishing itself, then, 'in relating itself to itself and in willing to be itself, the self rests transparently in the power that established it'.[74]

Despair is thus a universal sickness, the peculiar character of the wretchedness that Pascal had made the centre of his religious consciousness. The fact that most people go through life without becoming properly aware of their own despair does not mean that it is not just this despair which binds them to particular types of behaviour and blinds them to their own potentialities. Commonly people despair over something in particular, but 'in despairing over *something*, he really despaired over *himself*, and now he wants to be rid of himself'.[75] Despair, in this sense, is a kind of spiritual assertiveness, even when it asserts itself as the denial of man's spiritual character.

Despair manifests itself in a variety of forms which flow directly from the nature of the synthesis through which the self ought to be established. In the synthesis of finitude and infinitude, thus, the predominance of one term of the relation is a specific form of despair. Infinitude's despair is the lack of finitude: 'the fantastic, the unlimited'. The imagination is 'the medium for the process of infinitizing', and where this process is unchecked by any concrete limiting conditions it 'leads a person out into the infinite in such a way that it only leads him away from himself '.[76] This expresses itself as the 'abstract sentimentality' of care for a 'humanity' that 'inhumanly belongs to no human being', to abstract knowledge in which the self is squandered, and to the abstraction of the will, divorced from any present action. The excess of infinitude is a despair that afflicts an individual in any sphere of existence. It is not a purely aesthetic complaint. In some individuals, thus, there is a kind of 'religious intoxication' which is just as despairing as the wildest fantasy of any romantic young man. Equally, however, finitude's despair is the lack of finitude, a 'despairing reductionism, narrowness'. In this case the individual 'finds it hazardous to be himself ', and prefers 'to be like the others, to become a copy, a number, a mass man'.[77]

In terms of the synthesis of possibility and necessity, there is a similar twofold classification of despair. Probability's despair is the lack of necessity. The self has to be actualized as a necessity, and not simply played with as an abstract possibility. When it is not anchored in necessity the self 'flounders around in possibility', reduced to a series of images of itself, until finally 'these phantasmagoria follow one another in such rapid succession that it seems as if everything were possible', and the individual 'becomes a mirage'.[78] What is missing here is 'the power to obey, to submit to the necessity of one's life, to what may be called one's limitations'.[79] Necessity's despair, on the other hand, is to lose possibility, which is essentially to lose faith: 'The believer has the ever infallible antidote for despair – possibility – because for God everything is possible at every moment'.[80] To lack possibility may take the form of everything seeming to be absolute, necessary and fixed by some external power, or – more commonly – that everything has become trivial. This latter is the typically 'philistine-bourgeois mentality' of the Present Age, and denotes a complete loss of imagination.

The synthesis of the temporal and the eternal is not discussed further at this point, having served, in fact, as the primary mode of distinguishing the 'aesthetic' from the 'ethical'. The exaggerations of life conceived as the 'moment', or life equally devoid of content by representing itself as only the eternal, had already been profusely illustrated throughout the aesthetic works, and had been taken up in a systematic fashion by Vigilius Haufniensis in his *Concept of Anxiety*.

The psychology of the aesthetic which the pseudonyms had developed at considerable length in their 'imaginary psychological constructions' is here given a systematic and even a scholastic form. We can thus move through a series of 'potentiations' familiar from the earlier works: the despair of ignorance at having a self; the simplest and lowest form of despair in which the self is not recognized as spirit at all and the 'sickness' of despair goes unnoticed. Of the more advanced or conscious forms there comes first the despair of weakness; in despair not to will to be a self. Here despair is passive suffering, usually over external events, though in its most developed form it is despair over the sufferer's own weakness: this is a specifically spiritual development of an 'inclosing reserve' and depends upon a recognition of the eternal in the self. Finally there is the despair of strength rather than of weakness: defiance. This is 'the despairing misuse of the eternal within the self to will in despair to be oneself '.[81] Here despair is a self-consciously inflicted action, a kind of negative image of the self to which the self clings, unable to 'lose itself ' in the eternal and so regain itself in a non-despairing form.

The synthesis which is the 'self ' is described by Anti-Climacus in terms of progressive determinants. In becoming more and more 'itself ' it differentiates itself as an 'individual'. But this is by no means an 'asocial' conception. It does not represent a withdrawal from the world, but an increasing inclusiveness and enrichment of actuality qualified in terms of a personal 'point of view'. The pseudonyms, whatever their illusory understanding of themselves, distinguished themselves from the spiritless indifference of the modern crowd. The very conception and possibility of individualism, from a somewhat different perspective, is itself a social institution, a specific form in terms of which modern society is constructed, and in terms of which its characteristic tendencies are experienced. The consistent and at times extreme individualism of the pseudonyms can be viewed as part of their bourgeois critique of modernity. The distortions of character which they vividly bring to life exemplify the elaboration of a variety of 'first selves' which, in a more sophisticated way than the bourgeois philistinism of the crowd, represent the perversity of asocial individualism. The pseudonyms, though ridding themselves of many of the more obvious forms of vanity and envy which dominate the psychology of the crowd, are in fact under the sway of specific aspects of public opinion. The actualization of despair is a type of 'self-activity' which remains wrapped up in itself. It is an illusory form of action because it assimilates as its content the illusions of the age. But to actualize the self in a non-despairing form is simultaneously to challenge and transform the actuality of social life. The 'single one' is not only a social category, depending as it does on a relational network with others as a means to its own differentiation, it is a radical demand to overcome all those relations productive of illusory, despairing selfhood. In taking the claims of bourgeois liberalism seriously the pseudonyms turn bourgeois ideology against itself. The conventional requirement for self-actualization, in their hands, turns into an unsatisfied demand for the transformation of actuality.

Part III

Reduplication: towards a theomorphic discourse

In order for human finitude to be seen and expressed, a moment that surpasses it must be inherent in the situation, condition, or state of being finite. . . . The complete discourse on finitude is a discourse on the finitude and the infinitude of man.

Paul Ricoeur, *Fallible Man*

Chapter 7

The upbuilding: architecture of happiness

> All human speech, even the divine speech of the Holy Scriptures about spiritual matters, is essentially metaphorical.
>
> S. Kierkegaard, *Works of Love*

The pseudonymous works, whether written from aesthetic, ethical or philosophical viewpoints, are all indirect in form. In being attributed to different authors they appear before the public in a disguised form. The connection one with another is deliberately obscured; each is made to appear more independent than it is, and none bears the responsibility of expressing Kierkegaard's own views. Kierkegaard goes to extraordinary lengths to deny himself that outdated sense of godlike omnipotence over his creations which remains, in spite of everything, the enabling assumption of most modern forms of literary activity.[1] Kierkegaard, rather, like God in relation to the modern world, hides in his books, appearing only fugitively as an editorial assistant to other people's efforts. But there is something paradoxical in this reticence. In his directly written, autobiographical study *The Point of View for My Work as an Author*, unpublished during his lifetime, he declares clearly enough that the entire meaning of his authorship is summed up in the problem of how to become a Christian, and that he conceives the solution to this problem as lying in the emergence of the most precise and highly developed form of individualism. But if, in the modern world, to become a Christian is synonymous with becoming an individual (or if the latter is viewed at least as a necessary precondition of the former), why should Kierkegaard have insisted upon the puzzling fragmentation of himself in his work? Would his position not have been made more definite by the assumption of authorial responsibility, by demonstrating his individuality and earnestness as the singular creator standing behind the protean mass of words?

Kierkegaard's understanding of modern existence, however, makes of any such direct authorship a deeper and more damaging paradox than its alternative. Christianity, in the sense Kierkegaard wishes to attach to that term, is a hidden and potential reality within the non-Christian actuality of the Present Age. His aim as a writer is not to describe this hidden reality, but to provoke its coming into existence in his readers. It is not an intellectual appreciation of Christianity, but a reduplication of existence into Christian categories, which is the purpose of his writing. His method is firstly to present a series of 'thought experiments', through which the spiritual potential of the Present Age can be tested and explored. These aesthetic adventures capture the reader and, through a ruthless relativizing of each possible existence-sphere, confront the individual with the melancholic despair of secular life. The illusion of actuality, rather than depending on the authority of a single viewpoint, is communicated by sacrificing the privilege of authorship to a multiplicity of pseudonymous spokesmen. This is a dangerous method. Most obviously it runs the risk of allowing, and even encouraging, a purely aesthetic reading of the works.[2] Ideally a reader should 'work through' every position, bringing to life each successive form of despair before being guided (though making each transition only by an inexplicably activated leap), to the most radical of possibilities latent in human existence. To counteract the self-enclosed charm of each aesthetic position, therefore, each work is composed from more than one viewpoint, and is deliberately left incomplete.

Even allowing that the aesthetic works will intensify the experience of despair, which is the general characteristic of secular life, Kierkegaard, in giving up all pretensions to authorial supremacy, cannot defend himself against misreading. *Either/Or* achieved an immediate notoriety. It captivated the reader for just the wrong reasons, the very reasons (sensationalism, confession, literary brilliance, critical originality) that Kierkegaard recognized were the common aesthetic motives for reading. The difficulty was to spring the trap. The warning subtitle, *A Fragment of Life*, was easily ignored, and the carefully organized structure through which actuality might extend itself in the Present Age remained as hidden in the pseudonymous works as it did in life itself. It is not his maieutic deceptiveness, therefore, but Kierkegaard's fidelity to the truth that ultimately limits the effectiveness of the pseudonymous authorship. His obligation to portray actuality in all its psychological complexity is possible only because he has himself penetrated this reality and rejected as illusory the very charms to which the pseudonyms remained bound. The truth of the aesthetic works is the truth of the Present Age, the truth of despair, and the pseudonyms – as they must – represent the contemporary allure of melancholy.

Kierkegaard, thus, remains hidden in the aesthetic works primarily because a more fundamental truth is hidden in the contemporary world. It seems that the author can reveal himself only at the expense of distortion and misconception. Though the aim of the authorship is to present the reader with fresh and unexpected possibilities of inner transformation the only means at its disposal is the imaginary reconstruction of actuality itself. The reader is, therefore, seduced by just those illusions which, characteristically for modern life, trap the individual in despair.[3]

RECONSTRUCTIVE READING

Concurrently with the aesthetic production Kierkegaard published a series of short works under his own name. These *Upbuilding Discourses* are usually viewed as 'direct' religious works, and evidence for Kierkegaard's own claim that the entire authorship was guided from the beginning by a religious goal. The maieutic insincerity of the aesthetic works – 'my task is to get persons deceived . . . into religious commitment' – is, apparently, balanced by a parallel series of direct professions of a sincere, and perhaps even orthodox, Christianity.[4] The 'duplexity' of the authorship, however, is somewhat more complicated. If the aesthetic and philosophical works, on the basis of the experiences recounted by the pseudonymous writers themselves, cannot succeed in 'making men aware', the reader must be deeply suspicious of the seriousness of any 'direct' appeal. In what sense can their author claim these discourses to be 'upbuilding' or 'edifying'? The readers of the *Concluding Unscientific Postscript*, with its revised theory of irony and its evident admiration for the comic, might be forgiven the uncomfortable feeling that they have become the butt of some obscure joke, a feeling likely to be reinforced by a glance at the opening 'Preface' to the first of the *Upbuilding Discourses* which was published just a few weeks after *Either/Or*. Firstly we are told it is a discourse rather than a sermon because it 'lacks authority', and, even more obscurely, that, lacking any didactic purpose, it is an *upbuilding* discourse, and not a discourse *for* upbuilding. In fact it 'wishes to be only what it is, a superfluity, and desires only to remain in hiding, just as it came into existence in concealment'.[5] This seems anything but straightforward: is S. Kierkegaard, perhaps, just a pseudonym for Victor Eremita?[6]

With minor variations this self-deprecating preface is repeated in each volume of the *Upbuilding Discourses*. Each is addressed to 'that single individual (*hiin Enkelte*) whom I with joy and gratitude call *my* reader'.[7] Yet it is not *directed* towards this reader, who remains invisibly suspended within the public to which the pseudonymous authors, decked out in spectacular literary refinement, had *directly* appealed. All such efforts to find a reader, any reader, let alone an appropriate reader, are rigorously eschewed, and the entire business of communication between author and reader is left to chance. These discourses must simply wait upon their adventitious discovery by that

> favourably disposed person who reads aloud to himself what I write in stillness, who with his voice . . . summons forth what the mute letters have on their lips, as it were, but are unable to express without great effort . . . (and) rescues the captive thoughts that long for release.
>
> (*Discourses*, p. 49)

The pseudonymous works are conventional to the extent that they are written for an audience, and are intended to be read. The *Upbuilding Discourses*, it seems, are artificially preserved speeches, which ought to be listened to rather than read, but listened to, unusually, by oneself. Kierkegaard is, thus, speaking rather than writing. He is speaking to himself, and the reader, in listening to his or her own voice duplicating this speech, himself or herself becomes the author. The 'real' author once again disappears. These are at first sight melancholic texts, each, like the author who flees from them, 'inclosed in itself', alone with itself in a void.[8] Kierkegaard can put his name to these *Discourses* because, in being read aloud to oneself, the author is forgotten and the text becomes a medium for self-observation. The *Upbuilding Discourses*, thus, should not be viewed as a form of direct communication but rather as a different form of indirect communication.

Nor can they be distinguished by their subject matter. Both the pseudonymous works and the parallel series of *Discourses* are about religion, in the sense that their fundamental theme is the 'awakening' of the individual to his or her own obscured actuality (becoming Christian). And in both series the activity of writing is put to the service of transforming actuality, of uncovering its obscured potentiality for authentically Christian experience.

Equally, however, these *Discourses* cannot be assimilated to the (other) pseudonymous works. Their formally different characteristics are in fact reliable signs of a fundamental shift in perspective. Kierkegaard refers to the pseudonyms as works offered with 'the left hand' and the *Upbuilding Discourses* as those offered with 'the right hand', and his ideal reader as one who 'with the right hand accepts what is offered with the right hand'.[9] And what is offered is a 'reduplication' of the actuality bodied forth in the pseudonyms. The pseudonyms provide aesthetic and philosophical standpoints from which to view, and indeed construct, actuality. These shifting perspectives can all be more or less readily accommodated within the topological structure of the existence-spheres (aesthetic/ethical/religious) and the non-existence voids (ideality/sensuousness). For the pseudonymous writers this structure, depending upon their position within it, is only partially revealed. On closer examination the 'ethical' tends to be absorbed by the religious or dissolved into abstraction, giving rise to a new uncompromising either/or: either – the aesthetic; or – the religious. All the pseudonyms choose 'either'. Even in their most refined philosophical reflections (the works of Anti-Climacus) they exist aesthetically, and construct the distinction between the aesthetic and the religious as a 'thought-experiment'. For all the pseudonyms, religion exists as a possibility. Editorial remarks to the effect that Anti-Climacus is a Christian should obscure neither the judgement that he is a 'philosophical' Christian, nor, more importantly, that such remarks betray an *aesthetic* admiration for his advanced position.

In contrast to the entire bulk and variety of aesthetic works required to express what still remains a mere 'Fragment of Life', the *Discourses* compress the entire complexity of religiously qualified existence into a meagre series of slender like-titled volumes. And where the public had been assailed with every possible literary form, with massive volumes replete with the richest and most varied content, by a staggering multiplicity which continually suggested its further elaboration and complication, now the solitary reader, or rather speaker, overhears a single and monotonous voice: *Two Upbuilding*

Discourses (1843) is rapidly followed by *Three Upbuilding Discourses* (1843), *Four Upbuilding Discourses* (1843), *Two Upbuilding Discourses* (1844), *Three Upbuilding Discourses* (1844), *Four Upbuilding Discourses* (1844).

But what can it mean to 'upbuild'? *Either/Or* had concluded with an 'Ultimatum' in which the perpetual movement of the aesthetic was arrested by deliberating on 'the *upbuilding* that lies in the thought that in relation to God we are always in the wrong'.[10] It is, in fact, the first aesthetic work that introduces the notion of upbuilding, suggesting, in fact, that too sharp a distinction between the discourses and the pseudonymous works should not be drawn. *Or* had spilled over, so to speak, from the temporary refuge of the ethical and ended with an intimation of new religious categories. Judge William conceives of the upbuilding by analogy with human love. A wronged lover wishes to believe himself or herself to be mistaken; that, in fact, they have not been wronged and that their beloved is completely faithful. On a human scale this wish to be mistaken, to be in the wrong, involves a contradiction: the wish is counterposed by knowledge of the circumstances. Love, however, even on a human scale, is an 'infinite relationship', and when such a relationship is infinitely potentiated, and becomes a relationship with God, then the contradiction is dissolved and we are left only with the upbuilding: the thought that in relation to God we are continually in the wrong. The upbuilding is love, which acknowledges this truth without 'mental toil'. To seek God intellectually, on the other hand, would result in the thought that God is always in the right, and, paradoxically, would not be upbuilding, because the upbuilding is love, not thought which succeeds only in confirming the self in its own limitations.

The intimate connection between the upbuilding and love is explored in much greater detail in *The Works of Love*, which contains the fullest discussion of the most general sense that S. Kierkegaard (rather than Judge William) attaches to this now somewhat archaic expression. To *upbuild* in common language seems to refer to height, to growth, to an addition of some kind. But Kierkegaard distinguishes between this sense – which is to build *on* – and its meaning to build *up*, which is to construct afresh from the foundations. The *upbuilding* means to build 'from scratch'.[11] And since he is addressing his discourses to an already existing, if elusive, individual, the work of upbuilding must first of all be the work of dismantling and taking down what has previously been poorly constructed. It is a 'rebuilding', a building on firm foundations.[12]

This process of 'deconstruction' cannot be carried out through any aesthetic or philosophical form of reflection. The pseudonyms, equally, had held themselves apart from any speculative dialectic, and sought instead to trap the reader into a closer contact with actuality. The series of pseudonymous works test out the actual, and expand it within the consciousness and life of the reader. But actuality is full of illusions, so whichever route is chosen – the way of doubt or the way of anxiety – actuality, though it may be 'enlarged', cannot be inwardly transformed. Kierkegaard, as the author of the *Upbuilding Discourses*, assumes such an inward transformation has, in fact, already taken place, and seeks to redescribe actuality, to reconstruct it – to build it up – from its new foundations. The aim of the author is reduplication rather than reflection; not a reduplication of an existing condition of actuality, but a reduplication of the inwardness so well concealed in and obstructed by every aesthetic and philosophical perspective on the world. The pseudonyms, that is to say, start out from some position within actuality and explore all the possibilities of inward development inherent in that position; the *Discourses* redefine actuality by considering it exclusively in relation to the transcending reality of faith. They do not describe how such a transformation is effected (they do not contradict the pseudonyms), but they begin by supposing that such a transformation has indeed been effected. They assume, that is to say, that the intended reader has confronted the paradox without being offended.

Paradoxically, therefore, it is the pseudonymous works which display some residual homiletic purpose (though admitting their failure in this regard), while the explicitly 'upbuilding' works retain no trace of such an ambition. Rarely has 'preaching to the converted' been brought to such a refined point of self-awareness.

THE IMMEDIACY OF TRUST

The *Two Upbuilding Discourses* issued shortly after the publication of *Either/Or* thus extend and complete the comparison between the aesthetic and the ethical, not by building on a third, and definitive, category, the religious, but by a reduplication of the immediacy within which the young man has trapped himself.

Rather than contrast the spiritless chaos and melancholy of

boredom with the ethical seriousness of ideal values, therefore, Kierkegaard redefines the starting point of personal existence as the *expectation of faith*. When the immediate is brought into relation with the religious, with faith, momentary pleasure is transformed into eternal happiness. The good, in other words, is potentiated beyond the rational limits of any humanly calculable design.

Faith, thus, should not be talked about as if it were a good among other possible goods, albeit a greater and inherently more valuable good. The untransformed aesthetic has no conception of a transcending good, and views faith as no more than 'the highest' of human goods, therefore 'transient and capricious, bestowed only upon the chosen few, rarely for the whole of life'.[13] But religiously viewed, faith is absolutely different, a good of a different sort to any other, and a good in relation to which human life and conduct cannot remain unaltered. It is an infinite good, and as such it is infinitely available to all, with equal ease. The good of faith raises no difficulties of distributive justice, and as all can share equally in its benefit, the wish to possess it does not conflict with any ethical demand for fairness in its distribution. Indeed, in sharp contrast to all secular self-regarding desire,

> The person who wishes it for another person wishes it for himself; the person who wishes it for himself wishes it for every human being, because that by which another person has faith is not that by which he is different from him but is that by which he is like him.
>
> (*Discourses*, p. 10)

Faith simultaneously and paradoxically confers the most specific sense of individuality and the most general form of commonality: 'it is the only unfailing good'. This qualitative distinction means that in a more profound sense it cannot become the object of any rational calculation or earnest effort. It is a good which cannot be sought: 'it can be had only by constantly being acquired and can be acquired only by continually being granted.'[14] The reduplicated immediacy of the religious sphere, therefore, is found neither in the impotence of the romantic wish in which the self is abandoned 'to the anesthetizing dullness of sorrow',[15] nor in the rational earnestness of an ethical life which teaches 'that your wishes would not be fulfilled, that your desires would not be gratified, your appetites would not be heeded, your cravings would not be satisfied'.[16] It is fulfilled, rather, in the expectancy of faith. Whereas, for the aesthetic, the choice of despair is a wilful 'deepening' of melancholy productive of illusory self-images, the expectancy of faith is an effortless and unfounded trust in the authentic disclosure of actuality. As an aesthetic or a philosophical transition the religious retreats before every struggling advance. The *edifying* is an essentially religious category; it is already faith itself.

The aesthetic is preoccupied with the moment, with the vanishing nothingness of the present, while the ethical misconceives of itself as a unity extended in time. Both, however, are subverted by an unknown and uncontrollable future. 'The future is not', and this negativity continually disturbs the aesthetic moment with a disturbing vision of empty duration (boredom), and disarms every settled ethical value with its uncertain outcome (guilt). For each individual it 'presents itself externally as the enemy he has to encounter'.[17] Unaided, the person is defeated by the future, the whole of which remains an unfathomable mystery. The expectancy of faith is, therefore, a victory over the future. And it is in expectancy of faith that 'the soul is indeed prevented from falling out of itself', through doubt or anxiety, into sheer abstraction.[18] In contrast to this completely unprovoked trust in the future lies all 'wishing, hoping, longing for something, craving, coveting', which typifies the aesthetic, as well as the 'deep and crafty passion' of reasoned philosophical doubt and even the concentrated wilfulness of the ethical life.

This is an expectancy which flows from faith itself; if it does not it is merely wishfulness. 'The reason we so often go astray', claims the writer, 'is that we seek assurance of our expectancy.' But 'the person of faith demands no substantiation of his expectancy. . . . Time can neither substantiate nor refute it, because faith expects an eternity'.[19]

Timeless expectation of faith is a new immediacy. Its eternity, which can be neither wished for nor willed into existence, is not an object of thought or intellectual construct, but is grasped through love. Religiously transformed immediacy is simply the realization of love. But where the aesthetic had sought the ephemeral pleasure of the erotic, and the ethical could conceive love only within the form of marriage, Christian existence is suffused with God's *agape*. And the content of renewed immediacy is this changeless and universal love.

Thus, as distinct from any erotic particularity, he asks: 'What is it that is never changed though everything is changed? It is love, and that alone is love, that which never becomes something else.'[20] The endless availability of God's love, its unquenchable resourcefulness, transforms the egotism of the erotic into a form of self-love which, as it is also love of God, is spontaneously universal in its scope. It does not require ethical constraint, it is ethical in itself. Christian immediacy always 'bears the mark of God's love, without which it would become silliness or insipid philandering'.[21]

The aesthetic, including its ethical self-denials, is racked by continuous tension, by doubt and by dread, by irreconcilable difference. The immediacy of Christian love, however, sustains an entire world of inwardness without damaging contradictions. Love, thus, seeks out and discovers, it is the immediate awareness of all particularities, and, therefore, it 'discovers a multitude of sins'. Indeed, free of all self-delusion it discovers sin more readily than does either conventional wisdom or deliberative philosophical reflection. Yet, simultaneously and uncomprehendingly it conceals what it finds. This is, from a philosophical standpoint, 'simply foolishness', and the author asks on behalf of the speaker of the text, 'What is love? Is it a dream in the night that one has by sleeping? Is it a stupor in which everything is forgotten?'[22] But, he assures his especially receptive reader, 'love is no dream'. Where the dream, we might say, characterizes the fluid border between existence and non-existence, and is consequently charged with doubt and dread, love is an antidote to all 'light-minded or heavy-spirited anxiety'.[23]

The knowledge gained through love is concerned rather than indifferent or passionate. It is continually focused on actuality, and does not take the thinker away from existence because the 'sphere' of love is infinitely inclusive. The reduplication of love, in contrast to the reflection of abstract deliberation, is free of all 'doleful self-consuming'. The all-inclusive immediacy of love is exemplified in 'apostolic speech' which, far from being thoughtless, is

> concerned, ardent, burning, inflamed, everywhere and always stirred by the forces of the new life . . . everywhere witnessing to the powerful unrest of the spirit and the profound importance of the heart.
>
> (*Discourses*, p. 69)

Concern, rather than wonder (Socrates), doubt (Descartes), desire (Hegel) or melancholy (pseudonyms), sets in motion the process of expansion and differentiation of inwardness. It is the inverse of those characteristic forms of modern experience – 'self-inclosing reserve' and the frenzy of egotism – which stem from the sense of isolation within a void; it marks, therefore, the first genuine break with melancholy.

The 'inner strengthening' of concern is an enrichment of the self. Concern does not lead the self out of actuality, which conforms itself, so to speak, with the self 's own growth and development. The boundaries of the self, thus, remain coterminous with the boundaries of actuality. The differentiation of trust, expectancy, love and concern are not separated parts or sections of the self, but, rather, should be viewed as interrelated aspects of a single actuality.

The recalcitrant secular ego, which exists as the illusory separation of appearance and reality, and is sustained by the artificiality of contrived passions, cannot easily be renounced or overcome. As the activities of 'willing' or 'renouncing' are themselves part of the secular integument of the ego, all deliberative endeavours confirm, rather than negate, the illusory objects of desire. This is, religiously viewed, the central problem of the Fall. Rather than guiding human action, knowledge suspends itself in doubt, and creates its own fantastic and inhuman realm. Faith is distinct from knowledge not because of its irrationality but, primarily, by virtue of its availability as a gift. Faith cannot be sought, it can only be received; in one of Kierkegaard's favourite texts, 'every good and every perfect gift is from above'.[24]

Secular thought, 'distracted by life's confusing distinctions', is then reformed and, becoming an aspect of love, reduplicates itself as the 'likeness with God'. In stark contrast to the aesthetically conceived 'teleological suspension of the ethical', and its 'arrogant pride in difference', or the view of religious individuality as the 'exception', in religious immediacy 'every externality is discarded as imperfect, and equality is true for all'.[25]

Every 'upbuilding' view of life begins with this 'divine equality', which is founded in the non-reciprocal God-relation. No human can return the gift which is of ultimate value, so that in the face of this infinite indebtedness all humans gain equality. This again is a conception at odds with either an aesthetic pride in distinction or an ethical demand for universal standards of justice.

Nothing can be done, and nothing needs to be done, to acquire the infinite good of God's love. Indeed, trust and expectancy, the reduplication of immediacy, are difficult just because we disturb their groundless trust with human calculation and effort. Nor does our maintenance in its categories require anything other than patience, which is simply another aspect of expectancy. Patience is a form of continuity unknown both to the aesthetic (whose only continuity is in boredom) and to the ethical (which is preserved in the repetition of wilfulness). The religious is an eternity which is indifferent to the human preoccupation with continuity; but the delicate human contact with that which absolutely is, can, from the human side, always be disturbed. Religious immediacy, therefore, is preserved in patience, and, 'If a person does not use the help of patience, he may, with all his effort and diligence, come to preserve nothing else and thereby to have lost his soul.'[26] Impatience of any sort is inimical to spiritual growth:

> Not only did he lose his soul who danced the dance of pleasure until the end, but also the one who slaved in worry's deliberation and in despair wrung his hands night and day.
>
> (*Discourses*, p. 187)

Patience is the maintenance of the soul within the confines of actuality. It is, in one sense, both a form of deliberation and a species of anxiety. But where both doubt and anxiety tempt the individual out of himself or herself into abstraction, patience is the deliberative and anxious aspect of an all-inclusive religious immediacy and is, therefore, from a deeper point of view, neither doubtful nor anxious. Patience is continuous with the life it preserves. There is nothing ironic or mocking, nothing despairing in its persistence.

It is characteristic of both aesthetic wishfulness and ethical earnestness to conceive of life in terms of more or less distant goals, and the satisfactions of life in terms of 'reaching' these goals. But in sternly abandoning 'the fraudulence of wishes', the thought of salvation, which reason assimilates to wishfulness, has become frivolous:

> Eternal salvation seems to have become what the thought of it has become, a loose and idle phrase, at times virtually forgotten, or arbitrarily left out of the language, or indifferently set aside as an old-fashioned turn of speech no longer used but retained only because it is so quaint.
>
> (*Discourses*, p. 254)

But expectancy and patience 'pertain to a person essentially' and not to some particular condition of the world. The continuity of patience, therefore, is neither the instantaneous fulfilment of a wish nor a measurable 'progress' towards a goal. As the individual does nothing to gain the goal, 'his innermost life is equally important to him at every moment'.[27]

The thought of salvation, the genuine expectancy and the patience in which it is held, can never be indifferent. And in religiously transformed immediacy, there is no separation between the thought of salvation and salvation itself, both are called expectancy. The centrality of expectancy and patience in the *Upbuilding Discourses* manifests a profound shift in perspective. One of the most characteristic thoughts of all the pseudonyms (and one too easily attributed to both S. Kierkegaard and Søren Kierkegaard) is their insistence upon discontinuity. The existence-spheres are linked 'developmentally', but between one and another stretches an abyss that cannot be 'mediated'. The 'movement' from one sphere to another is effected by a non-rational, and therefore incomprehensible, leap. Yet in the *Discourses* there are no sharp divisions. Their author tells us directly that 'A sudden transition is a terrible hazard'.[28] Indeed, the aesthetic authors appear, from the new perspective, to be reckless. Their infatuation with the leap is the product of melancholy and provokes only a more tenacious form of despair. Expectancy, which is expectancy of salvation, is world-transforming but at the same time, rather than bewildering or engrossing, it is infinitely consoling. The aesthetic writers are, therefore, wishful rather than expectant:

> It is not the expectancy of the eternal but a superstitious belief in the future . . . the person does not rest in the trustworthiness of the eternal but dupes himself with the possibility of the future, which merely engrosses one as does the solving of riddles.
>
> (*Discourses*, p. 259)

While from an aesthetic viewpoint each existence-sphere is characterized by a negative and unstable disposition (boredom, guilt, sin), the religious reduplication of immediacy as patient expectation is 'the genuine joy of self-denial'.[29] This 'humble self-denial remains true to itself ', and is at once a process of self-realization and of self-annihilation.[30] What is abandoned is the secular ego, what he calls the 'first self ', which is composed of vain and illusory needs; and what is left, expanding as it were to take its place, is the 'deeper self ' of the genuine 'single one'. 'Self-denial' is the same as 'self-expression' or 'self-development', and is the only real form of 'self-knowledge'.

No Socratic questioning can throw the 'deeper self' into relief; its coming into existence is an act of worldly self-denial which is the unique possibility of religious simplicity and immediacy.

This bifurcation into a 'first self' and a 'deeper self' allows Kierkegaard to establish his position in relation to two important religious traditions. The first is mysticism. As early as *The Concept of Irony* he had expressed a deep distrust of the idea of mystical union as the goal of religious life.[31] The commitment of the pseudonyms, including the author of the *Discourses*, is to a religious transformation of actuality rather than any religiously inspired movement 'beyond' actuality. The annihilation of the first self should not be conceived, therefore, as the obliteration of an individual identity in some 'higher' state of consciousness. Quite the contrary, it is only the deeper self which is capable of containing within it the totality of qualitative differences of which the individual is actually composed.[32] The first self belongs to the world of appearances, and represents, in fact, the most stubborn of actual illusions.

The second major tradition is that associated with the idea of Christian 'works'. As a Lutheran, of course, Kierkegaard insisted upon the fundamental position that grace was an unearned gift. But he did not deny, any more than did Luther, the significance of 'works' of any sort. The prime example was the work of 'self-denial' as active *upbuilding*, that is as the tireless breaking down of the illusions of selfhood. The deeper self, however, does not act at all, and in relation to it works are of no significance.

Both these traditions, and Kierkegaard's reaction to them, are central to the author's discussion of the comfort of 'self-denial'. On the one hand,

> before this comfort can come, you must understand that you yourself are simply nothing; you must chop down the bridge of probability that wants to connect wish and impatience and desire and expectation with the object wished for, desired, and expected; you must renounce the worldly mentality's association with the future; you must retreat into yourself . . . sinking down into your own nothingness and surrendering yourself to grace and disgrace.
>
> (*Discourses*, pp. 306–7)

But, on the other hand, we are advised peremptorily to 'give up wishing; act'. We normally view action as an attempt to fulfil a wish, so the action referred to here is the action of self-denial. The first self is a product of desire, so self-denying action in relation to it is the renunciation of desire. The self 's entanglement in the vanity of appearances stems from the outgoing character of desire. The author is at one with Pascal in declaring that 'the eye aims its arrows outward every time passion and desire tighten the bowstring'. Self-denying action therefore is a struggle to free the 'deeper self' from being 'an instrument of war in the service of inflexible drives'.[33]

Real self-knowledge begins with the ascendancy of the deeper self, when it 'shapes the deceitful flexibility of the surrounding world in such a way that it is no longer attractive to that first self'.[34] The first self is not lost, but transformed in a new religious immediacy. The consolation of this new religious self-knowledge, which is knowledge of God, lies in action rather than in resignation:

> He does not want a person to be spiritually soft and to bathe in the contemplation of his glory, but in becoming known by a person he wants to create in him a new human being.
>
> (*Discourses*, p. 325)

The individual, in a deeper sense, becomes aware that 'he is capable of nothing at all'. And because of this, whatever the worldly sufferings into which the first self is drawn, the deeper self 'has nothing for which to reproach himself', and is for ever free of guilt.[35]

The inner transformation, the gaining of a specifically Christian immediacy, as the liberation of a deeper self, can now be seen as a continuous, if not actually progressive, process. Self-denial, viewed religiously, is a matter of resolution, which is 'waking up to the eternal'. Waking up, that is 'coming to' the self rather than a wide-awake decision, is both instantaneous and enduring. Thus, while 'the whole thing takes only a moment, just come to a resolution', equally resolution 'is a question not of boldly leaping out but of saving himself'.[36]

The enduring resolution of Christian inwardness appears, from an ethical standpoint, as 'precipitousness, immaturity, and haste'.[37] The cowardliness of the first self 'has won sagacity over to its side', and teaches caution.[38] But the unjustified and reckless foolishness of the deeper self is 'foolishness with regard to something in which there is nothing at all to win if one does not stake everything'.[39] The religious transformation, thus, is a transformation in the form, as well as in the aim, of resolution. Aesthetic enthusiasm and ethical wilfulness are a 'glittering delusion' in which 'resolution itself becomes a seducer and a deceiver instead of a trustworthy guide'.[40]

To 'waken up' the deeper self is also to 'venture the truth'. It is both to shake the individual free of all aesthetic sleepiness and, against any conception of ethical seriousness, it is to 'risk everything'.

A RELIGION OF THE HEART

During 1846 Kierkegaard wrote three longer discourses, *Upbuilding Discourses in Various Spirits*, or as one translator proposes, *in a Different Spirit*, or *in a Different Vein*.[41] They are, that is to say, *Upbuilding Discourses*, in a somewhat different sense to those that accompanied the pseudonymous works. Written after the first termination of the authorship in *Concluding Unscientific Postscript*, and not immediately published, they present an independent (though not direct) statement of the character of modern religiosity.[42]

These writings do not seem intended to be read aloud, they are much longer than the earlier series of discourses, but they are clearly meant to be read as if they had been composed by the reader himself or herself. The author, once again, 'wholly abandons' his work to that 'solitary individual . . . by whom it wishes to be received as if it had arisen within his own heart'.[43] Where the original series had opposed both aesthetic and ethical categories to a new, topologically simple religious immediacy described through mutually reinforcing and inclusive terms, these later pieces reconsider the relevance of differentiated stages to this immediacy. The inward transformation of Christianity, that is, bodies forth not simply a new 'totalizing' immediacy, but a new 'aesthetic', a new 'ethical' and, significantly, a new 'religious' sphere of actuality. These redefined spheres, as differentiated aspects of a religion of the heart, are all forms of Christian experience. In describing them the old terminology of the pseudonyms is abandoned, but in terms of its interrelated threefold structure, *Upbuilding Discourses in Various Spirits* bears an obvious relation to *Stages on Life's Way*.

Rather than begin again with the aesthetic, the first and longest discourse, *Purity of Heart is to Will One Thing*, might be seen as a new religiously inspired ethic.[44] Indeed it can be seen as a determined and overdue attempt to re-establish the ethical which had been assimilated by the earlier pseudonyms to the religious (ethico-religious), and, though granted a certain distinctiveness in the *Upbuilding Discourses*, had there been grouped jointly with the aesthetic against the religious (aesthetico-ethical). Does the ethical, then, have a genuine place within a religiously transformed actuality?

In terms of the earlier pseudonymous scheme of existence-spheres the ethical is defined through the action of the will, but is recognized primarily in the immediacy of guilt which is the inevitable after-effect of intentional acts. The religious form of will is introduced, therefore, in the transformation of guilt into remorse and repentance. The religious reduplication of remorse is a 'guide' to the emerging ethical consciousness of the Christian: 'He is not so quick of foot as the indulgent imagination, which is the servant of desire. He is not so strongly built as the victorious intention.'[45] Remorse, as all religious forms, is an expression of the eternal within the confines of human subjectivity. Its development into repentance, therefore, is a growing awareness of the eternal as a continuous human presence. Repentance is not simply a religious 'expression' for guilt – its translation into a new and arbitrary vocabulary – but, simultaneously, its unfailing consolation. Thus, 'what neither a man's burning wish nor his determined resolution may attain to, may be granted unto him in the sorrowing of repentance'.[46] Christian ethical consciousness begins in repentance rather than in the acknowledgement of any external, or autonomously fashioned, and binding norm; it is formed in sorrow rather than from a sense of 'ought'.

Equally, however, repentance is not to be confused with any form of aesthetic immediacy. It demands a maturity of heart, a calm mood, endurance in religious actuality. Superficially viewed repentance 'can easily be confused with its opposite, with the momentary feeling of contrition . . . with a painful agonizing sorrow after the world . . . with a desperate feeling of grief in itself, that is, with impatience'.[47] Sudden repentance lacks true inwardness, it is untouched by 'the inner anxiety of the heart' which religious immediacy, rather than negating, deepens and consoles.

It is this 'silent daily anxiety' that also distinguishes the Christian ethical consciousness from any socially useful imperative. 'The improvement towards society', typical of Judge William's ethical life-view, in other words, is not to be confused with 'the resigning of himself to God'.[48]

The coherence and character of the Christian ethic which emerges in repentance is defined both by the qualification of, and by the individual's relation to, the actuality that springs from it. Kierkegaard uses a Platonic formulation in discussing the ethical aspect of modern Christianity; its ethical actuality is the Good, and Christian repentance develops into a 'will to the Good'. But, since the Good is uniquely unity and simplicity, this is 'to will one thing'. The earlier *Discourses* had viewed the 'upbuilding' as a gradual uncovering of the deeper self, a self which cannot properly be thought of in terms of 'willing' at all. To 'will one thing', therefore, is not to will a specific good, or the general good, but to wilfully overcome the barriers that lie in the way of the spontaneous emergence of the Good in the form of the deeper self.

Properly to will one thing is to will the Good. To will 'one thing' which is not the Good, is to will an illusion of the Good, and is, therefore, to will diversity and changeableness. This he calls *double-mindedness*. In a typically Augustinian analysis Kierkegaard strengthens and broadens the earlier pseudonyms' critique of aesthetic immediacy. Quite apart from those who despairingly will diversity and 'see themselves in the magic mirror of possibility which hope holds before them while the wish flatters them', those who will pleasure as a principle still will multiplicity.[49] And not only to will pleasure, but to will honour, riches or power is characteristically double-minded. Thus honour, for example, is not one thing: 'worldly honour is a whirlpool, a play of confused faces, an illusory moment in the flux of opinions'. Its apparent unity is 'a sense deception, as when a swarm of insects at a distance seem to the eye like one body'.[50]

The deception of unity itself conceals the more vital illusion that the worldly goal has a reality of its own:

> the worldly goal is not one thing in its essence because it is unreal. Its so-called unity is actually nothing but emptiness which is hidden beneath the manyness. In the short lived moment of delusion the worldly goal is therefore a multitude of things . . . in the next moment it changes into its opposite.
>
> (*Purity*, pp. 59–60)

The double-minded, additionally, seeks a 'reason', other than its goodness, to will the Good: 'to will the Good for the sake of the reward is, as it were, a symbol of double-mindedness'.[51] Equally it is double-minded to will the Good from fear of punishment. Here the genuinely ennobling becomes superstitiously confused with the merely tempting.

The 'reward-centred man' is a contemporary commonplace, but the deeper deceptiveness of modern life is exemplified in 'the man who wills the Good and wills its victory out of self-centred wilfulness'.[52] This is a more subtle and resistant form of egotism, a type of impatience which 'effervesces' in the moment, and knows nothing of 'daily self-forgetfulness'.[53] And it is another typically modern form of egotism which limits commitment to the Good with the double-mindedness that 'dwells in the press of busyness'. Busyness 'is like a charm' in which the individual becomes entangled in 'the mass of connections, stimuli, and hindrances' that 'make it ever more impossible to win any deeper knowledge of himself '.[54] Busyness interrupts the time and the quiet in which the self can 'win the transparency' of its own deeper nature.

Religiously viewed, therefore, the ethical demand is continually directed inward, not because isolation has any special value of its own, but because 'the crowd' is the home of illusion and the source of self-deception. The overriding claim of morality is the obligation towards the deeper self: 'there is but one fault, one offence: disloyalty to his own self or the denial of his own better self '.[55] This is why the writer of the discourse must eschew all literary trickery in presenting his case. The merely clever or impressive has no more claim on the deeper self of the reader than has 'busyness' or any other form of double-mindedness. The 'exalted earnestness of the eternal' ought not to be confused with an aesthetically conceived 'aroused state of consciousness', and the genuinely edifying, therefore, requires 'neither the commendation of the majority nor the commendation of eloquence'.[56]

The upbuilding, therefore, has nothing to do with 'moralizing' in the sense of urging upon anyone the virtue of some specific value as a guarantor of correct conduct. Nor is the ethical, as purity of heart, the only form of the edifying. The religious transformation is a total remaking of actuality, so that the *Upbuilding Discourses in Various Spirits* seeks to make the reader aware of the deeper self also in relation to renewed aesthetics. Kierkegaard here exploits one of his favourite texts, inviting the reader to *Consider the Lilies.*[57]

This discourse is quite distinct from the long tradition of theologically inspired contemplations of nature. It is neither the design, nor the impressiveness, nor the beauty, nor the sublime incomprehensibility of nature that is the focus of the discourse, but its specific capacity to 'distract' the anxious. Where in the earlier pseudonymous works the aesthetic is portrayed as a dangerous multiplicity of immediate sensations and reflections, the new aesthetic discovers, through the prospect of nature rather than in the 'busyness' of human life, a positive value in distraction. Thus, where for the untransformed inwardness of melancholy distraction is always a self-defeating illusion in which melancholy itself is strengthened, the reduplicated deeper self can discover itself in every chance encounter with the world. The Gospel suggests specific images which, in their symbolic condensation of a human predicament, capture and calm the attention of a restless spirit.

The invitation to *Consider the Lilies* is a model for all 'upbuilding' discourses. It is addressed to the anxious, and any human intrusion on anxiety, by imposing upon it fresh comparisons with lesser or greater anxieties, serves only to reinforce its groundless sorrow. The discourse has no power to persuade but, like 'the lilies of the field and the birds of the air', distracts the anxious by holding itself apart from all comparisons. In observing (reading) them the anxious are comforted. If 'in his sorrow a man really observes the lilies and the birds', then, 'all by himself, unnoticed, from them learns something about himself '.[58]

The common 'neglected lily' serves as a symbol of a new religious immediacy; it grows effortlessly in its neglect, adorning itself without concern or anxiety over the judgement of others. The 'birds of the air', on the other hand, represent untransformed immediacy; it is 'the restless thought of comparison, which roams far and wide, inconstant and fickle, and acquires an unhealthy knowledge of difference'.[59] Yet correctly observed the birds also distract from and soothe anxiety, they teach a person 'to be content with what it is to be a man, to be content with what it is to be dependent, the creature as little capable of sustaining himself as of creating himself'.[60]

The double-meaning of distraction, and the ambiguity of the natural symbols of eternity, follow directly from the characteristic double-mindedness of modern life. For the anxious person, intent upon creating and sustaining himself through artificial differences, and 'to be himself his own Providence', distraction strengthens the first self. The care of the self becomes misconceived as the constant struggle to satisfy externally imposed needs. And the effort, in anxiety, to establish the self as autonomous in fact leads to its subordination under appearances. The desire for distraction follows from this illusory lack of freedom. For the religiously 'reduplicated' individual, however, distraction is a continuous sinking into the deeper self, a distraction into, rather than away from, reality.

The religious contemplation of nature as 'freedom from care' is a consolation for, rather than the abolition of, a deeper anxiety. Compared to the lily or the bird, the human being is created in the image of God, and to be spirit is 'man's invisible glory'. The consciousness of this likeness (worship) is a kind of anxiety in which the human preserves its superiority over natural creatures. The upbuilding in the vision of nature lies, therefore, both in the distraction from artificial differences among people, and in the arousal of the genuine and common difference between the human and the natural. The flight of the bird, thus, soothes and tranquillizes, and in its sight one 'forgets imaginary anxiety'. Yet the flight of the bird is an 'imperfect symbol' of faith. Its freedom from care only corresponds partially to the human potential for spirituality. Human perfection, which resides in a purely spiritual likeness to God, is invisible and continually provokes an inner tension in the painful awareness of the continuing abysmal difference between man and God. The careless indifference of the bird is an 'intermediary' between the secular anxiety of the human crowd, and the worshipful anxiety in which the individual carefully preserves the difference between the human and the divine.

Consider the Lilies represents an aesthetic essay 'in a new spirit', but, as the new Christian immediacy had been the central subject matter of *Eighteen Upbuilding Discourses*, it can be content with a less elaborate development than that provided for the ethical discourse that preceded it. The third discourse, *The Gospel of Sufferings*, is Kierkegaard's first attempt to describe the 'religious sphere' from a decisively Christian standpoint, and completes the transformation of the topological and anthropological perspectives introduced by the earlier pseudonyms.

For the 'aesthetic' writers the 'religious sphere' was conceived as the ultimate potentiation of the possibilities inherent in actuality. Restricted to the 'exceptional individual' the religious was viewed romantically as the endless prolongation of a moment of divine pleasure. And for Johannes Climacus, beginning with an 'ethical' (universal) conception of actuality, religion appeared before him as the impenetrable barrier of the Paradox and Offence. Beginning from either the aesthetic or the ethical, religion constituted 'another' sphere, a topologically specific region of reality, to which human beings were drawn, but into which they could not penetrate. Viewed anthropologically the pseudonyms saw the specific character of the religious 'sphere' in terms of the self-expansion of actuality against the constraining forces of non-existence (ideality and sensuousness), and for them Christianity was the conquest of doubt and anxiety. But from a religious perspective Kierkegaard had shown these views were all deceptions; self-generated illusions embedded in the structure of modern society. Religiously viewed, the aesthetic becomes 'patient expectation' and 'trust' rather than the moment, and the ethical becomes 'self-denial' rather than self-expression. And religiously viewed the 'religious sphere' similarly becomes inverted. Rather than hoping, in some persistent Hegelian delusion, that the religious will bring an end to the Offence, that in it the Paradox will be resolved and the inner tensions of actuality somehow transcended, the *Upbuilding* view is that these painful obstacles to any religious transition become, in the transition itself, the sources of a new religious joy. For the aesthetic, the ethical and the philosophical pseudonyms, that is to say, the religious is a dreamt-of sphere within which suffering (however defined) is abolished; but for the religiously transformed view of life the religious finds consolation and more in these sufferings, which are 'the joyous signs that the right way is being followed'.[61] And although 'there must be nothing that the follower is not willing to give up', and in a sense 'the greater the suffering the nearer the perfection', this is not to be thought of as a unique heroic event, but as a daily pursuit of self-denial.[62] Christianity does not alter anything outward: 'Humanly speaking, no new suffering has been added, nor, on the other hand, has any old suffering been taken away.'[63] Thus, 'A Christian may have to suffer exactly as he suffered before, but yet for a Christian the heavy burden has become light.'[64]

The patience of religious immediacy gains depth and inwardness in this transformation. Meekness is the religious sentiment commensurate with the burden made light, and, as a humanly unrewarded virtue, 'is the most distinctive mark of the Christian'.[65]

Religious suffering is *upbuilding*. Where it is impossible, religiously speaking, for one person to help another, suffering is essentially educative. In 'coming to know' through suffering human differentiation is not reintroduced, 'it is not a matter of aptitude'.[66] Suffering is an aspect of developing self-knowledge, and makes possible knowledge of the deeper self:

Suffering directs a man to look within. If it succeeds, the man will not despairingly resist, nor seek, for the sake of forgetfulness, to plunge into the distractions of the world, into astounding enterprises, into an all-embracing and undifferentiated knowledge.

(*Sufferings*, p. 56)

Suffering teaches the self-knowledge of obedience, and 'there is no obedience apart from suffering, no faith apart from obedience'.[67] Suffering, that is to say, like meekness, and faith, is an aspect of (rather than a topologically distinct region within) the religious reduplication of actuality.

Religiously, suffering brings joy rather than despair. For Kierkegaard, as indeed for the earlier pseudonyms, it is clear that 'reason cannot comprehend what can be gained by suffering'. But, from his different perspective, Kierkegaard is aware of a deeper connection between this inexplicable mystery and the notion that God is love. He distinguishes, thus, between the consequences of 'innocent suffering' which is doubt of others (Rousseau), 'guilty suffering' which is the self-doubt contained in the consciousness of sin (Anti-Climacus), and the 'religious suffering' which, in continually being aware that before God the human is essentially guilty, 'consists in absolute joy'. The suffering of the Christian is a voluntary acceptance of what is, in fact, an essential relation. The relation, of course, remains the same whether or not the individual becomes aware and accepts it. But in remaining unaware, the person is diverted into purely human, distractive, forms of suffering. Recognition of the inescapable guiltiness of the human before a loving God is the foundation of both religious suffering and the joy which it brings. Tribulation is the essential form of a Christian's joyful suffering, and 'inasmuch as tribulation is the way, doubt perishes'.[68]

Suffering is a form of self-knowledge, a way (though not a rational means) in which the deeper self is revealed. In this religious perspective S. Kierkegaard, as distinct from the passionate Johannes Climacus, views genuine self-knowledge as disinterestedness. It is, indeed,

the most difficult form of disinterestedness, to have no regard to one's own ideas of gain, and to the fertile excuses of one's passions, nor yet to the powerful bodings of a terror-struck imagination, in the consciousness of sin.

(*Sufferings*, p. 129)

It is only disinterested, however, because the deeper self is incapable of action and, therefore, has no interest beyond itself. Thus, though it is strictly speaking senseless to talk in the secular language of calculation, the situation might be 'rationalized' by saying that, as God's love is infinite, the tribulations inflicted by the form in which this love is accessible (suffering) are 'outweighed' by the benefit of religious reduplication which it brings about. Eternity is incommensurate with suffering, but from a human point of view it is true that 'the least part of the blessedness of eternity weighs infinitely more than the most prolonged earthly suffering'.[69]

A theomorphic reconstruction of actuality is traced in the upbuilding literature. Taken together, *Eighteen Upbuilding Discourses* and the *Upbuilding Discourses in Various Spirits* suggest that such a religious transformation deprives actuality of none of its content. The 'aesthetic', the 'ethical' and the 'religious' persist in it, but they have been 'deconstructed' into elements and then recombined according to a new pattern. Now there are no separated 'spheres', no abysmal 'gaps' in existence, and no moments of terrifying transition. The aesthetic, the ethical and the religious now coexist as a single totality viewed under different aspects. In a deeper sense, therefore, this reconstructed totality is religious through and through. All its organizing principles and characteristic forms, whether or not they serve the immediate interests of the aesthetic or the ethical, or even of the old 'religious', are religious in a new way. Their mode of interconnection, too, is quite new. And as there is now only a single 'existence-sphere', a topologically uniform simplicity, differentiation takes place in terms of temporal succession.[70] Trust, expectation, patience, self-denial, meekness, joy in suffering represent both a 'progress' in religious life, a deepening and maturing of Christian inwardness, and, equally, they are equivalent transformations each touching for a moment the secular life of the individual and remaking it inwardly. The individual, thus, should not be pictured as making steady 'progress' through these categories towards some 'ultimate' Christian consummation. These are simply the forms in which actuality now presents itself, and life becomes a continuous flux within them. The fundamental difference between the frenzy of the Present Age and this continuous modulation of inwardness is that all these latter forms, being touched by eternity, are equally Christian ways of existing, and, therefore, in a deeper sense, confirm the subject's non-melancholic selfhood.

It is characteristic of Kierkegaard's description of religious reduplication that all the paradoxes of the earlier pseudonyms give way to new forms which, without resolving or transcending their differences, contain them. In the Christian reduplication of immediacy there is no longer an *either/or*; the aesthetic *and* the ethical *and* the religious subsist as aspects of the totality of existence reflected in the single individual.

Chapter 8

Edification: the conquest of melancholy

Whoever seeks mere edification, and whoever wants to shroud in a mist the manifold variety of his earthly existence and of thought, in order to pursue the indeterminate enjoyment of this indeterminate divinity, may look where he likes to find all this. He will find ample opportunity to dream up something for himself. But philosophy must beware of the wish to be edifying.

G.W.F. Hegel, *Phenomenology of Spirit*

no one can have a true conception of God without having a corresponding conception of life and of oneself, or a true conception of oneself without a corresponding conception of God, or a true conception of life without a corresponding conception of oneself. A poetic creative fancy, or a conception at the distance of indifferent thought, is not a true conception. Neither does the conception of God come as an incidental addendum to that conception of life and of oneself. On the contrary, it comes and penetrates and crowns everything and was present before it became clear.

S. Kierkegaard, *Three Discourses on Imagined Occasions*

Christian reduplication dissolves into a single reality the topological distinctness of existence-spheres. This reconstructed totality has nothing outside itself, that is to say it has only God outside itself. Viewed anthropologically the human synthesis 'relates itself to itself' and does so 'before God', and religiously reduplicated there are no alien elements in this synthesis. There is no tendency within religiously reduplicated actuality towards either ideality or sensuousness, and, therefore, no 'transition zones' of doubt or anxiety. Actuality becomes 'all of a piece', a network of internal relations, which is wholly human in all its aspects. There is no part of actuality which is not completely human, and no aspect of the human which is not wholly actual.[1]

The Christian freedom from the misplaced doubt and anxiety

generated by the illusions of the public is the particular subject of the *Christian Discourses* which were published in 1848. Where *Upbuilding Discourses in Various Spirits* describes the deconstruction of the original existence-spheres and the reconstruction of a single sphere of Christian actuality, *Christian Discourses* proposes a distinctively Christian anthropology.[2] The two longest of its four sections return to themes introduced in *Upbuilding Discourses in Various Spirits*, namely a further meditation on the significance of the 'consider the lilies' text and a more general discussion of the central Christian category of joy.

The *upbuilding* significance of the 'lilies and the birds' is now treated more comprehensively by way of a three-part comparison of 'natural beings' (the lilies and the birds), secular human being (the heathen), and religiously reduplicated being (the Christian). Thus, in relation to any particular anxiety, the lilies and the birds remain untouched and unaware of its possibility, the heathen suffers it directly, and the Christian is 'cured' of it through the continuous 'spiritualization' of existence.

The bird, for example, 'is not anxious for the lower things which it does not seek, but neither does it seek the higher things'.[3] The heathen, however, is anxious over the distribution of every good, and, consequently, fears falling into any form of poverty, and, equally, becomes anxious over every abundance.[4] The anxiety of the heathen is rooted in the continuous process of comparing what they possess and want with what others possess and want to possess. The Christian's lack of anxiety in relation to either poverty or abundance is not ignorance of such matters, but the indifference which comes from 'the notion that possession is an illusion'. Anxiety is transformed into faith: 'the thought of eternity takes away the thought of possession'.[5] Similarly the bird is not anxious over the lowliness or highness of its social status, while the heathen, 'existing only before others, is perpetually tormented by the shifting boundaries of social valuation, and in 'his inmost being has become pithless and corroded'.[6] But the Christian exists continually 'before God' and thus learns the insignificance of social distinctions.

The bird is neither a self nor a potential self, and cannot know the anxiety of self-torment. The bird 'is not troubled by dreams' or by 'anxiety for the next day'. The bird lives 'in a persistent dream' into which the heathen would like to fall. But the heathen cannot shake off the insecurity of 'the next day', which is 'the grappling hook by which the prodigious hulk of anxiety gets a hold upon the individual's light craft'.[7] But for the Christian 'the next day' is non-existent: 'by the help of eternity' he lives 'absorbed in today'. And 'the more he is eternally absorbed in today, the more decisively does he turn his back upon the next day, so that he does not see it at all.'[8] The Christian lives as a 'contemporary with himself ', in an immediate relation with his or her own actuality; this is not to be confused with the 'care-freeness of the bird', which is simply the spiritless 'light-mindedness' of natural being. The more openly critical aspect of S. Kierkegaard's writing becomes obvious in the development of this complex comparison. The heathen develops aesthetic, ethical and even religious characteristics which, in 'elevating' him above natural being, produce obstacles to Christian reduplication. By 'heathen' he does not mean only, or even generally, 'primitive' or 'undeveloped'; his target lies much closer to home. Thus while primitively the heathen tries to negate the next day by 'sensuous absorption in today', and may even gain thereby a 'torpid security', the ethical demand which is normative for modern society is to live as it were in advance of oneself, to strive towards the actualization of the self through the realization of its goals. Hence it is the more refined and educated of people in modern society who, in speculative worry over the future, forget themselves:

> Most men, in feeling, in imagination, in purpose, in resolution, in wish, in apocalyptic vision, in theatrical make-believe, are a hundred thousand miles in advance of themselves, or several human generations in advance of themselves.
>
> (*Christian*, p. 77)

The Christian, on the other hand, loves 'to cram today with eternity and not with the next day'.[9]

Anxiety stems from the attempt to be wholly self-sufficient and independent; to make the first self of the heathen the sole generative power of actuality. But thus narrowly conceived human consciousness cannot help but detect 'other' elements in actuality and, anxiously and doubtfully, attributes them to an independent and alien nature or to a disembodied mind. Christian reduplication, on the other hand, is the transformation of both sensuous dread and temporal anxiety into a continuously developing need of God, and 'the Christian knows that a sense of the need of God is man's perfection'.[10]

The need of God, like anxiety, is an immediate relation to something outside actuality. But where the heathen's anxiety leads the person out of actuality into the spiritless nothingness of nature contiguous to it, the need of God, whose purity of being cannot be 'placed' adjacent to the human existence-sphere, serves only to confirm and 'deepen' actuality. The need of God does not lead the subject out of actuality but transforms all the determinants of the human realm.

In a similar way, where doubt propels the heathen consciousness beyond itself into fantastic abstraction, Christian reduplication relates consciousness and reflection immediately to itself. Reflection, which is an aspect of the totality of human being rather than a discrete activity within it, plunges the individual into his or her own existence. Dismay rather than doubt is the initial movement of Christian thought, and in it actuality gathers itself. Thought cannot conceive the absolute, and the need of God dismayingly confirms thought in itself. Dismay is a 'falling back on itself ', and thus the deepening, rather than the illusory extension, of actuality.

Christian self-understanding, which begins in dismay, is edifying, and thus continually reaffirms the essential relation between a wholly human existence and God. That there is sin is dismaying, that there is forgiveness of sins is edifying. And the edifying deepens into faith. The process of deepening, when it is described or is being talked about, appears to be the continuous development of a truth immanent in actuality. But, in actuality, it is a process which depends at every point on God's undeserved and freely offered grace. Even for the Christian, therefore, faith is the potentiation of dismay as well as the acceptance of grace:

> When faith is seen from the one side, the heavenly side, one sees in it only the highest reflection of blessedness; but seen from the other side, the merely human side, one sees sheer fear and trembling.
>
> (*Christian*, p. 182)

Faith is the possession of the ultimate good, but cannot be thought of as the possession of a 'thing' at all. It is, first of all, the possession of the self as a purely human being:

> If a man has *faith*, truly he has not thereby deprived others of anything. . . . By having faith he expresses the purely human, or that which is the essential possibility of every man.
>
> (*Christian*, p. 121)

The good of faith is 'essentially a communication', so that its individual possession is both a form of self-expression and a universal social bond. There is no contradiction, as there is in relation to all other goods, between selfish possession and a common benefaction. Here, as faith is a communication, possession is also sharing:

> The way, the perfect way of making others rich is to communicate the goods of the spirit, being oneself, moreover, solely employed in acquiring and possessing these goods.
>
> (*Christian*, p. 125)

Faith, which is the communication of faith, is a direct communication: 'But with regard to the true riches, the nature of which is communication, increase is neither more nor less than direct communication and the increase of it.'[11] This does not mean, however, that S. Kierkegaard's *Christian Discourses* can be regarded as a 'direct communication'. Quite apart from the question of the identity of S. Kierkegaard, the author admits at the end of the work that 'All our talk about God is of course human talk ... if we would not be completely silent, we must after all employ the human measuring-rod when we as men talk about God'.[12] And in terms of such a measuring-rod Christian faith may be represented as free and spontaneous communication, in contrast to the 'inclosing reserve' of human uncommunicativeness typical of the modern age.

In one of his late discourses, *Judge for Yourself*, S. Kierkegaard develops the notion that Christianity is not only in opposition to the 'bourgeois-philistinism' of modern secular life, but that, in actuality, it contains a whole series of oppositions. Because 'everything essentially Christian is a redoubling', he argues that 'every qualification of the essentially Christian is first of all its opposite'. The Christian seems to invert the secular order of values. Thus, 'in just a human view, elevation is only elevation and nothing more; Christianly it is first of all humiliation. So also with inspiration ... Christianly, inspiration is first of all becoming sober'.[13]

The secular mentality, which 'deifies sagacity' and submits every possible action to the calculation of probabilities, 'considers Christianity to be drunkenness', seeing in it nothing but a reckless venture. Christianity, on the other hand, interprets the human view of moderation as a melancholic intoxication; moderation is 'stupefying, makes one heavy, drowsy, sluggish, and apathetic'.[14] For Christianity, therefore, 'becoming sober' is 'venturing to relinquish probability'. Indeed, 'only by being before God can one totally come to oneself in the transparency of soberness'.[15] Christian soberness is an 'intoxicating' abandonment of 'the sensible, sagacious, and levelheaded':

> this will soon end with your tumbling like a drunk man into actuality, plunging yourself recklessly into reckless action without giving the understanding and sagacity the time to take into proper consideration what is prudent, what is advantageous, what will pay.
>
> (*Self-Examination*, p. 118)

But if one observed faith in another, a faith which is bound to express itself directly, one would see a person 'lost to, alienated from, and dead to all temporal, finite, earthly considerations'. Such a person would be 'unbearable – he would appear intoxicated'.[16] This expression evokes Erasmian 'Folly': 'the supreme reward for man is no other than a kind of madness'; and through Erasmus it suggests the recovery of a positive religious meaning for melancholy.[17]

The Danish term used extensively throughout the religious writings to refer to the 'happiness' or 'blessedness' of Christian faith is *Salighed*, from an Anglo-Saxon root *salig*, which in English means 'silly' or 'touched', so that the afflicted person becomes 'weak and helpless'.[18] Just as the anxious and doubtful become 'dizzy', so the Christian appears to be sheer 'dizziness' to the secular observer. From any perspective immanent within the Present Age

> becoming involved with God, with the infinite – nothing is more certain than that this is intoxication, that it is not so certain that someone staring into the waves from a ship or someone gazing down into the depths from a lofty place or from a lower place out into an infinite space where nothing limits the eye – that it is not so certain that he will become dizzy as the one does who becomes involved with God.
>
> (*Self-Examination*, p. 106)

This understanding forms the basis for a powerful attack on the 'toned-down' Christianity of the Present Age. To become sober means 'to come to oneself ', but in the Present Age there are two completely incompatible conceptions of the self: the secular life of the ego and the 'deeper self ' of Christian reduplication. Coming to oneself in the former sense takes one away from oneself in the latter sense, and *vice versa*. Although the deeper self has become obscured by the exotic whirl of the Present Age, its reality has not entirely slipped out of existence. Our melancholy is, after all, evidence of its continuing but 'unknown' presence, the sign of its absence. And though our melancholy cannot itself become a means to recover this abandoned selfhood, it forces us to acknowledge, in the form of occasional 'dizzy spells', the superficiality of our 'normal' wretchedness and the frightening proximity, rather than comforting distance, of a genuinely religious existence:

> The truth of the matter is this. All of us human beings are more or less intoxicated. But we are like a drunk man who is not completely drunk so that he has lost consciousness – no, he is definitely conscious that he is a little drunk and for that very reason is careful to conceal it from others, if possible from himself.
>
> (*Self-Examination*, p. 113)

We therefore choose to 'walk close to the buildings and walk erect without becoming dizzy'. Spiritually, that is to say, at the very point of realizing our intoxication 'sagacity and sensibleness and levelheadedness come to our aid'.

Again it is important to notice that the first self is not some universal natural creature, but is either the embodiment of solid bourgeois virtues of respectability or representative of contemporary European 'high culture'; neither is the deeper self some mystical nothingness in which the individual undergoes an ecstatic annihilation. The individual retains all his or her particular qualifications. Reduplication is not the abolition of actuality, but its inner transformation in which everything outer remains unchanged. In this context it is noticeable that the edifying, which strikingly 'mediates' between the pseudonyms and the first cycle of *upbuilding* discourses, and even finds a way of relating sobriety and drunkenness, also discovers a term between the 'movement' of the former and the 'stillness' of the latter. The *edifying* is restlessness but it is a restlessness in which nothing is changed. It is a restlessness

> which has to do with inward deepening. A true love affair is indeed a restless thing, but it never enters the lover's head to want to change things as they are.
>
> (*Self-Examination*, p. 21)

Kierkegaard at times, it is true, seems to express a more 'mystical' form of Christianity. He talks of worship as being 'lost in God', and of the 'bliss' in 'sensing God's strength'. He describes worship in terms of the passive voluptuousness of inner dissolution:

> God and the worshipper are adapted to one another, happily, blissfully, as never were lovers adapted to one another . . . the only wish of the worshipper is to become weaker and weaker. . . . The worshipper has lost himself.
>
> (*Christian*, pp. 136–7)

But as Christian reduplication 'contains' (in a new non-contradictory form) all possible secular distinctions within it, it contains both the conception of a self-annihilating mystical union with God and the conviction that 'only by being before God can one totally come to oneself in the transparency of soberness'.[19]

More generally, however, Kierkegaard maintains a critical attitude towards any notion of mystical indifference:

> A being which has no distinction within itself is a very imperfect being, it may be an imaginary being, such as the being of a mathematical point. A being which has the difference outside itself is an evanescent being. . . . Eternity, righteousness, has the distinction within itself.
>
> (*Christian*, pp. 215–16)

To be 'nothing before God', therefore, is not to lack all human distinction.

THE DIALECTIC OF CHRISTIAN LOVE

The *edifying*, another expression for the *upbuilding*, is not a discourse about existence but a discourse of existence given figurative expression in the 'whispering secrecy of the metaphorical'.[20] The cosmological ladder to God has been swept aside, so that God's presence lies, impenetrably concealed, in the human heart. Theology is thus transformed into an anthropology of self-knowledge, and the Christian life becomes a continuous struggle to uncover the deeper self which is the heart immediately transformed by the spirit's secret presence. Kierkegaard expresses this transformation, the *edifying*, in a number of ways, but suggests two compelling metaphors through which it might be grasped in its most general form.

The first describes reduplication from the perspective of the secular self as 'drunkenness' or 'madness'. Kierkegaard here exploits a long tradition of Christian Platonism which had found its most significant modern expression in Erasmus.[21] The second suggests the qualitative change of reduplication is experienced as love. Significantly Erasmus, explicitly invoking Plato, also links these two notions. Love is a kind of delirium in which the lover is 'taken out of ' the self: 'For anyone who loves intensely lives not in himself but in the object of his love, and the further he can move out of himself into his love, the happier he is.'[22] The most intense happiness, therefore, involves the destruction of that first self which clings to transient worldly forms. But, rather than become aware of this as an 'emptying' of the self, it 'fills out' the self with a new content.[23]

The association of drunkenness and dizziness with the happiness of salvation and of love, and the clear connection of both with a tradition of Platonism within which melancholy was deeply rooted, reveal the ambivalence of sorrow in Kierkegaard's later religious writings. 'Pleasure' has connected itself to the surface of life, and the aesthetic pseudonyms had demonstrated the ways in which the apparently reasonable pursuit of pleasure is self-defeating. But melancholy is not the 'result' of the unsuccessful search for pleasure. More significantly melancholy is sorrow over the loss of happiness which the pursuit of pleasure itself implies. This sorrow is, for the most part, barely conscious, but, insignificant as it might seem, it is this 'sorrow without reason' (the reason 'grief over the loss of happiness' is too fantastic to be seriously entertained, and is reduced to 'nothing') upon which the pursuit of pleasure is wrecked. Pleasure is no substitute for happiness, and it is this disparity which melancholy signifies. Melancholy is recollection, and repetition does not lie within its power.

This gives to sorrow a positive significance, without claiming for it a positive value. The experience of passive suffering, the affliction of passion, is not in itself a mode of appropriating religious truth, and S. Kierkegaard (though by no means all of his pseudonymous colleagues) sees nothing intrinsically valuable in sorrow and suffering. Melancholy 'deepens' and forms the self, but does not do so in terms of religious 'inwardness'. The positive significance of melancholy is in terms of its incommensurability with any humanly rational category. Try as we might we cannot rid ourselves of sorrow. It is the persistence of sorrow which destroys pleasure and the rational world of the first self. But the religious life is untouched by melancholy. It is the conquest of melancholy, the recovery of happiness without consequential regret over the 'loss' of the world.

The *edifying* discourses seek to describe this non-melancholic subjectivity. Having exhausted a variety of paradoxes, comparisons and mediations Kierkegaard turns finally to love as the central reality of religious experience.

Just as God's presence is revealed, for faith, only indirectly in signs, so love, which 'has an unfathomable connection with the whole of existence', is known only 'by its fruits'.[24] The *Works of Love* traces the connection among different forms of love and finds in them signs of God's love as their common source. But this source cannot itself be uncovered. Indeed, it is just the 'impenetrable' and 'unfathomable' character of 'love's secret life in the heart' and the various manifestations which justifies its use as a religious metaphor:

> As the quiet lake invites you to look at it, but by its dark reflection prevents your looking down through it, so the mysterious origins of love in the love of God prevents you from seeing its source; if you think you see it, then you are deceived by a reflection.
>
> (*Love*, p. 8)

This is, of course, also a description of melancholy, whose fathomless depths are so brilliantly reflected on the surface of modern life, and we are entitled to ask whether S. Kierkegaard has not, in fact, deceived himself into another aesthetic illusion. Is not 'reduplication' simply another 'existence-sphere' and ultimately, therefore, a mode of being already contained within the aesthetic magic of 'possibility'?[25] And is not the partial concealment of the signature, 'S.', rather than the personally revealing 'Søren', itself a residue of the aesthetic? He confides to his *Journal* (though why should we believe Søren in preference to his other pseudonyms?):

> For many years my melancholy has prevented me from being on terms of real intimacy with myself. In between my melancholy and myself lay a whole world of the imagination. That is, in part, what I rid myself of in the pseudonyms.[26]

And in another entry, referring to all his writings, he takes an even more decisive view: 'I always stand in an altogether poetical relationship to my work, and I am, therefore, myself a pseudonym'.[27] The *edifying* works, it seems, reveal the author as another pseudonym and therefore as another form of melancholy.

The reduplication of Christian love does not deny the reality of melancholy, in fact it confirms it as the 'dark ground' which is the presence of God for the human spirit. This changes nothing in the sense that the human still exists within an infinite void, yet, none the less, everything is changed: 'sorrow without cause' is transformed into 'senseless happiness' and, freed from despair over being free, human subjectivity restores to itself the depth and plenitude of its own reality. Melancholy, as an impenetrable 'inclosing reserve', is, in fact, an anticipation of religious reduplication rather than an obstacle in the path of its transformative realization.[28] And where melancholy gives rise to 'reflection', its reduplication as love bears the fruits of actuality. *Works of Love*, is, therefore, called 'Christian reflections', discourses which edify rather than instruct or divert.[29]

Christian love, like melancholy, springs from a hidden and inexhaustible source, and cannot directly reveal itself. Thus, 'as the love itself is invisible, a man must therefore believe in it'.[30] No human action 'unconditionally proves the presence of love, or unconditionally proves that love is not present'.[31] Earthly love, which is 'the beautiful fantasy of the infinite', and finds 'its highest expression in mysterious foolishness', is not an unambiguous sign of divine love.[32] The metaphor of earthly love is thus effective by way of difference as well as through similarity. This is nowhere clearer than in the Christian conception of love as a commandment. The 'divine primitiveness' of 'thou *shalt* love' is, claims S. Kierkegaard, something foreign to every human heart:

> What a difference between the play of the emotions and impulses and inclinations and passions . . . that glory celebrated in poetry, in smiles, or in tears, in wishing or in need . . . and that of eternity, the earnestness of the commandment in spirit and in truth, in sincerity and self-denial.
>
> (*Love*, p. 21)

The obligation to love, from a secular viewpoint, is a contradiction, but in faith it expresses the special character of divine love. As duty Christian love is placed beyond the changeable corruptibility of immediacy. There is no temptation, within a relation of obligation, to 'test' divine love. Love, in this sense, cannot change into hate, or suffer jealousy or the corrosion of habit.

The Christian is commanded to love the neighbour, and Kierkegaard argues that it is the commandment which itself creates the neighbour. Here Christianity and modern Romanticism are in striking opposition. The religious obligation to love creates a universal community of neighbours, while for the poetic it is the exclusiveness of passionate love which defines the unique character of the beloved. Christian love, thus, is not based on impulse, and it is seen as the suppression of a natural inclination only because of the fabulous conflation of Christianity and Romanticism. The 'passionate particularity' celebrated by the modern poet 'is essentially another form of selfishness'.[33] And it is passionate partiality which gives rise to 'the other I', the beloved, as a projection of secular self-love. The exclusive choice of passionate partiality is a 'prodigious wilfulness' in which 'arbitrariness is everywhere manifest'. Yet, from a secular viewpoint, the highest achievement of earthly love is the unrestricted mutuality, the merging, of the immediate I and the reflected I of the beloved. But the Christian obligation, which is indifferent to impulse, 'cannot make me into one with my neighbour in a united self '.[34]

The community of neighbours, therefore, is not an undifferentiated mass. The commandment is addressed to the individual, to each individual as a whole person, and neither to the community in general, nor to some specifically differentiated capacity for or principle of 'humanity' fabulously deposited in each person. For the reduplication of Christian love, the neighbour 'is the absolutely indistinguishable difference between man and man, or is the eternal resemblance before God'.[35] Christianity, that is to say, includes all, but 'has not *taken away* the *differences*' among people: 'For by being a Christian he is not exempt from the differences, but by triumphing over the temptation of the differences, he becomes Christian'.[36]

There is nothing exclusive in Christian love for the neighbour, nor does it represent, as does romantic love, a form of selfishness. Thus, while 'to love God is in truth to love one's self ', it is, simultaneously, to recognize the binding obligation to love the neighbour. Equally, to love the neighbour is self-love of a proper kind.

> To love oneself in the right way and to love one's neighbour are absolutely analogous concepts, are at bottom one and the same.
>
> (*Love*, p. 19)

This has nothing to do with human reciprocity, nor does it imply the emergence of a 'community of ends' in which all secular conflicts are resolved.[37] Rather than view 'humanity' as a spiritual intermediary between the individual and God, God is more truthfully seen as the 'mediation' among individuals. Kierkegaard concludes, therefore, that 'to love another man is to help him to love God, and to be loved is to be helped to love God'.[38] Love, that is to say, accomplishes what no discourse can; it edifies.

Christian reduplication, the commandment to love, transforms the immediacy of love into the immediacy of conscience: 'Christianity transforms every relation between men into a conscience-relationship, and thus also into a love relationship'.[39] This is not to be confused with either sympathy or admiration, both of which spring from purely human impulses. It is not the perfections in others that we must love, but others in themselves. Thus, while modern romantic love is a consoling fantasy, Christian love must:

> renounce all imaginative and overtrained ideas of a dream-world, where the object of love would be to seek and to find; that is, one must become sober, gain reality and truth by finding and remaining in the world of reality, as the sole appointed task.
>
> (*Love*, p. 130)

Love, thus, is an interpersonal medium, and not an exclusively personal attribute. It is 'the exact opposite of mistrust' in which the individual comes wholly to himself or herself through existing for others.

Christian love, in short, is the synthesis of, and the synthesizing power within, actuality. And there is nothing 'difficult' or 'obscure' in this. In a direct challenge to Johannes Climacus, S. Kierkegaard writes:

> Christianity is not a fairy tale, although the happiness it promises is more glorious than that of any fairy tale, nor is it an ingenious chimera which is intended to be difficult to understand, and which also requires one single condition, an idle head and an empty brain.
>
> (*Love*, p. 58)

Anti-Climacus, in *The Sickness Unto Death*, describes the self as a synthesis 'that relates itself to itself'. In the metaphorical language of upbuilding, however, the 'self-relating' synthesis of actuality is defined inwardly as Christian love. It is the binding obligation to love which breaks the solipsism of a purely self-generated existence-sphere. The inner movement of existence, rather than oscillating between itself and non-existence in doubt and anxiety, is then wholly contained within itself:

What love does, that it is; what it is, that it does – and at one and the same time: at the very moment it gives out of itself (the direction outward) it is in itself (the direction inward); and at the very moment it is in itself, it thereby goes out of itself, so that this outgoing and this return, this return and this outgoing, are simultaneously one and the same.

(Love, p. 227)

Love is not philosophical, it is not reflective, and therefore it does not grasp actuality through an act of conception. In love there is no 'gap' between the conception and constitution of actuality. Love's actuality is fully constituted in time; it 'draws itself out' as a developing intersubjectivity. It is an endless and effortless repetition. Love edifies, claims S. Kierkegaard, and the edifying is not another abstract term in a game of make-believe. In one sense Hegel was perfectly correct, philosophy must beware of the edifying. But, in another sense, it is only in relation to the edifying that human being comes into its own and 'fills out' actuality; only the edifying grasps the truth which philosophy seeks in vain. In Kierkegaard, claims his most significant 'philosophical' successor, 'something has been realized which in fact is *not* philosophy, something for which we as yet have no concept.'[40]

Inconclusive postscript: beyond despair

> Childlike simplicity did not observe what an infinite requirement is involved in being a Christian; therefore it could believe that this is possible; nowadays it is apparent that the requirement for being Christian is so enormous that humanness becomes satisfied with a relationship to it, a striving toward it.
>
> Søren Kierkegaard, *Journals*, 2: 1792

> I must get hold of my melancholy. . . .
>
> Søren Kierkegaard, *Journals*, 5: 6043

Kierkegaard's religious psychology of modern life cannot be readily expressed in terms of a few underlying and consistent ideas. The observational richness of his writing is itself a barrier to over-simplification. And, more significantly, the fact that he is himself part of what he wishes to describe means that there is no privileged 'position' from which he can observe and record the human world. Furthermore, although his own experience thus becomes an essential medium for gaining knowledge of the world, he finds that self-observation issues in deeply ambiguous and shifting 'categories'. The observing self is subject to continuous change so that Kierkegaard's psychology is 'incomplete' as well as 'indirect', and this follows simply from the unfinished character of human reality.

The ethnographic fidelity of Kierkegaard's work is conveyed through two features that remain fundamental to all his writing. First, the method of indirect communication protects the provisional and elusive character of all his psychological constructs. And, secondly, he describes and orders experience through a series of disparate and incompatible 'points of view' which cannot be 'added up' or harmonized.

Kierkegaard's own chosen form of simplification, therefore,

draws attention to, rather than obscures, the irreducible contrariness of actual experience. In particular he defines four separate perspectives, which are both the observational framework for, and the constitutive structure of, modern life.[1] These distinctive modes of differentiation might be termed, respectively, the *topological, anthropological, philosophical* and *theomorphic* points of view.

The *topological* viewpoint has become the most familiar, and indeed frequently appears to be the only, 'Kierkegaardian' framework. However, the differentiation of 'existence-spheres' – the aesthetic, the ethical and the religious – is itself an aspect of the 'maieutic art' practised by the earliest pseudonyms and is, therefore, the expression of untransformed immediacy. In this perspective the 'ethical' and the 'religious' are essentially life-views contained within the 'aesthetic' as its immanent possibilities. The pseudonymous writers themselves realize that the tripartite division into 'stages' is, in fact, a series of aesthetic self-projections. The ethical, thus, loses all claim to autonomy, while the religious is romanticized in the unreality of the 'exceptional individual'. In addition to these products of melancholic self-inclosure, the pseudonyms detect, through doubt and dread, 'other' realms of being which lie outside the immediacy of the existence-spheres. In an *anthropological* perspective, therefore, human experience is described in relation to forms of 'non-existence' which condition its content. Actuality, that is to say, is established as the 'space' between sensuousness and the ideality of pure concepts. And it is in the dialectical expansion of actuality (rather than in any aesthetically conceived leap) that the self emerges as a structured unity. This primitive identity of the self, viewed *philosophically*, wrecks itself in passion and offence. It is caught in a continuous process of rising up from, and falling back into, actuality; attracted towards, and repulsed by, the absolute. Described from these three different viewpoints, melancholy emerges not only as a common theme for the pseudonymous authors but as the central experience of modern life. Counterposed to all of these perspectives, therefore, is a *theomorphic* description of selfhood which is actually (and not just imaginatively) 'beyond despair'.

The aim of the authorship is to provoke, and not simply to describe, authentic selfhood. But the complexity of the indirect, pseudonymous method results in two strikingly different views. The pseudonyms present a picture of 'developing' selfhood, or rather the development of a variety of possible selves, each of which is marked by a specific 'tension'. The 'existence-sphere' is stretched between contradictory poles, and the self emerges within the midst of these contradictions. In contrast to all such aesthetic 'potentiations', the 'last pseudonym' S. Kierkegaard regards theomorphic selfhood as a radical possibility; a possibility for, but not an immanent tendency within, actuality. This selfhood corresponds to the traditional Christian promise of happiness. It is both the 'highest' form of selfhood, and the form in which Christianity can exist for the modern world. The first view is primarily an exploration of modern melancholy, in all the inner richness of its varied forms; the second invokes a structurally and topologically distinct non-melancholic selfhood. For the first, a series of critical psychological studies leads to the view that 'subjectivity is truth', for the latter, distrustful of the social passions, 'subjectivity is untruth'.

The *Upbuilding Discourses* are continuous with the pseudonymous authorship; just as the theomorphic self both coexists with, and continually transcends, all other possibilities of existence. Its possibility, thus, can be detected in all other forms of actuality, and this possibility is characteristically expressed within each perspective. But it would be misleading to view the pseudonymous description of these forms as 'leading to' theomorphic selfhood. The transcending possibility of Christianity, in other words, does not confer upon human existence a 'finished' form. Christianity, for Kierkegaard, is life (not doctrine or conviction) and, therefore, must be continuously unstable. Inasmuch as the incompleteness of the self can be viewed melancholically, then Christianity is simply the 'highest' form of despair. In Kierkegaard's view, however, Christianity is neither the finished structure of experience nor a vision of totality, wholeness and unity. It is rather (philosophically) a continuous transition, and (theomorphically) a perpetual deepening of selfhood.

These two forms of selfhood are discontinuous. Thus, although Kierkegaard claims in *The Point of View for My Work as an Author*, that he was, from the beginning, a 'religious' writer, Christian faith cannot provide a conditioning norm through which the variety of aesthetic possibilities can be reduced to a logical order. The pseudonyms are usually read sequentially, and it is difficult to avoid the impression of an internal 'development' of some kind. Johannes Climacus, it is assumed, is somehow 'nearer' to Christianity and thus to authentic selfhood than is the young man of *Either*. However, as faith (theomorphic selfhood) is 'uncaused happiness', it is a permanently available possibility whose actualization does not depend on any preparatory 'training'. The developmental sequence of pseudonymous works is conditioned by aesthetic considerations alone, and, in relation to religious faith, the multiplicity of these possibilities falls back into the disorder typical of the Present Age. The aesthetic writers are not linked 'developmentally', other than in terms of purely secular bourgeois (if not 'bourgeois-philistine') conventions, though each consistently develops a possibility 'floating' on the surface of modern life.

Pervasive wretchedness is, for the most part, easily understood; it continuously flows from injustice. For the European bourgeoisie there were obvious advantages in assimilating the misery consequent on injustice to the 'uncaused sorrow' of melancholy. An important strand in the whole development of idealist philosophy after Kant, as well as in literary Romanticism, succeeded beyond all expectation in providing such a service. The pervasiveness of melancholy, and its apparent pre-adaptation to modern life, became the focus, not only of attacks upon Enlightenment optimism, but, more significantly, of secular and religious demands for self-actualization.[2] At the same time radical implications of these same intellectual and artistic movements became increasingly apparent.[3] Kierkegaard can be interpreted in the context of either tradition; as, in part, either a romantic conservative or as a philosophical radical.

DISILLUSIONMENT

This brings the authorship into a closer relation with the ideological ferment of the 1840s, the period during which the call of 'Left Hegelians' for the practical 'completion' of Hegel's philosophy came into prominence.[4] Exploiting the spiritual radicalism of Hegel's own earlier works against the conservatism of his official followers after his death, they attempted to reclaim for philosophy the entire territory of practical life.

More significantly, perhaps, striking similarities between the pseudonyms' attack on the Hegelian system and the writings of the young Marx have been pointed out on a number of occasions.[5] Neither is content with a simple criticism of Hegel's thought or with a general appeal to his forgotten revolutionary spirit, but propose a comprehensive 'critique' of the 'German ideology'. What unites them is an effort less to expose the error than to uncover the truth which is hidden in the 'system'. And for Marx, as well as the pseudonyms, that truth is 'existential'; Hegel's philosophy is important for them just because it so accurately and profoundly expresses the character of the modern age. Systematic abstraction is the result of the most rigorous application of human reason to the task of analysing the real character of modern experience. It is, indeed, nothing other than the emergence of a rational spirit from entanglement with its own history. But, in becoming reflexively conscious of itself, the critics claimed, reason fails to grasp its own limitations and expresses its 'findings' as if they were universal truths of 'spirit'. The historical sensitivity of the *Phenomenology* gives way to the new scholasticism of the *Logic*, and philosophy becomes 'detached' from the very reality from which it sprang. Hegel, creating a limitless and ideal domain of unchallenged speculative truth, thus gives expression to a specifically bourgeois interest in misleadingly universal and abstract language as the realization of a generalized 'human spirit'.

Both Marx and the pseudonyms insist that the actuality of modern life is itself a distorted and illusory social form, and Hegel's philosophy is the most consistently developed expression of this distortion. It is the Present Age which is the 'real foundation' of Hegel's philosophy, and it is, therefore, the transformation of this conditioning possibility, rather than the realization of his philosophical vision, which confronts the genuinely 'interested' individual as an urgent task. The call for a 'disillusioned' philosophy, for a critical understanding of actuality which is conditioned by the undeveloped 'potentiality' obscured by modern conditions, is at the same time the demand for a new way of life. 'Truth', at least humanly interesting truth, is for neither an 'objective' and 'indifferent' form of knowledge. Kierkegaard, of course, in terms of contemporary political issues, was conservative, if not reactionary. The apparent split between Kierkegaard's private views, expressed in letters and *Journal* entries, and the (unconventional) radicalism of the pseudonyms offers further evidence of his dialogical skill. Efforts to 'harmonize' the pseudonyms with each other and with their creator leads here, as elsewhere, to considerable difficulties. It is not necessary, in other words, to argue that 'Kierkegaard's' view of modern individualism, coupled with his ideological devotion to 'subjectivity', directs any radical tendencies in his work into a harmless retreat into inwardness which leaves nothing changed.[6] Quite apart from the bitter attack on the Danish church, the pseudonyms' challenge to bourgeois-philistinism is perfectly genuine, the disclosure of the deeper self is potentially destructive of all established authority, and the ambition to revitalize actuality with the sharpest of spiritual tensions undermines every facile ecclesiastical or secular apologetics of the Present Age. At the same time the pseudonyms reject contemporary political radicalism as simply another symptom of the spiritless crowd's susceptibility to the chaotic enthusiasm of a romantic ego.

Clearly, in spite of their at times parallel attack on Hegel, Kierkegaard and Marx are not easily compared.[7] For Marx, it might be suggested, melancholy is borne on the face of the commodity. The modern world is a world of commodities, objects created only to be alienated into an impersonal process of exchange. The human spirit is deposited in these objects, and then it is lost, transformed into an oppressive and strange world of pure objectivity. They are distant, aloof, impenetrable and are qualitatively identical. The commodity is set apart, and appears unreal. The commodity is a melancholic object because through it we are turned into something 'alien'. It can be owned, which is only to say someone has the exclusive right to send it on its way again by selling it, but it cannot be possessed. Our desire for objects springs directly from the melancholy engendered by their mode of creation. It is the mysterious 'use value' that replenishes our desire. In wanting objects we want what they 'contain': 'the object produced by estranged wage-labour is not simply a material thing but the objectification of the worker's subjectivity.'[8] For Marx the problem of modern society is not an issue of distributive justice, but one of overcoming 'alienation'. For Marx the entire world of modern experience has a melancholic aura because all our needs are met, and can only be met, through contact with the cold and inhospitable world of commodities. But for Kierkegaard there is no particular set of objects which 'mediate' the melancholy of modern life, which is an immediate experience of every aspect of existence. The inexplicable sorrow which comes upon us – so like a mournful loss, yet we remain unaware of what we have lost – is rationalized, but not explained, as the loss of spirit which is the real process of modern production. Melancholy is objectless and every effort to create an appropriate object in which it might be reflected is to be resisted.

His melancholy seems to fatally compromise his critique of modernity. Kierkegaard's works can appear either as nostalgia for a vanished world of cosmological certainty, or as a vanishing inwardness which conceals an uncomfortable apologia for the most fundamental conditions of the Present Age which he claimed to despise. The persistence of melancholy, in this perspective, is due neither to the appropriation of the essentially human power of labour nor to the unavoidability of 'externalization' or 'objectification', and it cannot, therefore, be 'cured' by their reappropriation as either 'property' or as 'things'.[9] Melancholy, rather, in first making the world spiritless, turns the commodity into a dead and narrowly useful 'object'. For Kierkegaard the world of modern things cannot be the *locus* of melancholy, which lies in the misrelation between happiness and pleasure rather than in a misrelation between subject and object. Indeed, 'the world of things is for him neither part of the subject nor independent of it. Rather this world is omitted.'[10] Critics have frequently noted the characteristic 'loss of the world' in his work, and viewed it as representative of his own position of social detachment. His writings, then, retain a certain value only because they exemplify the new cultural role of *flâneur*, and express with unmatched vivacity and fullness the modern bourgeois *intérieur*.[11]

But such criticisms do little justice to the care with which the varied authorial personae are interrelated. For Kierkegaard it is a philosophically naive longing to regain direct participation in the world of things as substance, rather than an open acceptance that, for the modern world, the 'thing' can be nothing more than 'the existing bearer of many existing yet changeable properties', that might more accurately be termed nostalgia.[12] None of Kierkegaard's pseudonyms express any wish to be returned to the immediacy of the premodern world, in which things directly bodied forth distinctive spiritual essences. The 'absence' of the world in the authorship is, in fact, a revealing symptom of the literal 'abstraction' of the Present Age. The view that 'things' can be the real bearers of spiritual value is implicitly dismissed by the pseudonyms as a sentimental longing for a premodern, if not imaginary religious community and worldview. Modern things, which are the product of spiritless relations, cannot be anything other than secretive and melancholic objects.

This is not to say that melancholy is a changeless foundation of the human condition. Kierkegaard responds, as specifically as Marx, to the conditions of the Present Age, and in discovering its melancholy interprets its specific features historically. The melancholy of modern life is not the same as premodern melancholy, and it cannot be overcome by rational, or at least deliberative, action because 'reason' and 'deliberation' are themselves suffused with its mournful indifference.[13]

PLAY

The self is a spiritual synthesis and, as such, is 'beyond' despair. But the elements of which it is composed, in isolation or as a simple mixture of unconnected parts, are experienced as despair. The pseudonyms present a view in which it seems to be that all experience other than the experience of individuated selfhood is despair; that the self, and only the self, is the synthesis which is beyond despair. Perhaps surprisingly they nowhere explicitly discuss the possibility of regarding play as a 'selfless' but non-despairing 'existence-sphere'. Possibly because of its centrality for the Romantic movement, from which he wanted to distinguish the pseudonyms decisively, Kierkegaard denies himself the creation of a wholly playful pseudonym, nor does he include play as a 'category' in his more didactic works.

Yet the entire authorship is playful. The 'maieutic art', whatever else it might be, is a game of 'let's pretend'. It is Kierkegaard's favourite game. He adopts first one and then another pseudonym; mask succeeds mask at a moment's notice or with no notice at all. And not the least paradoxical aspect of his extraordinary production is that this playfulness should be put at the service of a profoundly melancholic pursuit of the 'single individual'.

In retrospect, indeed, play, rather than aesthetic immediacy, might seem to be the obvious starting point for the authorship; play might be construed as a primordial and undifferentiated 'existence-sphere'. Following Rousseau's pioneering recollection of childhood, Schiller and others saw play as a privileged mode of human being. In the play-world there is no disjunction between appearance and reality; everything is just as it seems.[14] There is nothing hidden and inward in play, and therefore no possibility of deception. It is a transparent world in which each participant is wholly 'absorbed'; there is no melancholic distance between the 'inner' world of the self and an external reality, between one self and another self. Schiller, viewing modern experience as riven between finite 'sensuous drives' and the infinite 'formal drives' of reason, seeks a new aesthetic unity founded upon a preconceptual impulse to play. In play the disunited fragments of human existence can be unified:

> it is play alone, which of all man's states and conditions is the one which makes him whole and unfolds both sides of his nature at once . . . man only plays when he is in the fullest sense of the word a human being, and he is only fully a human being when he plays.[15]

While it persists play is an all-embracing and exhaustive reality. There is nothing 'beyond' it, just as there is nothing hidden within it. In pseudonymous terms play is pure actuality. In play the ideal and the sensuous interpenetrate each other so completely that they 'feel' the same. There is a perfect 'synthesis' which 'relates itself to itself'. And as this synthesis contains within itself every possible inner transformation, doubt and anxiety remain completely unknown to it. Indeed, if doubt or anxiety is introduced into the play-world from the outside (they cannot be generated within it), then play is immediately destroyed.

The fundamental characteristic of play is trust in existence. From the viewpoint of play itself, however, this is not an enabling precondition bestowed upon reality by potentially suspicious participants, but is, rather, the enfolding actuality of the absolute.[16] The play-world simply exists, and exists simply. Nothing 'holds it up', because, for it, there is no 'void' into which it might collapse. Play lacks nothing, wants nothing, and, therefore, is undisturbed by passion or offence. It is tensionless activity, the continuous and effortless movement of insincere wishes, a movement to and fro without purpose or intention, a movement that 'renews itself in constant repetition'.[17] The error of the pseudonyms, following Schiller, is to invoke the unity of the play-world through the differentiated, and thus partial, reality of the aesthetic. The modern aesthetic, as the pseudonyms demonstrate, is so impregnated with the character of the Present Age, that, in representing human unity and wholeness, it succeeds only in furthering its fragmentation. This does not mean that play cannot be considered as an originating 'existence-sphere' which, like Anti-Climacus in relation to Johannes Climacus, stands 'before' the Present Age, and is therefore 'prior' to any of the pseudonymous works.

Indeed, if play, rather than melancholy, were to be regarded as the initial, and non-arbitrary, existence-sphere then it becomes tempting to regard the religious 'sphere' as a rediscovered play-world. Play, like faith, is a gift. Neither can be deliberately instituted. Neither is sustained by intentional activity. Both are corrupted by social passions. Both exist 'in themselves' and remain incommensurable with any autonomous human self-image. And Kierkegaard himself points out that:

> the increase in inwardness in the relationship to God is indicated by the fact that it goes backward for a person. . . . Therefore one does not begin by being a child and then become progressively more intimate as he grows older; no, one becomes more and more a child.
>
> (*Journals*, 1: 272)

And Johannes Climacus claims that Christianity is 'the idea of childlikeness raised to the second power'.[18] Christianity restores the playful character of actuality, where the aesthetic makes us more melancholic over its loss.

If the analogy is pressed, both are impermanent. As neither reason nor desire can lead to play or faith, the player or the religious individual may just as readily find themselves, without reason, deprived of their world and plunged into melancholy. Children habitually find they cannot play, that they remain stubbornly 'bored', then, inexplicably, find themselves once again at play and cannot remember the despairing interlude. Similarly, it might be argued, Kierkegaard, in presenting the religious interstitially with his many pseudonymous works, suggests that 'faith' is an impermanent condition. It is not achieved 'once-for-all' but, like play, 'happens' from time to time for those who remain open to its unadvertised possibility.

Its symmetry with faith – before and after melancholy – might even suggest that play be favoured as a 'systematic' starting point for Kierkegaard's varied approaches. It seems less strained to argue that play, rather than melancholy, is the 'anticipation' of Christian faith. Indeed, he almost does begin with play. There is something playful in irony, and Socrates, after all, was frequently accused by his Sophist opponents of lacking 'seriousness'. The limitless freedom of both irony and play subvert any attempt to 'fix' their own conceptual boundaries. But if Hegel's definition of irony as 'infinite absolute negativity' suggests something of its peculiarity, then play might be viewed as 'infinite absolute positivity'; as thoughtless trust in, rather than as systematic suspicion of, existence. And, for Kierkegaard, it would be as dangerous to begin with play as it had been to begin with irony. If we begin with either we can go no further. Play, like irony, is 'self-inclosing', and like irony (but unlike melancholy) is free of all inner contradiction. Both play and irony, thus, are 'indifference spheres', made up of endlessly circulating forms within which no categorical differences can emerge.

Johannes Climacus, in viewing faith as 'infinite absolute paradox', comes closer than any other of the pseudonyms to the completion of a Kierkegaardian 'system'. If the rejection of irony and, by implication, of play is borne in mind then this 'system' might be represented as a triangle 'enclosing' existence. The points of this triangle are internally consistent, exhaustive and mutually exclusive 'reflections' upon existence. Each, that is to say, pre-supposes and, in different ways, each transcends existence. Thus, in addition to the variety of 'points of view' from which existence in relation to its religious possibilities might be described, it might also be analysed from the perspective of the inner potentiality of and for play or irony. Play is the 'innocent' or 'natural' form of sensuousness, the recollection of which gives rise to anxious pleasure. Irony is the transcending freedom of thought in grasping pure forms of being, which, when tied to the limitations of existence, becomes universal doubt. And existence in relation to faith becomes despair. Kierkegaard's psychology is centred on despair, whereas, it might be suggested, Freud's view of modern life is reconstructed from the recollection of the play-world, and Proust's from the intuition of pure forms. Play and irony are, thus, 'non-existence' rather than 'existence' spheres, and, for Johannes Climacus (if not for S. Kierkegaard) this is true also of faith. Human reality then becomes, within this more inclusive 'system' of transcending categories – which cannot be directly related one to another – a continuous movement first towards one then towards another possible 'apex' of the triangle. From within the triangle, that is to say, from within the limitations of actuality, each point of the triangle might appear to be 'the highest', and human reality can appear so structured as to tend 'naturally' towards each in turn.

THE PERSISTENCE OF DESPAIR

This potentiation of the pseudonyms' anthropological perspective suggests a 'postmodern' but non-aesthetic reading of Kierkegaard. The human is continuously self-transcending, but is not, by virtue of this natural disposition, essentially a 'religious' being. There are present in existence, rather, incompatible tendencies towards different transcending forms. The endless mobility, contrariness and incompleteness of human self-realization is due, not to human absorption in the limited horizon of secular life, but to the irreconcilable differences among transcendental forms themselves. Or, rather, as transcendental forms must remain humanly unknowable, the relation of human ends to transcending forms is bound to appear, from the human side, contradictory.

These considerations give added weight to Johannes Climacus's repeated assertion that he wants to make it difficult to become a Christian, to make people aware of just how difficult this is. There are two distinct sources of difficulty and, consequently, two distinct 'reasons' for the persistence of despair. First is the incommensurability of faith to any human capacity or activity. Faith cannot become the end of human activity, consciously worked for, hoped for, reasoned towards, wished, desired or longed for, nor can it be sought in any other way. It resists all human endeavour to appropriate its ultimate good. Secondly, however, the human tendency towards play and irony reveals (at least) other ways in which the absolute may be present for us, and, as we have no means of deciding among these forms we can only trust first one and then another as they absorb us. We are forced into 'the straitjacket of existence', waiting on periodic and unpredictable 'escapes' into religious categories, the poetic inspiration of Platonic forms or the inner freedom of sensuous play.

Johannes Climacus asks 'what use is Christianity?' and points out the absurdity of such a question. The absolute simply is, and is not 'for' anything. It is, however, worth reinforcing the other side of his question and its implied answer. If faith is not useful, then nor is it pleasant, good or truthful; yet faith is persistently misrepresented as a projection of just these human values. It is in this respect that the pseudonyms' perspective is most sharply distinguished from Feuerbach's contemporary 'anthropological transformation' of the 'religious sphere' into eccentric human self-consciousness. Neither, however, can faith be represented as unpleasant, evil or untruthful, and attempts to do so, as for example among the more radical of eighteenth-century *philosophes*, are equally inept. If we were to be granted faith as a permanent condition would we be happy? Certainly this is, for the western tradition, the very definition of happiness. Equally, however, we would be happy in a perpetual state of play, or in inspired contemplation of pure forms. Each transcending reality momentarily confers eternity upon the human subject caught in its trance. But we would not, in any of these cases, be racked with pleasure or glow with the inner satisfaction of grasping a truth or realizing a good. All human satisfactions stop short of happiness, which is qualitatively set aside as an ungraspable otherness. The human in relation to each transcending form is a limitation, or absence, or contradiction; it is despair. And the charms of existence, as the 'Diapsalmata' have it, are only the anguish of its despair viewed from another angle.

If the consciousness of self-transcendence is melancholy, ought we then to renounce religion, and have done with faith, as with play and philosophy? Ivan Karamazov's 'Grand Inquisitor', after all (neatly inverting Kierkegaard's 'Attack upon Christendom'), has Christ put to death a second time in order to preserve the small measure of human comfort the church has secured in the face of God's transcendental terrorism.[19] And Nietzsche's madman declares the death of God as a final liberation of humanity. Kierkegaard's response (in advance) to these radical (defiant) proposals is twofold. Human pleasure, goodness and truth, as well as despair, are constructed from its hidden relation with the absolute. To destroy the absolute would be to destroy the good with the evil. And, more significantly, the absolute, as absolute, could not be destroyed or even renounced. Existence is so structured that it forms within us images which tend towards its transcending realities. The urge to renounce and destroy these images (defiance) is simply one other such tendency which, properly understood, constitutes a stage in human existence. Indeed the closer we come to the absolute the deeper the despair we experience. Thus boredom is 'almost' play, irony 'almost' grasps the plastic reality of pure forms, and sin is 'almost' faith. There is, thus, a hidden complicity between melancholy and the 'reduplication' of existence which is its conquest. Both are spiritual inversions of the inverted form of existence which is the Present Age. And both, therefore, propose themselves as critiques of Modernity.

Melancholy persists as the 'normal' state of the human heart.[20] But there are two ways in which modernity 'conquers' melancholy: firstly, and deceptively, in spiritless disregard of the human prompting towards self-transcendence, in the insistent assertion that life is 'nothing but' the satisfaction of artificially created and stimulated wants; and secondly, in the awareness of moments of blissful release from this 'nothing but'.

Notes

INTRODUCTION

1 This is by no means an original insight, e.g. Price (1963), Dupré (1964). It is perhaps surprising that Tillich (1967), p. 166, treats Kierkegaard's melancholy as a purely personal affliction.

1 MELANCHOLY: THE DEPTH OF MODERN LIFE

1 Cf. *Stages*, pp. 199–200; *Journals*, 5: 5913, 6: 6166. It has been suggested that Kierkegaard's melancholy developed quite late, distorting his view of his own childhood (Henriksen (1951), pp. 45–6). Biographical disputes are not central, however, to an understanding of the role of melancholy in his writings.

2 Cf. the opening 'Diapsalmata' in *Either/Or.* 'What is a poet? An unhappy person who conceals his profound anguish in his heart but whose lips are so formed that as his sighs and cries pass over them they sound like beautiful music.' In an early *Journal* entry (5: 5141) he confirms the view that, in public, he was noted for his vivacity: 'I have just now come from a gathering where I was the life of the party; witticisms flowed out of my mouth; everybody laughed, admired me', but immediately on leaving '[I] wanted to shoot myself '. His father was also gifted with this 'mental-spiritual elasticity enabling him to hide his melancholy' (*Journals*, 5: 5913).

3 *Point of View*, p. 76.

4 Ibid. This is not to deny that Kierkegaard was able to use the circumstances of his childhood partially to 'make sense' of his own melancholy. He recalls, for example, in a letter to his sister-in-law Henriette in 1844, that when he was a child, his father often forbade him to go out but would take him on an 'imaginary walk' to Frederiksberg (*Letters*, 112).

5 Biographical investigation/speculation has been a staple of the Kierkegaard literature, but little decisive or conclusive beyond what he revealed of himself in his works has been established. See, for example, Allen (1935), Haecker (1937, 1948), Lowrie (1938), Martin (1950),

Hohlenberg (1954), Paulsen (1955), Rohde (1963), Brandt (1963), Carnell (1965), Thompson (1974). Henriksen (1951) contains useful reviews of the Scandinavian literature. Grimault (1965) discusses a variety of medical/psychiatric hypotheses purporting to account for Kierkegaard's melancholy. Fenger (1980) provides a vigorous antidote.

6 *Point of View*, p. 79.

7 In the context of the development of modern society the inner connection, hinted at here, between melancholy, religious suffering and the critique of conventional forms of social consciousness, is also alluded to by Kierkegaard's contemporary, Karl Marx. In his Introduction to the *Critique of Hegel's Philosophy of Right*, Marx declares: '*Religious* suffering is at one and the same time the *expression* of real suffering and a protest against real suffering' (Marx (1975), p. 244).

8 Klibansky, Panofsky and Saxl (1964), p. 9; Jackson (1986), pp. 19–20; Screech (1991), pp. 22–36. In fact there were a variety of humoral theories, all in various ways elaborating on the Empedoclean 'elements' of earth, air, fire and water; see Lloyd's 'Introduction' to the *Hippocratic Writings* (1978).

9 Ibid., p. 12.

10 *Phaedrus*, 244d.

11 This is generally held to be a Pseudo-Aristotelian work. The translation is by W.S. Hett, in The Loeb Classical Library.

12 Klibansky, Panofsky and Saxl (1964), p. 41.

13 Quoted in Roccatagliata (1986), p. 199.

14 Ibid., p. 200.

15 Ibid.; Jackson (1986), pp. 43–4.

16 Klibansky, Panofsky and Saxl (1964), p. 88.

17 Wenzel (1960), p. 5; Bloomfield (1952), p. 59.

18 Quoted in Wenzel (1960), p. 5.

19 Quoted by Thomas R. Heath in Appendix to vol. xxxv of Aquinas (1964–81), pp. 189–92.

20 Kuhn (1976), p. 50; Wack (1990). Kierkegaard himself draws attention to the spiritual affinity between *acedia* and the inner isolation of the modern individual. In a marginal note to an entry on *acedia* he remarks: 'This is what my father called: A *quiet despair*' (*Journals*, 1: 739, 740).

21 Robert Grosseteste, a thirteenth-century Bishop of Lincoln, wrote an influential treatise *On Light*, Reidl (1942), in which the western metaphysics of light is given a distinctively Christian interpretation. Light is both a corporeal form and the eternal Word. See McEvoy (1982), Southern (1986), Ferguson (1990), pp. 119–20.

22 Flaubert's *The Temptation of St Antony* seems far from fanciful in the light of similar and related examples offered by King III (1983).

23 Aquinas (2a2ae. 35, 4): 'he is sad about the divine good. It is this which is of the essence of spiritual apathy.'

24 Lovejoy (1960) is a classic analysis; see also Gurevich (1985), pp. 41–92.

25 Hugo de Folieto, quoted in Klibansky, Panofsky and Saxl (1964), p. 107.

26 Mâle (1958), for a perceptive account in relation to architecture.

27 This background has been sympathetically reconstructed by a number of outstanding scholars; influential examples include Walker (1958), Yates (1964), Wind (1967), Garin (1976, 1978), Debus (1978, 1987), Shumacher (1972), Couliano (1987).

28 Ficino (1988), p. 111.

29 From *Theologia Platonica*, bk. 14, quoted in Kristeller (1943), p. 208.

30 Kristeller (1943), p. 173.

31 Quoted in ibid., p. 211. See also Petrarch (1991), 3, pp. 323–9, 4, pp. 358–86. Petrarch's descriptions of *tristitia* and *miseria* seem less 'modern' than Ficino's, and still draw on the theme of darkness: 'In such times I take no pleasure in the light of day, I see nothing, I am as one plunged in the darkness of hell itself ' (4, p. 359). More generally see Kinsman (1974), McClure (1990).

32 Klibansky, Panofsky and Saxl (1964), p. 250; Wittkower (1963).

33 Ficino (1988), pp. 113–15.

34 Benjamin (1977), p. 153. The imagery of 'blackness', of course, persisted, and took on new meanings of its own. Thus one modern melancholic, Ellen West, writes that 'Melancholy lies over my life like a black bird' (quoted in May *et al.*, (1958), p. 264).

35 Cassirer (1963), Trinkaus (1970).

36 Ancient writers also talked of heaviness in relation to melancholy, but referred usually to the 'density' of the vapour produced by black bile, rather than to its inherent 'gravity'.

37 Timothy Bright, *A Treatise of Melancholie* (1586), quoted in Hunter and Macalpine (1963), p. 38.

38 Thomas Elyot, *The Castel of Helthe* (1530), quoted in Jackson (1986), p. 81.

39 Goethe, quoted in Kuhn (1976).

40 Burton (1932), 1, p. 140.

41 Kristeva (1989), pp. 3–4.

42 Ibid.

43 Baudelaire (1989), p. 110.

44 Koyré (1957).

45 Koyré (1978), p. 3.

46 Nicholas Cusanus (1954), p. 8.

47 Ibid., pp. 74–5.

48 Johnson (1937).

49 Benjamin (1977), p. 139.

50 Newton (1931), p. 400. Cf. Freudenthal (1986).

51 Blumenberg (1983, 1987), for a highly sophisticated discussion of modernity in terms of 'Copernicanism' in its broadest terms. It must be stressed that it is only in retrospect that there appears to be a decisive shift in worldview. Copernicus, Kepler, Galileo and Newton were all, in different ways, and to differing degrees, involved in efforts to 'save' traditional cosmology from the destructive 'conventionalism' of modernity (Bechler (1991)).

52 Weber (1930), p. 104.

53 Richter (1839), pp. 61–2.

54 Schelling, quoted in Price (1963), p. 45.
55 Klibansky, Panofsky and Saxl (1964), p. 234.
56 This is already evident in Petrarch's recommendation of introspection, inspired by reading Augustine's *Confessions*. The emergence of Renaissance individualism implied, as Garin (1965), p. 21, points out, 'the rediscovery of the whole richness of the inner life'.
57 Babb (1951), Mueller (1952), Nordstrom (1962), Webber (1968), Lyons (1971), Fish (1972), Lepenies (1992).
58 Burton (1932), 1, p. 39.
59 Fox (1976).
60 'A good divine either is or ought to be a good physician, a spiritual physician at least' (Burton (1932), 1, p. 37).
61 Fish (1972), p. 314, remarks:

> It is not simply that Democritus Jr. seems incapable of a sober discourse, but that sober discourse itself is an impossibility given the world the preface reflects and describes. The strategy of inclusion, which collapses speaker, reader, and a thousand or more 'authorities' into a single category of unreliability, extends also to every aspect of what we usually think of as 'objective reality'.

62 Burton (1932), 1, p. 21. Writers on *acedia* had recommended work and sociability as distractions from solitary gloom. Bishop Grosseteste even urged a glass of wine as a *penance* on a melancholic friar (Clarke (1975), p. 116).
63 For a long time both Montaigne and Burton were admired (or disparaged) as 'essayists' and, consequently, their books were read unsystematically. More recently scholars have paid greater attention to their overall design. On Montaigne, see particularly Screech (1991) and Starobinski (1985), and on Burton, Fox (1976) and Vicari (1989).
64 Screech (1991).
65 Burton with Montaigne and Rousseau, among many others, characterize discourse as an imaginary journey, or, more accurately, as a journey of the imagination. Modern philosophy, like modern life, is ceaseless travel, and is, therefore, melancholic in character (Abbeele (1992)). In contrast to Ficino's espousal of a metaphysics of rest, for example, Montaigne remarks '*being* consists in motion' (1991, p. 434).
66 Burton (1932), 1, p. 257. Similarly Montaigne (1991), 'On Idleness', warns that our minds, 'If we do not keep them busy with some particular subject which can serve as a bridle to rein them in, they charge ungovernably about, ranging to and fro over the wastelands of our thoughts.'
67 Burton (1932), 1, p. 406.
68 Ibid.
69 Ibid., 3, p. 30.
70 Ibid., 3, p. 141.
71 Ibid., 3, p. 398–9. This particular form of religious melancholy is central to Weber's (1930) thesis, which he illustrates primarily from the writings of Baxter. Bunyan's *Grace Abounding to the Chief of Sinners,*

or Swedenborg's *Heaven and its Wonders* are perhaps more familiar, and more apposite, to the 'pathological' development of the Puritan tradition. For a comprehensive and insightful discussion, see Bercovitch (1975), King III (1983).

72 Burton (1932), 3, p. 400.

73 Ibid., 2, p. 313. Cf. Montaigne (1991), p. 5.

74 On Pascal's achievements in mathematics see Broome (1965), pp. 46–74. Characteristically, although holding 'geometry to be the highest exercise of the mind', he confesses, in a letter to Fermat, that 'for my own part, I would not as much as walk down the street for geometry's sake'; quoted in Goldmann (1964), pp. 50–1. Davidson (1993) argues for the centrality of a geometric mode of thought, understood in the more general sense of an 'art of the mind', to Pascal's reflections.

75 Goldmann (1964), p. 27. See also Freudenthal (1986).

76 Pascal, quoted in Goldmann (1964), p. 56.

77 Pascal (1966), p. 114.

78 Ibid., p. 200.

79 Ibid., p. 131. Melzer (1986), p. 87, argues that it is at this point that Pascal cuts himself off from all previous formulations of the 'cosmological argument'. He uses the 'argument from wretchedness' to save himself from the solipsism of a world of self-reflecting signifiers: 'God speaks to humans not through the signs of the order of creation but through the message of his punishment which he transcribes in their souls.' Significantly the *Pensées*, echoing Augustine and Petrarch, classifies both pleasure and pain in opposition to happiness.

80 Pascal (1966), p. 131.

81 Ibid., p. 427.

82 Ibid., p. 134.

83 Ibid., p. 136. Martin Luther, another acute religious sensibility intimate with melancholy, similarly advises those who are sad to 'seek whatever relief you can' Luther (1967), 54: pp. 74–7. For a psychoanalytic view of Luther's melancholy see Erikson (1962), pp. 120–1.

84 Ibid., p. 136.

85 Pascal (1966), 136. Influenced by Kierkegaard directly, rather than Pascal, Heidegger also recognizes the modern significance of boredom: 'Profound boredom, drifting here and there in the abysses of our existence like a muffling fog removes all things and men and oneself along with it into a remarkable indifference. This boredom reveals being as a whole' (quoted in Bigelow (1987), p. 120). Interestingly Kretschmer (1936), p. 161, also talks of 'the soft muffled gloom of the interior'.

86 Pascal (1966), p. 143.

87 Ibid., 148.

88 Ibid.

89 Ibid., 418.

90 Ibid., 686.

91 Ibid., 423.

92 Ibid., p. 424.
93 Ibid., p. 201.
94 Pascal (1850), 2, p. 240.
95 Pascal (1966), 564. And, ibid., 978: 'The nature of self-love and of this human self is to love only self and consider only self.' This is quite distinct from the 'Social passions' founded on vanity and false self-representations:

> Human relations are only based on this mutual deception: and few friendships would survive if everyone knew what his friend said about him behind his back, even though he spoke sincerely and dispassionately. Man is therefore nothing but disguise, falsehood and hypocrisy, both in himself and with regard to others.

96 'Not infinity itself, but man in the grasp of infinity, is the subject matter of Pascal's meditation' (Lönning (1962), p. 56).
97 Though it is most frequently interpreted in this way. See, for example, Unger (1975), Blumenberg (1983), Cascardi (1992), Kolb (1986).
98 Pascal (1850), 2, p. 132.
99 Ibid.
100 Ibid.
101 Ibid., p. 133. A consideration which makes reading an equivocal activity. Thus, Pascal (1966), 689: 'It is not in Montaigne but in myself that I find everything I see there.'
102 Pascal (1850), 2, p. 209.
103 Pascal (1966), 688.
104 Ibid.
105 Ibid., 919.
106 Coleman (1986), pp. 194–7.
107 *Journals*, 5: 5761. The fact that melancholy as an experience and as a literary/scientific term has been radically transformed does not mean, as one commentator suggests, that 'melancholy is obsolete' (Harré (1986), p. 222).
108 Taylor (1989), pp. 187–8.
109 Montaigne (1991), p. 434.
110 Lepenies (1992), p. 109.
111 Hoffmann (1992), p. 20.
112 Tieck (1831), pp. 43, 90, 175.
113 Kristeva (1989), p. 4. Characteristically the clarity of detached and disinterested images does not amount to a coherent and meaningful 'picture' of reality. Modern melancholy, thus, is also described as an 'oppressive, imageless world-view' (May *et al.* (1958), p. 272).
114 Starobinski (1989a); Bloch (1986), 3, pp. 835–7.
115 Proust (1983), 1, p. 199; Kristeva (1989), p. 6.
116 Late in his authorship Kierkegaard was sceptical of the success of his earlier works in bringing his melancholy into focus: 'I must get hold of my melancholy. Up to now it has been deeply submerged and my enormous intellectual activity has helped to keep it there' (*Journals*, 5: 6043).

2 IRONY: THE ROMANCE OF DISTANCE

1 Kirmmse (1990), pp. 77–99.

2 Bigelow (1987), p. 117; Taylor (1989), 185–98.

3 *Stages*, p. 356. Cf. Alexander Blok, writing in 1908: 'All the most lively and sensitive children of our century are stricken by a disease unknown to doctors and psychiatrists. It is related to disorders of the soul and might be called "irony" ' (quoted in Glicksberg (1969), p. 4).

4 *Irony* has more recently been reassessed, and used as a key text for the understanding of Kierkegaard's work as a whole. See Manheimer (1977), Schleifer and Markley (1984), Smyth (1986), Bigelow (1987), Agacinski (1988), Gouwens (1989).

5 *Journals*, 5: 5061–87; *The Concept of Irony*, pp. 21–6; this project was formulated more clearly during a summer visit to Gilleleie, in North Sjaelland, during 1835, shortly after the death of his mother, when he reflected deeply on his own future. 'What I really need is to get clear about *what I must do*, not what I must know . . . the crucial thing is to find a truth which is truth *for me*, to find *the idea for which I am willing to live and die*' (*Journals*, 5: 5100).

6 The term is taken from Bakhtin (1973) who coined it to describe Dostoevsky's ability to represent the independence of his fictionalized characters.

7 For a critical view of Kierkegaard's poetic talent see Adorno (1989), pp. 5–9.

8 Mackey (1971).

9 *Journals*, 4: 4281 (probably written in 1850). This judgement reveals the extent to which he later felt he had been unable, at that point, sufficiently to free himself from Hegel. Equally, it might be argued he had not freed himself from Romanticism. Thus, while it is plausible to argue, like Mesnard (1948) and Wahl (1949), following the lead of Bohlin (see Henriksen (1951)), that Kierkegaard used Hegel to defeat the Romantics, and the Romantics to defeat Hegel, neither assault was completed with *Irony*, which retains strong overtones of both positions.

10 Kierkegaard scholars have, on the whole, been happy to take this judgement at face-value. *Irony*, consequently, has been neglected or discussed, as in Thulstrup (1980), exclusively in the context of Kierkegaard's relation to Hegel. Apart from some recent interest noted above (see Note 4) older studies by Mesnard (1948) and Wahl (1949) remain important exceptions to the general trend. For an overview of literary theories of irony see Thomson (1926), Knox (1961), Glicksberg (1969), Muecke (1970), Booth (1974), Enright (1986), and particularly Wernaer (1966). Literary critics have made little use of Kierkegaard's work. Booth's attitude is typical; after a laudatory (ironic?) preface ('*The Concept of Irony* is to me one of the most interesting and profitable books ever written on an abstract idea' (1974, p. xii)), Kierkegaard's book is ignored. For a more sympathetic treatment see Thorslev (1984).

11 *The Concept of Irony*, pp. 8–12.

12 Behler (1993) for an excellent overview. Wheeler (1984) provides a useful collection of translated texts central to these issues.

13 Exemplified, for example, in the 'uncanny' atmosphere of the stories of Hoffmann or Kleist.

14 Hegel (1892), 3: p. 507.

15 Thorslev (1984), p. 175; Wheeler (1984), pp. 145–50.

16 Hegel (1892), 3: p. 507.

17 Hegel (1975), 1: p. 66.

18 Quoted in Pattison (1992), p. 1. Fichte stresses, however, that this ideal of absolute inner freedom is a virtually unattainable ideal; and that the actual experience of the 'I' is always of a relation between itself and the 'non-I' (Fichte (1988), p. 152). See Neuhouser (1990).

19 Neuhouser (1990).

20 Smyth (1986), p. 103.

21 Vlastos (1971), p. 4. The same writer, however (ibid., p. 12), insists that we should not see Socrates as 'a bundle of incompatible roles precariously tied together by irony'. It was this recognition that 'Irony is the form of a paradox', that Friedrich Schlegel admired in Socrates (Schlegel (1971), p. 149). Vlastos (1991), pp. 21–44, argues that Kierkegaard misinterprets Socrates by reading back into the early Platonic dialogues an intention to deceive which was not originally present. See also Guthrie (1971).

22 Plato, *Phaedo*, 99E.

23 Ibid.

24 Friedländer (1958), 1: Ch. 1.

25 Ibid., p. 19.

26 Zeller (1885), p. 103.

27 *Irony*, p. 9.

28 One of the leading 'theoreticians' of Romanticism, Friedrich Schlegel ((1971), pp. 151–6), none the less expresses very clearly what Kierkegaard himself drew from Socrates:

> Socratic irony is the only involuntary and yet completely deliberate dissimulation. . . . It is meant to deceive no one except those who consider it a deception. . . . It contains and arouses a feeling of indissoluble antagonism between the absolute and the relative, between the impossibility and the necessity of complete communication.

29 Ibid., p. 12.

30 Ibid., p. 17.

31 Ibid., p. 58.

32 Ibid., p. 64.

33 Ibid., p. 72.

34 Ibid., p. 132.

35 For a recent discussion of these works as biographical sources see Waterfield's 'Introduction' to Xenophon (1990).

36 This can be seen as an early formulation of what was to become his attack on Hegel. Thus *Irony*, pp. 133–4: 'Clouds superbly characterize the utterly flabby thought process, continually fluctuating, devoid of

footing and devoid of immanental laws of motion.' Clouds also characterize the ancient conception of melancholy. In satirizing intellectual pretension it is a superb 'comedy of self-assertion' (Dover (1972)).

37 *Irony*, p. 149.

38 Ibid., p. 152.

39 Bigelow (1987), p. 117.

40 Ibid., p. 175.

41 Ibid., p. 173.

42 Beckman (1988) argues that, quite apart from its radical philosophical and psychological dimensions, there is a distinctive religious element in Socratic thought.

43 In Socrates 'the whole of existence has become alien to existence' (*Irony*, p. 259).

44 Thus, for example: 'Irony is a demand, an enormous demand, because it rejects reality' (*Irony*, p. 213).

45 And to realistic surprise at sharing with just one of his brothers the distinction of surviving into adulthood.

46 *Irony*, p. 261.

47 Though they remain distinct:

> In doubt, the subject continually wants to enter into the object, and his unhappiness is that the object continually eludes him. In irony, the subject continually wants to get outside the object, and he achieves this by realizing at every moment that the object has no reality.
>
> (*Irony*, p. 257).

48 *Fragments*, pp. 130–2, itself a continuation of early *Journal* characterizations of the 'Faustian doubter'.

49 Yack (1986), Beiser (1992).

50 A point of view expressed forcefully in Hegel's Jena writings (1948).

51 The ironist cannot attain 'the true bliss in which the subject is not dreaming but possesses himself in infinite clarity, is absolutely transparent to himself, which is possible only for the religious individual, who does not have his infinity outside himself but inside himself ' (*Irony*, p. 298).

52 For Novalis, for example, 'intellect is but a dream of feeling' (quoted in Wernaer (1966), p. 45), a view Kierkegaard could never endorse.

53 As early as 1836 he noted in his *Journals*, 2: 1677: 'For the ancients the divine was continually merged with the world; therefore no irony.'

54 *Irony*, p. 64.

55 Neubauer (1980), p. 62. Cf. Coleridge (1983), 1, p. 81.

56 Thomas Mann (1983), p. 419; though Mann could never be accused of mysticism he admits to the conservative tendency of his intellectually demanding ironic art.

57 Ibid.

58 *Journals*, 2: 1462.

59 Agacinski (1988), pp. 33–6.

60 *Irony*, p. 268.

61 There is some irony in the subsequent adoption, among a group of existentialist writers, of Kierkegaard as an intellectual progenitor of a 'philosophy of the will' of which he would have been contemptuous.

3 REFLECTION: ON THE SURFACE OF MODERNITY

1 In Thompson (1972).

2 Mann (1983), p. 423.

3 The 'real' and the 'non-real', for modern society, therefore, bear something of the character of the more primitive distinction between the 'sacred' and the 'profane': Durkheim (1915), pp. 23–47, Ferguson (1992), pp. 2–12.

4 Some more recent literature focuses on the social aspect of Kierkegaard's thought – Elrod (1981), Perkins (1984), Westphal (1987), Kirmmse (1990), Connell and Evans (1992) – but tends to emphasize the 'second' authorship rather than view the writings as a whole in this context. For a 'social' interpretation of the 'aesthetic' writings some earlier commentators are still more significant: Lukács (1974, originally 1909), Adorno (1989, originally 1933), Löwith (1964).

5 For example Smit (1965), Sponheim (1968). Almost all commentators discuss this problem as a question of the relation between the 'real' author and his many pseudonyms. The approach adopted here is restricted to outlining relations among the pseudonyms.

6 Fenger (1980), p. 152, Lowrie (1938), 1: pp. 191–231, Thompson (1974), pp. 106–16.

7 Møller's review may have lacked profundity, but it did contain at least one suggestive comment: 'Writing and producing seem to have become a physical need for him, or he uses it as medicine' (*Corsair*, p. 100).

8 Kierkegaard admired Goldschmidt's novel, *En Jøde*, published under the pseudonym Adolf Meyer.

9 *Corsair*, p. xiv.

10 *Purity*, p. 158.

11 Ibid., p. 195.

12 *Journals*, 6: 6593.

13 *Lilies*, p. 46.

14 *Anxiety*, p. 42.

15 Kirmmse (1990); the book-length 'Part One' is an important and illuminating study of Kierkegaard's intellectual and social milieu, and clearly defines his commitment to bourgeois modernism, as distinct from the Present Age.

16 Fenger (1980), pp. 4–5, Kirmmse (1990), pp. 136–68. Martensen was one of Kierkegaard's teachers, and it was his enthusiastic lectures on Hegel that roused the latter's intense opposition. Martensen's enthusiasm soon faded, as can be gauged from his later published works (Martensen (1866, 1873, 1885)). Kierkegaard, however, remained hostile and many of the acerbic comments directed at 'the

professor' are intended for Martensen. Somewhat unfairly, Martensen (1873), pp. 206–20, treats his former student's 'reckless polemic against speculation' as a somewhat inferior brand of the fashionable 'religious individualism' which he claimed was better exemplified in the writings of Alexander Vinet. But Kierkegaard would have agreed with many of Martensen's criticisms of Vinet which, in some respects, repeat Kierkegaard's own criticism of Adler (Vinet (1843a, 1843b, 1852, 1859)).

17 Grundtvig attracted a considerable following in rural Denmark (Kirmmse (1990), pp. 198–237, Hovde (1948), 1: pp. 321–40).

18 Jensen (1983), p. 38. For Grundtvig, Scandinavian myth represented 'another spiritual element than that which had been introduced by Christianity' (Thaning (1972), p. 73); see also Todberg and Thyssen (1983).

19 Hovde (1948), 1: p. 96.

20 Ibid., p. 95. And, ibid., p. 337: 'Grundtvig had a social philosophy based upon history and religion, which championed nationalism and democracy, and was directed toward the highest ideals of middle class capitalism.'

21 Barton (1986), p. 373.

22 Thulstrup (1984), p. 161. Conflict between the Grundtvigians within the church and the established authorities came to a head over the issue of child baptism. During the eighteenth century full citizenship rights had been conditional upon confirmation: Jones (1986). Grundtvig urged the abandonment of any element of force in the performance of the sacraments, and the separation of the very close relations between church and state. Bishop Mynster, who had been a personal friend of Kierkegaard's father, finally taking action against unorthodox ministries, had offending priests removed, but significantly took no action against Peter Christian Kierkegaard (Kirmmse (1990) pp. 119–24).

23 Such was the dominance of ecclesiastical culture in Denmark that radical politics was also conducted in religious language. In his first journalistic writings, while still a student, Kierkegaard had rejected left-wing alternatives proposed by H.N. Clausen and Orla Lehmann; (*Polemical*, pp. xx-xxii). For readings of Kierkegaard's writings in the more immediate context of Danish religious politics see Elrod (1981) and particularly Kirmmse (1990).

24 Funkenstein (1986), Ferguson (1990).

25 Rousseau (1973), p. 6.

26 Ibid.

27 Ibid., p. 7.

28 Ibid.

29 Rousseau (1953), p. 337. This was a project fraught with 'quite incredible difficulties'. The more so since, unlike Montaigne or Burton before him, he counted friendship an obstacle to the conquest of melancholy: 'If I had shaken off the yoke of friendship as well as that of public opinion, I should have accomplished my purpose' (ibid., p. 338).

30 Ibid., p. 332.
31 Rousseau (1911), p. 249. Rules of conduct cannot be derived from philosophy: 'I find them in the depths of my heart, traced by nature in characters which nothing can efface.'
32 Ibid., p. 30. In this context he remarks that 'all children are afraid of masks'.
33 Ibid., p. 330.
34 Rousseau (1953), pp. 29–30: 'I had not yet sufficient reasoning power to realize the extent to which appearances were against me. . . . There ended the serenity of my childish life.'
35 Starobinski (1988), p. 27. Rousseau (1984), p. 40:

> *Amour de soi-même* is a natural sentiment, which prompts every animal to watch over its own conservation, and which, directed in man by reason and modified by piety, produces humanity and virtue. *Amour-propre* is only a relative, artificial sentiment, born in society, prompting every individual to attach more importance to himself than to anyone else and inspiring all the injuries men do to themselves and to others; it is the true source of honour.

36 Starobinski (1988), p. 27. This accounts for the variety of contradictory motives he finds for his actions: Ginzburg (1991), p. 187.
37 Ginzburg (1991).
38 Rousseau (1911), p. 298.
39 Starobinski (1988), p. 41. But, as Grimsley (1966), p. 79, points out 'withdrawal from society was not simply a means of retreating from others but also of finding an opportunity for recovering the freedom and independence he deemed necessary for true self-affirmation'.
40 Rousseau (1979), p. 88.
41 Ibid., p. 123.
42 Ibid., p. 88. The implicit distinction between solitude and loneliness was quickly taken up. Loneliness was productive of pathological distortion of feeling, while solitude was an essential aspect of healthy self-development. Zimmerman (1852), p. 96, writing in 1773, however, was willing to defend 'that *philosophic melancholy* which solitude inspires'.
43 Rousseau (1979), p. 89.
44 Ibid., p. 107.
45 Ibid., p. 108.
46 Ibid.
47 Ibid., p. 112.
48 Starobinski (1988), p. 69.
49 Yack (1986), a tendency continued in twentieth-century 'existentialist' writers, e.g. Jaspers (1971), beginning with remarks reminiscent of those to be found in *Two Ages*, defends a view of existence as 'self-positing'.
50 Blumenberg (1987), using Kant's phrase, views the entire development of modernity in terms of the gradual unfurling of the consequences of Copernicanism.
51 See Pippin (1991). Habermas elects Hegel to the key role, Johannes Climacus opts for Descartes.

52 Kant (1988), p. 34.
53 Yack (1986).
54 Ibid., p. 83.
55 'Kant's theoretical and practical philosophy are both equally groundless unless they both arise from the principle of the original autonomy of the human spirit' (Tillich (1974), p. 44).
56 Kant (1974), p. 31.
57 Ibid., p. 101.
58 Ibid., p. 102.
59 'Historical Introduction' to *Two Ages*.
60 *Polemical*, p. 74. Kierkegaard had apparently been impressed by the book on a first reading but later changed his view, and there is an element of self-criticism in his strictures against the novelist; *Polemical*, p. xxvi, Andersen (1955), p. 88. In a later work, Andersen refers to Kierkegaard as 'a dripstone-cistern of humour and good sense' (Andersen (1857), p. 297). Andersen, to a large extent, agreed with Kierkegaard's literary judgement. Reviewing his own work in 1839 he finds the same weakness as had Kierkegaard: 'he knows how to embellish and arrange thoughts and feelings, but lacks creative power ... it is nothing more than a poetic embellishment of experienced facts' (Bredsdorff (1975), p. 138).
61 *Two Ages*, p. 61, emphasis in original.
62 Ibid., p. 68, emphasis in original.
63 Ibid. Kierkegaard's reaction to the 1848 revolutions is expressed in a letter to Kolderup-Rosenvinge (*Letters*, 186): 'And purely political movement ... is a vortex, cannot be stopped, and is a prey to the illusion of wanting a fixed point ahead ... my opinion about the whole European confusion ... which appears to be purely political, will turn out suddenly to be religious.' The more recent scholarly interest in Kierkegaard's 'social philosophy' – Perkins (1984), Westphal (1987), Kirmmse (1990) – represents a considerable advance over earlier views; cf. Stark in Lawson (1970), still evident in Malantschuk (1980) and Mullen (1981). As a result *Two Ages* now seems to be a much more significant work; it should also be noted that the much later 'discourses', *For Self-examination* and *Judge for Yourself!* were *Recommended to the Present Age*.
64 For example Tocqueville (1968), 2: pp. 652–7.
65 *Two Ages*, p. 69.
66 Ibid.
67 Ibid., p. 81.
68 Ibid., pp. 81–2. Perkins (1984), p. 128, suggests the analysis of envy in *Two Ages* is in some ways comparable with Nietzsche's conception of *ressentiment*. It is perhaps closer to Rousseau's notion of *amour-propre*.
69 *Two Ages*, pp. 98–9.
70 Ibid., pp. 101–2. Many of Kierkegaard's complaints against the 'Present Age' were made at about the same time by Thomas de Quincey, in his 'Suspira de Profundis', originally published in *Blackwoods Magazine* in 1845. De Quincey (1966), pp. 113–14, talks of 'the gathering agitation of our present English life', of a 'fierce condition of eternal hurry' leading 'towards the vortex of the merely human'.

71 *Two Ages*, p. 102.
72 The English text adopts the title *On Authority and Revelation*. It is a heavily edited version of the original manuscript, to which Kierkegaard added very many corrections over an extended period. Kierkegaard's plans for publication indicate a late decision to present it under the pseudonym Petrus Minor. It is considered here only in relation to *Two Ages*, as a further illustration of his polemical relation to the crowd.
73 *Adler*, p. 5.
74 Ibid., p. 12.
75 Ibid., p. 31.
76 Ibid., p. 57.
77 As proposed, for example, by Lyotard (1984).

4 REVOLUTION OF THE SPHERES: A TOPOLOGICAL FANTASY

1 *Postscript*, I, p. 626. This tendency is most marked in biographical interpretations of Kierkegaard's writings. Even more dubious, however, is the widespread recent philosophical interest in the authorship, which, after noting its 'polyonymity', proceeds by ignoring its implications. The books ascribed to Johannes Climacus and Anti-Climacus (because they are of most interest to contemporary philosophers?), thus, are frequently regarded as Kierkegaard's own views, in spite of Kierkegaard's personally signed and forthright denial of this appended to the *Postscript* in 'A First and Last Declaration'.
2 Taylor (1975) has been influential in reviving interest in the 'theory of the stages'. He discusses a number of different, but by no means incompatible, approaches: that they represent stages in Kierkegaard's own development, or epochs of world history, or ideal possibilities, or generalized stages in the development of the self. See also Malantschuk (1971), Elrod (1975), Dunning (1985). Taylor (1980) provides a contextually richer study which emphasizes the centrality of the 'aesthetic' to an understanding of modern experience. See also Eagleton (1990), and for specific studies of the aesthetic in Kierkegaard, George (1965), Shmuëli (1971), Gouwens (1989), Pattison (1992a). Hartshorne (1990) usefully emphasizes the authorial independence of each of the pseudonyms. The 'aesthetic' has become a central interest for recent studies of Kant's philosophy, e.g. Saville (1987), Ferguson (1992), Guyer (1993), and it now seems more plausible to link Kierkegaard and Kant as 'philosophers of the aesthetic' rather than as moral philosophers.
3 'I have lost all my illusions. In vain do I seek to abandon myself to joy's infinitude. . . . My soul has lost possibility' (*Either*, p. 41).
4 Moretti (1987) provides an interesting analysis of youth as a symbol of modernity in the classical *Bildungsroman*. See also Bruford (1962), p. 174. The literary archetype was established by Goethe in his *Wilhelm Meister*. Mackey (1971), p. 274, acutely remarks of *Either/Or* that it is 'a *Bildungsroman* but without *Bildung*'.

5 Hegel (1969), pp. 67–73, concludes, however: 'The beginning is no pure nothing, but a nothing from which something is to proceed. . . . The beginning, therefore, contains both, being and nothing, is the unity of being and nothing.'

6 Schlegel (1971) p. 189 (*Athenaeum Fragment*, 206): 'A fragment, like a miniature work of art, has to be entirely isolated from the surrounding world and be complete in itself like a porcupine.' And, as quoted in Lacoue-Labarthe and Nancy (1988): 'Each fragment stands for itself and for that from which it is detached.' For helpful discussions, from a variety of viewpoints, of fragmentation in German Romantic literature see Wernaer (1966), Taylor (1970), Cooke (1976, 1979), McFarland (1981), Thorslev (1984), Wheeler (1984), Kuzniar (1987), Ziolkowski (1990), Behler (1993). Though rejecting both the *Bildungsroman* and the *fragment* as literary models adequate to his own project, Kierkegaard clearly adapted both as vehicles for various aspects of his own mode of 'psycho-cultural' analysis.

7 *Either*, p. 65.

8 Ibid.

9 Thus, for example, the human body is viewed as the 'proper object' of painting, Lessing (1874), p. 131. And more generally it relies on Hegel's *Aesthetics*, in arguing that the specific character of music as a non-spatial form of representation is peculiarly suited to the expression of sensuousness. Thus, Hegel (1975), 2: p. 891: 'what alone is fitted for expression in music is the object-free inner life, the self without any further content. . . . Its content is what is subjective itself'. See Wicks, in Beiser (1993), p. 358.

10 Kierkegaard, a founder member of the University Music Society, was a frequent visitor to the opera. *Don Giovanni* was first performed in Copenhagen in 1836, and frequently thereafter. Kierkegaard confesses that Mozart's music 'diabolically gripped me'. The 'young man's' close relation to the Romantic movement is once again apparent. Hoffmann, for example, had written extensively on musical theory, and had himself devoted an essay to Mozart's *Don Giovanni*, which he called 'the opera of all operas'. Hoffmann treated music as 'the mysterious Sanskrit of nature, translated into sound', and the author's conception of music as the 'immediate-sensuous' is close to the idea of 'nature' expressing itself in human feeling. See Hoffmann (1989), pp. 94, 398. More generally the structure of *Either/Or* may owe something to Hoffmann's popular novel *The Life and Opinions of Kater Murr* (1969), published in 1819, a work to which Hoffmann's name is appended as an 'editor', and purports to be a 'fragmented biography', written on sheets of loose paper, accidentally come to light, which the editor has reassembled in the form of a loose dialogue between an intelligent tomcat and his master. Additionally Paul de Man (1993), pp. 112–13, suggests a connection between the notion of 'repetition' and Hoffmann's tale 'Princess Brambilla'; but the latter, like Gogol's 'The Nose' and innumerable later stories of 'doubles', is better viewed as a case of 'hysterical' splitting of the personality. Kierkegaard writes of melancholy as 'hysteria of the spirit', as a symptom, in other words,

which 'repetition' might cure. Kierkegaard wrote of Hoffman that he felt 'related to him in many ways', but that his 'grief about the world' had not yet 'despairingly swung around to its opposite', to the fantastic (*Letters*, 5, p. 53). The more distant literary model, for both, was no doubt *Wilhelm Meister* (Billeskov Jansen in Bertung (1989), pp. 19–30).

11 For a discussion of the 'young man's' misunderstanding of Mozart see Zelechow, in Pattison (1992b), pp. 64–77.

12 *Either*, p. 75.

13 Ibid., p. 76.

14 Ibid.

15 Thus, for example, Goethe (1989), p. 67: 'all my active energies have been cast down into restless listlessness, and I can neither be idle nor accomplish anything.'

16 Garber (1982).

17 *Either*, p. 101.

18 Ibid., p. 56.

19 Ibid., p. 61.

20 The specifically modern characteristic of the secret as an 'adornment of the personality' was later taken up by Simmel (1950), pp. 330–44.

21 *Either*, p. 173.

22 Ibid., p. 184; 1 Peter 3: 4.

23 *Either*, p. 206.

24 Ibid., p. 222.

25 Ibid., p. 290.

26 Ibid., p. 291.

27 Ibid., p. 298.

28 Ibid., p. 299.

29 Ibid., p. 300.

30 In a similar fashion the notion of 'crisis' is taken up in a later essay (on Heiberg's wife, who was a celebrated actress), *The Crisis and a Crisis in the Life of an Actress.*

31 *Either*, p. 234.

32 Ibid., p. 238.

33 This, again, is a completely modern conception. It has nothing in common with, for example, the eighteenth-century novel in which chance plays a central role as a plot device, but has no 'deeper' significance.

34 *Either*, p. 308.

35 Ibid., p. 306.

36 Ibid., p. 385.

37 Ibid., p. 384.

38 Ibid., p. 381.

39 Ibid., p. 36.

40 Ibid., p. 26.

41 McCarthy (1978) has drawn attention to Kierkegaard's use of both Danish terms, normally translated by the single English word 'melancholy'. He distinguishes them (ibid., p. 56) as follows: '*Melancholi* being lighter, having a certain sweetness and the association of passivity which the word also has in English; *Tungsind*

being deeper, however, more intense, closer to brooding, and with an
element of reflection present in it.'

42 *Or*, p. 8.
43 Ibid., p. 11.
44 Ibid., p. 17.
45 Ibid., p. 7.
46 Ibid., p. 56.
47 Ibid., p. 88.
48 Ibid., p. 138.
49 Ibid., p. 144.
50 Ibid., p. 160.
51 Ibid., p. 166.
52 Ibid., p. 164.
53 Ibid., p. 169. Bruford (1975), p.73, views this as a central element in
   the classical *Bildungsroman*: 'A single free resolution is needed to be a
   human being: anyone who has so resolved, will always remain truly
   human; if he fails, he has never been so at all.' But it would be
   misleading to view *Either/Or* as a *Bildungsroman*; for the 'ethical'
   pseudonyms the decisiveness of 'choice' is *continually* before the
   individual, and within the work as a whole there is no conclusive
   development.
54 *Or*, p. 191.
55 Ibid., p. 211.
56 Ibid., p. 213.
57 Ibid., p. 223.
58 Ibid., p. 222.
59 Ibid., p. 251.
60 Ibid.
61 Ibid., p. 258.
62 Kierkegaard regarded himself, at the time of writing, as 'beyond' both
   positions, but his own more developed stance was far from being a
   neutral platform from which he could offer a dispassionate and
   objective description of the 'stages' through which he had already
   passed.
63 It is, of course, possible to interpret *Either/Or* as an 'authentically'
   ethical work which should be judged in an appropriate external
   context. This raises a number of interesting issues, such as the relation
   between Judge William's ethical views and those of, say, Kant, but this
   not only tends to allow *Or* too easy a victory over *Either*, it obscures the
   relationship that develops among the pseudonyms. For none the less
   interesting suggestions along these lines see Stack (1977), Hannay
   (1982).
64 The phrase 'marionette theatre' is from Jolivet (1951). The subtitle to
   Repetition has been translated in the new Princeton edition as *A Venture
   in Experimenting Psychology*, in preference to Lowrie's *An Essay in
   Experimental Psychology*. The former has the advantage (apart from
   distancing itself from modern laboratory studies in psychology) of
   drawing attention to Kierkegaard's method of 'imaginative
   construction' of characters and situations which is used throughout

the 'aesthetic' works. For an extended defence see the editors' note, *Repetition*, pp. 357–62.

65 *Repetition*, p. 131.

66 Deleuze (1968) goes a long way towards justifying this claim.

67 For the bourgeois worldview the 'ego', like 'nature', existed in a timeless moment (Meyerson (1930)).

68 *Repetition*, pp. 132–3.

69 Neubauer (1980), pp. 41–2: 'The philistines know only their everyday life and have become estranged from their essential self, forgetting that man is not merely a common sense being, but by virtue of his "higher self", also a citizen of an invisible order.' See also Pfefferkon (1988).

70 *Repetition*, p. 138.

71 Ibid., p. 145.

72 Ibid., p. 150.

73 Ibid., p. 186.

74 Ibid., p. 201.

75 Ibid., p. 133.

76 Ibid., p. 148.

77 Ibid., p. 229. This is another attack on Romanticism, in which the 'poetic' and the 'religious' are promiscuously joined. There is here, as elsewhere in the aesthetic writings, a strong element of self-reproach as well. In a letter to his friend Emil Boesen he writes 'I think I can turn anything into a poetic subject' (*Letters*, 50).

78 Many commentators persist, however, in trying to assimilate *Fear and Trembling* to a rational ethical discourse. See, e.g., Mooney (1991).

79 *Fear*, p. 33.

80 Ibid., p. 32.

81 Ibid., p. 34.

82 Ibid., p. 47.

83 Ibid., p. 37.

84 Ibid., p. 39.

85 Ibid., p. 55.

86 *Stages*, p. 9.

87 Ibid., p. 10.

88 Ibid., p. 12.

89 Ibid., p. 13.

90 Ibid., p. 31.

91 Ibid., p. 36.

92 Ibid., p. 48.

93 Ibid., p. 59.

94 Ibid., p. 71.

95 Ibid., p. 76.

96 Ibid., p. 77.

97 Ibid., p. 102.

98 Ibid., p. 109.

99 Ibid., p. 163.

100 Ibid., p. 174.

101 Ibid., p. 195.

102 Ibid., p. 196.
103 Ibid., p. 197.
104 Ibid., p. 209.
105 Ibid., p. 216.
106 Ibid., p. 257.
107 Ibid., p. 309.
108 Ibid., p. 316.
109 Ibid.
110 Ibid., p. 340.
111 Ibid., p. 342.
112 Ibid., p. 351.
113 A *rapprochement* between Hegel and Kierkegaard has also been suggested by some recent reinterpretations of Hegel, influenced particularly by the work of Kojève and Hyppolite, itself influenced by Heidegger and, thus, distantly by Kierkegaard himself. See, for example, Solomon (1983).
114 Adorno (1989), pp. 40–6.

5 BETWEEN EXISTENCE AND NON-EXISTENCE: AN ANTHROPOLOGICAL DIGRESSION

1 *Journals*, 4: 217: 'If Hegel had written his whole logic and written in the preface that it was only a thought experiment, in which at many points he still steered clear of some things, he undoubtedly would have been the greatest thinker who has ever lived. As it is he is comic.' The close association between Johannes Climacus and Hegel is revealed in another entry (4: 1575) dated January 1839: 'Hegel is a Johannes Climacus who does not storm the heavens as do the giants, by setting mountain upon mountain – but enters them by means of his syllogisms.'
2 *Sickness*, p. 13. It is worth noting that it is through this 'third term' that the pseudonyms maintain the historical and social character of 'selfhood'; actuality as a 'second-order' reality includes social relations within it. The emerging 'selfhood', therefore, is not the product of an act of isolated reflection.
3 From an extensive literature see, for example, van Peursen (1966), Moltmann (1971), Pannenberg (1985).
4 'So today I have expressly rid my mind of all worries and arranged for myself a clear stretch of time' (Descartes (1985), 2: p. 12).
5 Thus, for Kierkegaard, Spinoza implicitly plays a counterpart to Hegel. He charges Spinoza's whole 'introflected method' with duplicity, and with a misplaced conception of motion, which belongs uniquely to the domain of human action (*Journals*, 4: 4319).
6 Hegel (1975), 1: p. 49.
7 Ibid., p. 38.
8 The work remains unfinished but clearly takes the form of an intellectual biography, written, presumably, by one or other of the pseudonyms.
9 *Climacus*, p. 117.

10 Ibid.

11 Ibid., p. 116.

12 Ibid., p. 119; unlike the earlier aesthetic writers: 'He did not pay any attention to people and did not imagine that they could pay any attention to him.'

13 Ibid., p. 118.

14 St John Climacus (1959). Kierkegaard may have found some consolation in the work; recalling his early envy of Heiberg's preeminent position in Danish cultural life, the following is apt: 'A condemned man who has heard the death sentence will not worry about how theatres are managed' (Climacus (1959), p. 15).

15 Ferreira (1991) suggests a non-ironic interpretation of the choice of Climacus as a pseudonym, arguing that the imagery of the ladder is a useful corrective to that of the 'leap'. This approach, however, seems to ignore the essentially modern context of the pseudonymous writings. Similarly Law (1993) ignores the historical context in claiming Kierkegaard for 'negative theology'.

16 *Climacus*, p. 119.

17 Ibid.

18 Ibid., p. 123.

19 Ibid., p. 19.

20 Adorno (1989), p. 11, is forthright: 'Kierkegaard's realm is ruled by logical immanence in which everything must find its place, come what may.'

21 A traditional view; see, for example, Jerome (1933), given powerful expression by Hegel in his analysis of lordship and bondage (Hegel (1977), pp. 111–19).

22 Ferguson (1992), pp. 13–16. This is also the central point of Marx's criticism of Feuerbach, that the latter's philosophy of sensuous spirit was, in the end, just another *concept* of a human being.

23 *Journals*, 5: 5383.

24 Ibid., 1: 100.

25 Freud, in his 1915 'metapsychological' essay 'Instincts and their Vicissitudes' writes: 'an "instinct" appears to us a concept on the frontier between the mental and the somatic, as the psychical representative of the stimuli originating from within the organism and reaching the mind' (Freud (1957), 14: pp. 121–2). For general comparisons between Kierkegaard and Freud see Cole (1971), Nordentoft (1978).

26 The relationship between anxiety and psychic 'splitting' was taken up later in the nineteenth century, particularly among French psychologists, most significantly Pierre Janet (Ellenberger (1970), pp. 331–417).

27 *Anxiety*, p. 42.

28 Green and Dupré, both in Perkins (1985), argue that Haufniensis's view of anxiety as 'fear of nothing' is closely related to Schelling's philosophy. The formula 'sympathetic antipathy and antipathetic sympathy' recalls Schelling's *Naturphilosophie*: 'attractive and repulsive forces constitute the *essence* of matter itself' (Schelling (1988), p. 165).

But, for Schelling, the gradual 'disentangling' of spirit from sensuousness is a wholly self-motivated movement of the 'I', which contains, from the beginning, its own *telos*. Schelling's view of the relationship between melancholy and self-development is based, however, on a Platonic doctrine of 'recollection' rather than 'repetition', and depends upon a self-positing 'I'. In a fine passage (Schelling (1988), p. 10), for example:

> At that time man was still at one with himself and the world about him. In obscure recollection the condition still floats before even the most wayward thinker. . . . Nor would it be conceivable how man should ever have forsaken that condition, if we did not know that his spirit, whose element is *freedom*, strives to make *itself* free, to disentangle itself from the fetters of Nature and her guardianship, and must abandon itself to the uncertain fate of its own powers, in order one day to return, as victor and by its own merit, to that position in which, unaware of itself, it spent the childhood of its reason.
>
> See Marx (1984), pp. 58–83.

29 Ibid., p. 49.
30 These compressed formulas are taken almost verbatim from Karl Rosenkranz, a student of Hegel's, whose *Psychologie* was published in 1837 (Nordentoft (1978), p. 21).
31 Ibid., p. 50.
32 *Postscript,* p. 544.
33 Of many descriptions see particularly the elder Henry James, quoted in King (1983).
34 Onians (1988); Schilder (1964), pp. 113–15, draws a specific parallel between nausea and dizziness. Hoberman, in Perkins (1987), pp. 185–208, treats vertigo as a 'metaphorical equivalent' of anxiety. He claims that 'Prior to Kierkegaard, anxiety is not even a distinct, let alone a crucial, category of experience'. After Kierkegaard, for Nietzsche, Freud, Heidegger and Sartre it is obviously central. 'Spatiality' has been taken up particularly within 'phenomenological psychology', itself indirectly influenced (via Heidegger) by Kierkegaard. Thus Strauss (1966). Minkowski (1936, 1970), following Bergson, examines the moral and aesthetic significance of 'high' and 'low' in bodily terms.
35 *Anxiety,* p. 88.
36 Ibid.
37 *Fragments,* p. 139.
38 *Postscript,* 1: 361; *Fragments,* p. xviii. It must be remembered that *Fragments* is another 'imaginative construction' and thus has an aesthetic character. There is considerable irony in Kierkegaard creating a 'pagan' philosopher whose dialectical grasp of existence, which was 'designed' to demonstrate the inability of philosophy to 'raise' itself into religious categories, could be mistaken by his contemporaries for a genuinely religious sensibility. Roberts (1986) is one of the few commentators to take account of this irony.

39 Nielsen (1983), p. 41.
40 *Fragments*, p. 73. Kierkegaard, as Johannes Climacus, was considerably influenced by Trendelenburg's analysis of Aristotle's metaphysics in this discussion. See Malantschuk (1971), pp. 132–3.
41 *Fragments*, p. 74.
42 Ibid., p. 75.
43 Ibid., p. 81.
44 Allison (1966).
45 *Fragments*, p. 44.
46 Ibid., p. 45. The paradox is neither 'improbability' (Evans (1978), p. 89) nor a 'formal contradiction'; it is 'beyond' reason rather than 'irrational' (Evans (1983), pp. 217–25). Pojman (1984).
47 *Sickness*, p. 77.
48 Ibid., p. 101.
49 One is reminded of Dostoevsky's obsessive characters, thus, Shestov (1969), p. 21: 'Dostoevsky is Kierkegaard's double'. See Ferguson (1990), pp. 209–15. There is also a close relation to de Sade; what is at issue is not 'giving way' to 'nature' but imbuing it with spiritual potency. Only thus does 'sensuous nature' becomes 'discernible in the form of a propensity to act' (Klossowski (1992), p. 17).
50 *Anxiety*, p. 30.
51 Ibid., p. 32.
52 Ibid., p. 33. See Perkins (1985), p. 55.
53 *Journals*, 4: 3964.
54 *Anxiety*, p. 38.
55 Ibid., p. 119.
56 *Anxiety*, p. 105.

6 THE RELIGION OF INWARDNESS: AN OFFENSIVE PHILOSOPHY

1 *Practice*, p. xiii. And *Journals*, 6: 6433:

> Johannes Climacus and Anti-Climacus have several things in common; but the difference is that whereas Johannes Climacus places himself so low that he even says that he himself is not a Christian, one seems to be able to detect in Anti-Climacus that he considers himself to be a Christian on an extraordinary high level. . . . I would place myself higher than Johannes Climacus, lower than Anti-Climacus.

2 *Fragments*, p. 49.
3 *Sickness*, p. 116.
4 *Postscript*, p. 17.
5 Lessing (1956), pp. 51–3; Allison (1966), Barth (1972), pp. 234–65.
6 Reimarus (1970), p. 40. Though formally assimilating all 'revealed religion' to 'natural religion', Reimarus rejected the idea that the 'truth of Christianity' could be viewed philosophically. Thus, the intention of Jesus' preaching 'is directed toward a change of mind,

toward sincere love of God and the neighbour, toward patience, gentleness, self-denial, and the suppression of all evil will'. See also Reimarus (1971).

7 *Postscript*, p. 28.

8 Ibid., p. 29. Adams (1987), pp. 44–6, makes the point that 'probable beliefs' are not converted into faith on the basis of a rational, or irrational, 'decision'; that Johannes Climacus is concerned to show (as had Pascal in his discussion of the wager) the difference between empirical beliefs and what might be termed 'convictions'. Growing interest among analytical philosophers in the work of Kierkegaard has concentrated on the writings attributed to Johannes Climacus, e.g. Evans (1978), Pojman (1984), Bell (1988). This is a welcome reversal of the neglect, or hostility, which was previously commonplace. However, such an approach, which remains insensitive to the contextual issues of the authorship, tends to be somewhat narrow in its focus.

9 Ibid., p. 29.

10 As it was for Grundtvig (Todberg and Thyssen (1983), pp. 12–13).

11 *Postscript*, p. 52.

12 Ibid., p. 80. Hamann and Herder had similarly criticized Kant. For them the 'purism of thought' was a dangerous fiction; all thought was 'embodied' in specific cultural forms, most significantly it was bound to a particular language. See Smith (1960); Herder (1969); Beiser (1987), pp. 16–43, 127–64.

13 *Postscript*, p. 73.

14 Ibid., p. 95.

15 In this Kierkegaard was particularly influenced by Trendelenburg, see Malantschuk (1971), pp. 82–4.

16 Johannes Climacus was, no doubt, as unfair to Hegel as were the other pseudonyms. On the basis of Hegel's earlier theological writings or his later lectures on the philosophy of religion, a quite different reading of the *Phenomenology* becomes plausible. See Hegel (1948, 1988), Fackenheim (1967), Brazill (1970), Harris (1972), Solomon (1983), Olson (1992). It must be remembered that the Danish interpreters of Hegel were conservative, and that the writings of Bauer, Strauss and Feuerbach had little or no influence; Thulstrup (1980), pp. 74–5.

17 *Postscript*, p. 118.

18 Ibid., p. 130.

19 Ibid., p. 132.

20 Ibid., p. 190. Fichte's version of idealism was a model of pure self-determination (Neuhouser (1990)). 'The *self posits itself*, and by virtue of this mere self-assertion it *exists*', and at the same time 'the self posits the not-self as limited by the self ' (Fichte (1970), pp. 97, 122). The self strives towards a rational mastery over all its self-posited elements, and Fichte sees the 'vocation of man' as a search for unity within the multiplicity of representations flowing from his 'productive imagination'. Each person aims 'to be at one with himself; he should never contradict himself ' (Fichte (1988) p. 149).

21 *Postscript*, p. 195.

22 Ibid., p. 197.

23 Lukács (1975), p. 532, argues that, for Hegel, the problem of knowledge stems from his conception of 'objects' as 'externalizations' of spirit which are, consequently, deprived of autonomy. Climacus might well have agreed.

24 Hamann had also used Socrates as a model of inwardness: 'The ignorance of Socrates was sensibility. But between sensibility and a proposition is a greater difference than between a living animal and its anatomical skeleton' (Smith (1960), p. 181).

25 *Postscript*, p. 203.

26 Ibid., p. 204.

27 Ibid., p. 243.

28 Ibid., p. 249.

29 Ibid., p. 302.

30 Ibid., p. 301.

31 In this, Kierkegaard's view is similar to that of the young Marx who regarded Hegel's philosophy as an ideology; that is, not simply as an intellectual error, but as a distortion which springs directly from the actual conditions of existence. See, for example, Marx (1975), pp. 243–57, Löwith (1964), pp. 137–44.

32 *Postscript*, p. 350.

33 Ibid., p. 351.

34 Ibid., p. 353.

35 Ibid., p. 577.

36 Ibid., p. 387.

37 Ibid., p. 399.

38 *Fragments*, p. 49.

39 *Postscript*, pp. 434–45.

40 Ibid., p. 453.

41 Ibid., p. 457.

42 Ibid., p. 499.

43 Ibid., p. 557.

44 Ibid., p. 563.

45 Ibid., p. 531.

46 Ibid., p. 532.

47 *Practice*, p. xi.

48 Ibid., pp. 288–96. 'The fact that there is a pseudonym is the *qualitative* expression that it is a poet-communication, that it is not I who speaks but another, that it is addressed to me just as much as to others' (ibid., p. 293).

49 Ibid., p. 207; *Journals*, 6: 6501.

50 *Practice*, p. 26.

51 Ibid., p. 48.

52 Ibid., p. 23.

53 Ibid., p. 30.

54 Ibid., p. 62.

55 Ibid., p. 35.

56 Ibid., pp. 35–6. 'Mr. Goodman' is a benign character in a popular Danish children's story.

57 Ibid., p. 62.
58 Ibid., p. 67.
59 Ibid., p. 81.
60 Ibid., p. 123.
61 Ibid., p. 124.
62 Ibid., p. 135.
63 Ibid., p. 143.
64 Ibid., p. 114.
65 It is perhaps here, rather than in relation to the dialectical rigour of the *Postscript*, or the final attack on the Danish church, that one might talk of the 'anti-Christianity of Kierkegaard' (Garelick (1965)). But here, also, it is the 'monstrous illusion' of the Present Age which is the real target (Bouwsma (1984)).
66 *Practice*, p. 151.
67 Ibid., p. 159.
68 Ibid., p. 127.
69 Ibid., p. 120.
70 Ibid., p. 122.
71 *Sickness*, p. 6.
72 Ibid., p. 13.
73 Ibid.
74 Ibid., p. 14.
75 Ibid., p. 19.
76 Ibid., p. 31.
77 Ibid., p. 33.
78 Ibid., p. 36.
79 Ibid.
80 Ibid., pp. 39–40.
81 Gadamer (1975), p. 93; and pp. 91–9 for an important discussion of play.

7 THE UPBUILDING: ARCHITECTURE OF HAPPINESS

1 Kierkegaard, of course, is not alone in his attempt to undermine such an assumption. See, for example, Smyth (1986).
2 As exemplified, for example, by Sartre, in Thompson (1972).
3 Hence the primary interest in Kierkegaard has been either aesthetic or philosophical, rather than religious.
4 *Journals*, 6: 6533.
5 *Discourses*, p. 49. Anti-Climacus, significantly, writes *for* upbuilding.
6 Sløk (1954) suggests that Kierkegaard is not only 'a profoundly unreliable author', but that 'it would not be unfair to assert that this "S. Kierkegaard" by a reverse twist is also a pseudonym'; quoted in Hartshorne (1990), p. 92.
7 *Discourses*, p. 49.
8 Ibid., p. 231.
9 Ibid., p. 179. An expression used in a somewhat different way by Lessing (1956), p. 43: 'If God held all truth in his right hand and in his

left the everlasting striving after truth . . . with humility I would pick the left hand.'

10 *Or*, p. 346. Hannay in fact translates the title of this concluding section as 'The Edifying', rather than 'Ultimatum'.

11 *Love*, pp. 171–2.

12 Heidegger (1962), p. 5, develops a similar metaphor in relation to 'rebuilding' metaphysics.

13 *Discourses*, p. 10.

14 Ibid., p. 14.

15 Ibid., p. 36.

16 Ibid., p. 22.

17 Ibid., p. 18.

18 Ibid., p. 23.

19 Ibid., p. 27.

20 Ibid., p. 56.

21 Ibid., p. 75.

22 Ibid., p. 73.

23 Ibid., p. 84. This is, of course, a precise description of melancholy.

24 James 1: 17–22.

25 *Discourses*, pp. 141–2; cf. *Fear*, p. 63.

26 *Discourses*, p. 157.

27 Ibid., pp. 221–2.

28 Ibid., p. 257.

29 Ibid., p. 287.

30 Smit (1965) interprets the entire authorship as a dialectic between 'self-positing' and 'self-abdication' but argues that they remain unresolved polarities in his thought.

31 *Irony*, p. 64.

32 A point brought out, in relation to the western mystical tradition, particularly well by Screech (1988).

33 *Discourses*, p. 308.

34 Ibid., p. 314.

35 Ibid., p. 333.

36 Ibid., pp. 347–9.

37 Ibid., p. 357; *Journals*, 4: 4519.

38 *Discourses*, p. 358.

39 Ibid., p. 360.

40 Ibid., p. 363.

41 A.S. Aldworth and W.S. Ferrie: 'Introduction' to *Sufferings*.

42 The delay in publication, which affected a number of works, was connected with his protracted indecision over his possible future as a country pastor.

43 *Purity*, p. 27.

44 The different ethical views advanced in *Purity of Heart* and *Fear and Trembling* have been noted by several authors, e.g. Collins (1954), Walker (1972), Rudd (1993), and have been the focus of attempts to relate (by agreement or disagreement) Kierkegaard to Kant. However, as these texts are ostensibly by different authors, it is hardly surprising that there is no agreement on Kierkegaard's 'real position'.

45 *Purity*, p. 39.
46 Ibid., p. 32.
47 Ibid., pp. 43–4.
48 Ibid., p. 44.
49 Ibid., p. 61.
50 Ibid., p. 58.
51 Ibid., p. 73.
52 Ibid., p. 99.
53 Ibid., pp. 102–3.
54 Ibid., p. 108.
55 Ibid., p. 140.
56 Ibid., p. 195.
57 Matthew 6: 24. *Consider the Lilies* is the second part of *Edifying Discourses in a Different Spirit.* In the following year Kierkegaard published a quite separate discourse entitled *The Lilies of the Field and the Birds of the Air*, an English translation of which appears in Lowrie's edition of *Christian Discourses.*
58 *Lilies*, p. 15.
59 Ibid., p. 23.
60 Ibid., p. 32.
61 *Sufferings*, p. 23.
62 Ibid., pp. 18, 23.
63 Ibid., p. 34.
64 Ibid., p. 38.
65 Ibid., p. 43.
66 Ibid., p. 52.
67 Ibid., p. 64.
68 Ibid., p. 120.
69 Ibid., p. 125.
70 Malantschuk (1971), p. 310.

8 EDIFICATION: THE CONQUEST OF MELANCHOLY

1 S. Kierkegaard's *upbuilding* is thus distinct from the 'faith' of either Johannes Climacus or Anti-Climacus, as for both those writers 'faith occupies a peculiar, paradoxical position at once within and beyond the field of conflicting interpretations' (Smith (1981), p. 41).
2 Sløk (1954).
3 *Christian*, p. 21.
4 Hence Petrarch (1991) offered secular consolation for 'Fortune, Fair and Foul'.
5 *Christian*, p. 31.
6 Ibid., pp. 44, 60.
7 Ibid., pp. 74–5.
8 Ibid., p. 76.
9 Ibid., p. 78.
10 Ibid., p. 67.
11 Ibid., p. 125.

12 Ibid., p. 299.
13 *Self-Examination*, p. 98.
14 Ibid., p. 107.
15 Ibid., p. 106.
16 Ibid., p. 113.
17 Erasmus (1971), p. 206.
18 Khan (1985), pp. 87–8.
19 *Self-Examination*, p. 106.
20 *Love*, p. 169.
21 Erasmus (1971), p. 206.
22 Ibid.
23 Mackey (1971), p. 124, describes this more generally: 'The world of the *Edifying Discourses* might seem to be the world upside down. It is a world in which every value honoured among men is subverted, every thought that passes for consequent among men is undermined.'
24 *Love*, p. 8.
25 Westphal, in Connell and Evans (1992), suggests this amounts to a new existence-sphere, a 'Religion C' which in some sense lies 'beyond' the 'Religion B' of Anti-Climacus. However, the fact that the 'upbuilding' literature is signed, and makes no reference to the pseudonymous works, suggests it is better viewed in contrast to the entire pseudonymous production, rather than as an addition to it. It is also not uncommon, of course, to misread the *edifying* literature as a continuation of Kierkegaard's (Climacus's) 'philosophy', as, e.g., Thomte (1948), p. 124.
26 *Journals*, vol. 641.
27 Ibid., vol. 484.
28 Dupré (1964), p. 35; Price (1963), p. 50.
29 In his extensive survey Singer (1987), pp. 38–49, reads 'Kierkegaard' directly and non-contextually. As a result he stresses the earlier aesthetic works as the more significant contribution to an understanding of modern love.
30 *Love*, p. 11.
31 Ibid., p. 12.
32 Ibid., p. 16.
33 Ibid., p. 44.
34 Ibid., p. 47.
35 Ibid., p. 56.
36 Ibid., p. 58.
37 As suggested by Elrod (1981).
38 *Love*, p. 99.
39 Ibid., p. 111.
40 Heidegger (1988), p. 13.

INCONCLUSIVE POSTSCRIPT: BEYOND DESPAIR

1 The self is incomplete but not unstructured. Swenson (1945), p. 27, is perfectly justified in claiming that the central significance of

Kierkegaard's psychology is 'to have shown us . . . that the life of the spirit has a structure as definite as the law-governed, inorganic universe, and an organization as specialized as that of the highest living thing'.

2 Beiser (1987, 1992).

3 Yack (1986).

4 Løwith (1964), Brazill (1970), Kolakowski (1981), Stepelevich (1983).

5 Westphal (1987).

6 Adorno, Eagleton (refs)

7 Löwith (1964) stresses their divergent attacks on Hegel. Marx turning Hegel 'back on his feet' but retaining his conception of the 'end of history' as an absolute, while Kierkegaard dissolves this dialectic through his insistence on the continuously present and insurmountable contradictoriness of experience. But, again, it depends which pseudonyms are taken to be 'normative' for 'Kierkegaard's' view.

8 L. Colletti, 'Introduction' to Marx (1975), p. 51. Compare *Grundrisse* (Marx (1973)), pp. 514–15.

9 Lukács (1975) argues for the critical distinction between the specific damaging form of 'alienation' based on commodity production, and the harmless inevitability of 'objectification'.

10 Adorno (1989), p. 29.

11 Ibid., pp. 40–6.

12 Heidegger (1967), p. 34.

13 From a somewhat different perspective Mackey, in Thompson (1972), points to a 'loss of the world' in Kierkegaard's writings. But this 'acosmism' is altogether appropriate to the realities (as well as the appearances) of the Present Age: see also Mackey (1986), pp. 114–15. Buber (1947), p. 65, similarly complains: 'It cannot be that the relation of the human person to God is established by the substration of the world.'

14 Nordentoft (1978) treats the 'spheres' as a theory of 'developmental psychology' and, consequently, places *The Concept of Anxiety* at the conceptual starting point of the authorship. This is one way of relating Kierkegaard to Freud; see also Cole (1971).

15 Schiller (1967), pp. 105–7.

16 Erikson (1963), pp. 239–43, recognizes the importance of trust, but views it in relation to an already existing ego.

17 Gadamer (1975), p. 93; pp. 91–9 for an important discussion of play.

18 *Postscript*, p. 591.

19 Shestov (1969), p. 21, remarks 'Dostoevsky is Kierkegaard's double'; it is illuminating to view Dostoevsky's huge characters as Kierkegaardian pseudonyms.

20 A change in terminology, from 'melancholy' to 'depression', and a new 'sociological' account of its origins, is only the latest in a long series of failed attempts to assimilate 'sorrow without cause' to 'reasonable unhappiness' (Brown and Harris (1978)). Not that the notion of 'depression' is without significance, see particularly Coyne (1985), Klein (1988), pp. 262–89.

Bibliography

WORKS BY SØREN KIERKEGAARD

Søren Kierkegaard (1938) *The Journals of Søren Kierkegaard*, trans. and ed. Alexander Dru, Oxford.

—— (1938) *Purity of Heart is to Will One Thing*, trans. Douglas V. Steere, New York.

—— (1940) *Christian Discourse*, trans. Walter Lowrie, London and New York.

—— (1940) *Stages on Life's Way*, trans. Walter Lowrie, Princeton, New Jersey.

—— (1940) *Consider the Lilies*, trans. A.S. Aldworth and W.S. Ferrie, London.

—— (1941) *Concluding Unscientific Postscript*, trans. David F. Swenson and Walter Lowrie, Princeton, New Jersey.

—— (1941) *Repetition*, trans. Walter Lowrie, Princeton, New Jersey.

—— (1941) *Training in Christianity*, trans. Walter Lowrie, Princeton, New Jersey.

—— (1941) *For Self-Examination and Judge For Yourselves!*, trans. Walter Lowrie, Princeton, New Jersey.

—— (1944) *Attack Upon 'Christendom'*, trans. and ed. Walter Lowrie, Princeton, New Jersey.

—— (1946) *Works of Love*, trans. David F. Swenson and Lillian Marvin Swenson, Princeton, New Jersey.

—— (1954) *Fear and Trembling and The Sickness unto Death*, trans. Walter Lowrie, Princeton, New Jersey.

—— (1955) *Gospel of Sufferings*, trans. A.S. Aldworth and W.S. Ferrie, London.

—— (1955) *On Authority and Revelation*, trans. and ed. Walter Lowrie, Princeton, New Jersey.

—— (1957) *The Concept of Dread*, trans. Walter Lowrie, Princeton, New Jersey.

—— (1959) *Either/Or*, trans. David F. Swenson and Lillian Marvin Swenson, 2 vols, Princeton, New Jersey.

—— (1962) *The Point of View for My Work as An Author*, trans. Walter Lowrie, New York.

—— (1962) *Philosophical Fragments*, trans. David Swenson and Howard V. Hong, Princeton, New Jersey.

—— (1965) *The Concept of Irony*, trans. Lee M. Capel, Bloomington and London.

—— (1967) *Crisis in the Life of an Actress*, trans. Stephen Crites, London.

—— (1967–78) *Søren Kierkegaard's Journals and Papers*, trans. and ed. Howard V. Hong and Edna H. Hong, 7 vols, Bloomington and London.

—— (1978–??) *Kierkegaard's Writings*, projected 26 vols, Princeton, New Jersey. The following published volumes have been referred to in the text:

—— (1978) *Two Ages*, trans. and ed. Howard V. Hong and Edna H. Hong.

—— (1978) *Kierkegaard: Letters and Documents*, trans. and ed. Henrik Rosenmeier.

—— (1980) *The Sickness Unto Death*, trans. and ed. Howard V. Hong and Edna H. Hong.

—— (1980) *The Concept of Anxiety*, trans. and ed. Reidar Thomte in collaboration with Albert B. Anderson.

—— (1982) *The Corsair Affair*, trans. and ed. Howard V. Hong and Edna H. Hong.

—— (1983) *Fear and Trembling/Repetition*, trans. and ed. Howard V. Hong and Edna H. Hong.

—— (1985) *Philosophical Fragments/Johannes Climacus*, trans. and ed. Howard V. Hong and Edna H. Hong.

—— (1987) *Either/Or*, trans. and ed. Howard V. Hong and Edna H. Hong, 2 vols.

—— (1988) *Stages on Life's Way*, trans. Howard V. Hong and Edna H. Hong.

—— (1989) *The Concept of Irony/Notes of Schelling's Berlin Lectures*, trans. and ed. Howard V. Hong and Edna H. Hong.

—— (1990) *Early Polemical Writings*, trans. and ed. Julia Watkin.

—— (1990) *For Self-Examination/Judge For Yourself!*, trans. and ed. Howard V. Hong and Edna H. Hong.

—— (1990) *Eighteen Upbuilding Discourses*, trans. and ed. Howard V. Hong and Edna H. Hong.

—— (1991) *Practice in Christianity*, trans. and ed. Howard V. Hong and Edna H. Hong.

—— (1992) *Concluding Unscientific Postscript to Philosophical Fragments*, trans. and ed. Howard V. Hong and Edna H. Hong, 2 vols.

—— (1993) *Three Discourses on Imagined Occasions*, trans. and ed. Howard V. Hong and Edna H. Hong.

—— (1985) *Fear and Trembling*, trans. Alastair Hannay, Harmondsworth.

—— (1989) *The Sickness Unto Death*, trans. Alastair Hannay, Harmondsworth.

—— (1989) *Prefaces*, trans. William McDonald, Tallahassee.

—— (1992) *Either/Or*, trans. and ed. Alastair Hannay, Harmondsworth.

268 Bibliography

OTHER WORKS

Abbeele, George van den (1992) *Travel as Metaphor*, Minneapolis and Oxford.
Abrams, M.B. (1971) *Natural Supernaturalism: Tradition and Revolution in Romantic Literature*, London.
Adams, Robert Martin (1966) *Nil: Episodes in the Literary Conquest of Void during the Nineteenth Century*, Oxford and New York.
Adams, Robert Merrihew (1987) *The Virtue of Faith*, Oxford and New York.
Adorno, Theodor W. (1989) *Kierkegaard: The Construction of the Aesthetic*, trans. and ed. Robert Hullot-Kentor, Minneapolis.
Agacinski, Sylviane (1988) *Aparté: Conceptions and Deaths of Søren Kierkegaard*, trans. and Introduction Kevin Newmark, Tallahassee, Florida.
Allen, E.L. (1935) *Kierkegaard: His Life and Thought*, London.
Allison, Henry E. (1966) *Lessing and the Enlightenment*, Ann Arbor, Michigan.
Andersen, Hans (1857) *To Be, or Not To Be*, trans. Mrs Bushby, London.
—— (1955) *The Mermaid Man: The Autobiography of Hans Christian Andersen*, trans. Michael Maurice, London.
Aquinas, St Thomas (1964–81) *Summa Theologiae*, London.
Arbaugh, George E. and Arbaugh, George B. (1968) *Kierkegaard's Authorship*, London.
Athanasius, St (1950) *The Life of St. Anthony*, trans. Robert M. Meyer, London.
Babb, Lawrence (1951) *The Elizabethan Malady: A Study of Melancholia in Elizabethan Literature 1580–1640*, East Lansing, Michigan.
—— (1959) *Sanity in Bedlam: A Study of Robert Burton's 'Anatomy of Melancholy'*, East Lansing, Michigan.
Bakhtin, Mikhail (1968) *Rabelais and His World*, trans. Helene Iswolsky, Cambridge, Mass., and London.
—— (1973) *Problems of Dostoevsky's Poetics*, trans. R.W. Rostel, New York.
Barth, Karl (1933) *The Epistle to the Romans*, trans. Edwyn C. Haskyns, Oxford.
—— (1972) *Protestant Theology in the Nineteenth Century*, trans. Brian Cozens and John Bowden, London.
Barton, H. Arnold (1986) *Scandinavia in the Revolutionary Era, 1760–1815*, Minneapolis.
Baudelaire, Charles (1972) *Baudelaire, Selected Writings on Art and Artists*, trans. and Introduction P.E. Charvet, Harmondsworth.
—— (1989) *The Flowers of Evil*, ed. Marthiel and Jackson Mathews, New York.
Bechler, Zev (1991) *Newton's Physics and the Conceptual Structure of the Scientific Revolution*, Dordrecht, Boston and London.
Beckman, James (1988) *The Religious Dimension of Socrates' Thought*, Waterloo, Ontario.
Behler, Ernst (1993) *German Romantic Literary Theory*, Cambridge.
Beiser, Frederick C. (1987) *The Fate of Reason; German Philosophy from Kant to Fichte*, Cambridge, Mass.
—— (1992) *Enlightenment, Revolution, and Romanticism; The Genius of Modern German Political Thought, 1790–1800*, Cambridge, Mass.

—— (ed.) (1993) *The Cambridge Companion to Hegel*, Cambridge.
Bell, Richard H. (ed.) (1988) *The Grammar of the Heart: New Essays in Moral Philosophy and Theology*, San Francisco.
Benjamin, Walter (1973) *Charles Baudelaire; A Lyric Poet in the Era of High Capitalism*, trans. Harry Zohn, London and New York.
—— (1977) *The Origins of German Tragic Drama*, trans. John Osborne, London and New York.
—— (1992) *Illuminations*, trans. Harry Zohn, London.
Bercovitch, Sacvan (1975) *The Puritan Origins of the American Self*, New Haven and London.
Bertung, Birgit (ed.) (1989) *Kierkegaard – Poet of Existence; Kierkegaard Conferences 1*, Copenhagen.
Bigelow, Pat (1987) *Kierkegaard and the Problem of Writing*, Tallahassee, Florida.
Bloch, Ernst (1986) *The Principles of Hope*, trans. Neville Plaice, Stephen Plaice and Paul Knight, 3 vols, Oxford.
Bloomfield, Morton W. (1952) *The Seven Deadly Sins*, East Lansing, Michigan.
Blumenberg, Hans (1983) *The Legitimacy of the Modern Age*, trans. Robert M. Wallace, Cambridge, Mass., and London.
—— (1987) *The Genesis of the Copernican World*, trans. Robert M. Wallace, Cambridge, Mass., and London.
Booth, Wayne C. (1974) *A Rhetoric of Irony*, Chicago and London.
Bouwsma, O.K. (1984) *Without Proof or Evidence*, ed. and Introduction J.L. Craft and Ronald E. Hustwit, Lincoln, Nebraska, and London.
Brandt, Frithiof (1963) *Søren Kierkegaard, 1813–1855: his Life, his Works*, trans. A.R. Born, Copenhagen.
Brazill, William J. (1970) *The Young Hegelians*, New Haven and London.
Bredsdorff, Elias (1975) *Hans Christian Andersen; The Story of His Life and Work 1805–75*, London.
Brown, G. and Harris, T. (1978) *The Social Origins of Depression*, London.
Brown, James (1955) *Subject and Object in Modern Theology*, London.
Bruford, W.H. (1962) *Culture and Society in Classical Weimar: 1775–1806*, Cambridge.
—— (1975) *The German Tradition of Self-Cultivation: 'Bildung' from Humboldt to Thomas Mann*, Cambridge.
Buber, Martin (1947) *Between Man and Man*, trans. Ronald Gregor Smith, London.
Bunyan, John (1987) *Grace Abounding to the Chief of Sinners*, Harmondsworth.
Burton, Robert (1932) *The Anatomy of Melancholy*, 3 vols, London.
Carnell, Edward John (1965) *The Burden of Søren Kierkegaard*, Grand Rapids, Michigan.
Cascardi, Anthony J. (1992) *The Subject of Modernity*, Cambridge.
Cassirer, Ernst (1963) *The Individual and the Cosmos in Renaissance Philosophy*, Oxford.
Climacus, St John (1959) *The Ladder of Divine Ascent*, trans. Archimendrite Lazarus Moore, London.
Cole, J. Preston (1971) *The Problematic Self in Kierkegaard and Freud*, New Haven and London.

Coleman, Francis X.J. (1986) *Neither Angel Nor Beast: The Life and Work of Blaise Pascal*, New York and London.

Coleridge, Samuel Taylor (1983) *Biographia Literari I*, ed. James Engell and W. Jackson Bate, Princeton and London.

Collins, James (1954) *The Mind of Kierkegaard*, London.

Connell, George B. and Evans, C. Stephen (eds) (1992) *Foundations of Kierkegaard's Vision of Community: Religion, Ethics and Politics in Kierkegaard*, New Jersey and London.

Cooke, Michael G. (1976) *The Romantic Will*, New Haven and London.

—— (1979) *Acts of Inclusion: Studies Bearing on an Elementary Theory of Romanticism*, New Haven and London.

Couliano, Ioan P. (1987) *Eros and Magic in the Renaissance*, trans. Margaret Cook, Chicago and London.

Coyne, James C. (ed.) (1985) *Essential Papers on Depression*, New Haven and London.

Crites, Stephen (1972) *In the Twilight of Christendom; Hegel vs. Kierkegaard on Faith and History*, Chambersburg, Pennsylvania.

Croxall, T.H. (1948) *Kierkegaard Studies*, London and Redhill.

—— (1956) *Kierkegaard Commentary*, London.

Cusanus, Nicholas (Nicholas of Cusa) (1928) *The Vision of God*, trans. Emma Gurney Salter, Introduction by Evelyn Underhill, London and New York.

—— (1954) *Of Learned Ignorance*, London.

Davidson, Hugh M. (1993) *Pascal and the Arts of the Mind*, Cambridge.

Debus, Allen G. (1978) *Man and Nature in the Renaissance*, Cambridge.

—— (1987) *Chemistry, Alchemy and the New Philosophy 1550–1700*, London.

Deleuze, Gilles (1968) *Différence et répétition*, Paris.

De Man, Paul (1993) *Romanticism and Contemporary Criticism*, Baltimore and London.

Descartes, René (1985) *The Philosophical Writings of Descartes*, trans. John Cottingham, Robert Stoothoff and Dugald Murdoch, 2 vols, Cambridge.

Dickey, Laurence (1987) *Hegel: Religion, Economics, and the Politics of Spirit 1770–1807*, Cambridge and New York.

Diem, H. (1959) *Kierkegaard's Dialectic of Existence*, trans. H. Knight, Edinburgh.

Dilthey, Wilhelm (1985) *Poetry and Experience, Selected Works, vol. 5*, ed. Rudolph A. Makkreel and F. Rodi, Princeton, New Jersey.

Dover, K.J. (1972) *Aristophanic Comedy*, London.

Dufrenne, Mikel (1973) *The Phenomenology of Aesthetic Experience*, trans. Edward S. Casey, Albert A. Anderson, Willis Domingo and Leon Jacobson, Evanston, Illinois.

Dunning, Stephen N. (1985) *Kierkegaard's Dialectic of Inwardness*, Princeton, New Jersey.

Dupré, Louis (1964) *Kierkegaard as Theologian*, London and New York.

Durkheim, Emile (1915) *The Elementary Forms of the Religious Life*, trans. Joseph Ward Swain, London.

Eagleton, Terry (1990) *The Ideology of the Aesthetic*, Oxford.

Ellenberger, F. Henri (1970) *The Discovery of the Unconscious: The History and Evolution of Dynamic Psychiatry*, New York and London.

Eller, Vernard (1968) *Kierkegaard and Radical Discipleship: A New Perspective*, Princeton, New Jersey.

Elrod, John W. (1975) *Being and Existence in Kierkegaard's Pseudonymous Works*, Princeton, New Jersey.

—— (1981) *Kierkegaard and Christendom*, Princeton, New Jersey.

Enright, D.J. (1986) *The Alluring Problem: An Essay on Irony*, Oxford and New York.

Erasmus, Desiderius (1971) *The Praise of Folly*, trans. Betty Radice, Harmondsworth.

Erikson, Erik H. (1962) *Young Man Luther: A Study in Psychoanalysis and History*, New York and London.

—— (1963) *Childhood and Society*, Harmondsworth.

Evans, C. Stephen (1978) *Subjectivity and Religious Belief: An Historical, Critical Study*, Grand Rapids, Michigan.

—— (1983) *Kierkegaard's 'Fragments' and 'Postscript': The Religious Philosophy of Johannes Climacus*, Atlantic Highlands, New Jersey.

Fackenheim, Emil L. (1967) *The Religious Dimension in Hegel's Thought*, Bloomington, Indiana, and London.

Fenger, Henning (1980) *Kierkegaard, The Myths and Their Origins: Studies in the Kierkegaardian Papers and Letters*, trans. George C. Schoolfield, New Haven, and London.

Ferguson, Frances (1992) *Solitude and the Sublime: Romanticism and the Aesthetics of Individuation*, New York and London.

Ferguson, Harvie (1990) *The Science of Pleasure: Cosmos and Psyche in the Bourgeois World View*, London.

—— (1992) *Religious Transformation in Western Society: The End of Happiness*, London.

Ferreira, M. Jamie (1991) *Transforming Vision: Imagination and Will in Kierkegaardian Faith*, Oxford.

Feuerbach, Ludwig (1957) *The Essence of Christianity*, trans. George Eliot, New York and London.

—— (1972) *The Fiery Brook: Selected Writings of Ludwig Feuerbach*, trans. and Introduction Zawar Hanfi, New York.

Fichte, J.G. (1970) *Science of Knowledge*, trans. and ed. Peter Heath and John Lachs, New York.

—— (1978) *Attempt at a Critique of All Revelation*, trans. and Introduction Garrett Green, Cambridge.

—— (1988) *Fichte: Early Philosophical Writings*, trans. and ed. Daniel Breazeale, Ithaca, and London.

Ficino, Marsilio (1988) *Three Books on Life*, trans., Introduction and notes Carol V. Caske and John R. Clark, Binghamton, New York.

Fish, Stanley E. (1972) *Self-Consuming Artifacts*, Berkeley, California.

Flaubert, Gustave (1980) *The Temptation of St Antony*, trans. Kitty Mrosovsky, Harmondsworth.

Fox, Ruth A. (1976) *The Tangled Chain: The Structure of Disorder in the 'Anatomy of Melancholy'*, Berkeley, California.

Freud, Sigmund (1957) *Papers on Metapsychology: Standard Edition vol. XIV*, trans. James Strachey, London.

Freudenthal, Gideon (1986) *Atom and Individual in the Age of Newton*, Dordrecht.

Friedländer, Paul (1958) *Plato*, trans. Hans Meyerhoff, 3 vols, London.

Funkenstein, Amos (1986) *Theology and the Scientific Imagination: from the Middle Ages to the Seventeenth Century*, Princeton, New Jersey.

Gadamer, Hans-Georg (1975) *Truth and Method*, London.

Garber, Frederick (1982) *The Autonomy of the Self from Richardson to Huysmans*, Princeton, New Jersey.

Garelick, Herbert M. (1965) *The Anti-Christianity of Kierkegaard: A Study of 'Concluding Unscientific Postscript'*, The Hague.

Garin, Eugenio (1965) *Italian Humanism: Philosophy and Civic Life in the Renaissance*, trans. Peter Munz, Oxford.

—— (1976) *Astrology in the Renaissance, the Zodiac of Life*, London.

—— (1978) *Science and Civic Life in the Italian Renaissance*, trans. Peter Munz, Gloucester, Mass.

Geismar, Eduard (1938) *Lectures on the Religious Thought of Søren Kierkegaard*, Augsburg, Minneapolis.

George, A.G. (1965) *The First Sphere: A Study in Kierkegaard's Aesthetics*, London.

Giddens, Anthony (1991) *Modernity and Self-Identity: Self and Society in the Late Modern Age*, Cambridge.

Ginzburg, Lydia (1991) *On Psychological Prose*, trans. and ed. Judson Rosengrant, Princeton, New Jersey.

Glicksberg, Charles I. (1969) *The Ironic Vision in Modern Literature*, The Hague.

Goethe, J.W. von (1989) *The Sorrows of Young Werther*, trans. Michael Hulse, Harmondsworth.

Goldmann, Lucien (1964) *The Hidden God*, London.

Gouwens, David J. (1989) *Kierkegaard's Dialectic of the Imagination*, New York.

Greenblatt, Stephen (1980) *Renaissance Self-Fashioning: From More to Shakespeare*, Chicago and London.

Grimault, Marguerite (1965) *La Mélancolie de Kierkegaard*, Paris.

Grimsley, Ronald (1966) *Søren Kierkegaard and French Literature*, Cardiff.

—— (1973) *Kierkegaard: A Biographical Introduction*, London.

Grundtvig, N.F.S. (1984) *A Grundtvig Anthology: Selections from the Writings of N.F.S. Grundtvig (1783–1872)*, trans. Edward Broadbridge and Niels Lyhne Jensen, Cambridge.

—— (1989) *What Constitutes Authentic Christianity*, trans. and ed. Ernest D. Nielsen, Philadelphia.

Gurevich, A.J. (1985) *Categories of Medieval Culture*, trans. G.L. Campbell, London.

Guthrie, W.K.C. (1971) *Socrates*, Cambridge.

Guyer, Paul (1993) *Kant and the Experience of Freedom*, Cambridge.

Habermas, Jürgen (1987) *The Philosophical Discourse of Modernity*, trans. Frederick Lawrence, Cambridge.

Haecker, Theodor (1937) *Søren Kierkegaard*, trans. Alexander Dru, London and New York.

—— (1948) *Kierkegaard the Cripple*, trans. C. Van O. Bruyn, Oxford.

Hamilton, Kenneth (1969) *The Promise of Kierkegaard*, Philadelphia and New York.

Hannay, Alastair (1982) *Kierkegaard,* London.

Harré, Rom (1986) *The Social Construction of Emotion,* Oxford.

Harris, H.S. (1972) *Hegel's Development: Towards the Sunlight 1770–1801,* Oxford.

—— (1983) *Hegel's Development: Night Thoughts (Jena 1801–1806),* Oxford.

Hartshorne, M. Holmes (1990) *Kierkegaard's Godly Deceiver: The Nature and Meaning of the Pseudonymous Writings,* New York.

Hegel, G.W.F. (1892) *Lectures on the History of Philosophy,* trans. E.S. Haldane, 3 vols, London.

—— (1948) *Early Theological Writings,* trans. T.M. Knox, Chicago.

—— (1956) *Philosophy of History,* trans. J. Sibree, New York.

—— (1969) *Hegel's Science of Logic,* trans A.V. Miller, London and New York.

—— (1975) *Aesthetics: Lectures on Fine Art,* trans. T.M. Knox, 2 vols, Oxford.

—— (1977) *Hegel's Phenomenology of Spirit,* trans. A.V. Miller, Oxford.

—— (1988) *Lectures on the Philosophy of Religion: One-Volume Edition, The Lectures of 1827,* ed. Peter C. Hodgson, Berkeley, Los Angeles, and London.

Heidegger, Martin (1962) *Kant and the Problem of Metaphysics,* trans. James S. Churchill, Bloomington, Indiana.

—— (1967) *What is a Thing?* trans. W.B. Barton Jr and Vera Deutsch, New York and London.

—— (1978) *Being and Time,* trans. John Macquarrie and Edward Robinson, Oxford.

—— (1988) *Hegel's Phenomenology of Spirit,* trans. Parris Emad and Kenneth Maly, Bloomington, Indiana.

Henriksen, Aage (1951) *Methods and Results of Kierkegaard Studies in Scandinavia: A Historical and Critical Survey,* Copenhagen.

Herder, J.G. (1969) *J.G. Herder on Social and Political Culture,* trans., ed. and Introduction F.M. Barnard, Cambridge.

Hoffmann, E.T.A. (1969) *The Life and Opinions of Kater Murr,* trans. and ed. Leonard J. Kent and Elizabeth C. Knight, Chicago and London.

—— (1973) *Selected Writings of E.T.A. Hoffman,* trans. and ed. Leonard J. Kent and Elizabeth C. Knight, Chicago and London.

—— (1989) *E.T.A. Hoffmann's Musical Writings,* ed. and Introduction David Charlton, trans. Martyn Clark, Cambridge.

—— (1992) *The Golden Pot and Other Tales,* trans. Ritchie Robertson, Oxford.

Hohlenberg, Johannes (1954) *Søren Kierkegaard,* trans. T.H. Croxall, London.

Hovde, B.J. (1948) *The Scandinavian Countries 1720–1865: The Rise of the Middle Classes,* 2 vols, Ithaca, New York.

Huizinga, Johan (1970) *Homo Ludens,* London.

Hunter, Richard and Macalpine, Ida (1963) *Three Hundred Years of Psychiatry 1535–1860,* London.

Hyppolite, Jean (1974) *Genesis and Structure of Hegel's Phenomenology of Spirit,* Evanston, Illinois.

Jackson, Stanley W. (1986) *Melancholia and Depression: From Hippocratic Times to Modern Times,* New Haven and London.

Jaspers, Karl (1971) *Philosophy of Existence*, trans. and Introduction Richard F. Grabau, Philadelphia.

Jensen, Niels Lyhne (ed.) (1983) *A Grundtvig Anthology*, trans. Edward Broadbridge and Niels Jensen, Cambridge and Copenhagen.

Jerome, St (1933) *Select Letters of St Jerome*, trans. F.A. Wright, London and New York.

Johnson, Francis R. (1937) *Astronomical Thought in Renaissance England*, London.

Johnson, Howard A. and Thulstrup, Niels (eds) (1962) *A Kierkegaard Critique*, New York.

Jolivet, R. (1951) *Introduction to Kierkegaard*, trans. W.H. Barber, New York.

Jones, W. Glyn (1986) *Denmark: A Modern History*, London.

Kant, Immanuel (1928) *The Critique of Judgement*, trans. James Creed Meredith, Oxford.

—— (1933) *Immanuel Kant's Critique of Pure Reason*, trans. Norman Kemp Smith, London.

—— (1956) *Critique of Practical Reason*, trans. Lewis White Beck, New York and Toronto.

—— (1974) *Anthropology from a Pragmatic Point of View*, trans. and Introduction Mary J. Gregor, The Hague.

—— (1979) *The Conflict of the Faculties*, trans. Mary J. Gregor, Lincoln, Nebraska, and London.

—— (1988) *Fundamental Principles of the Metaphysics of Morals*, trans. T.K. Abbott, Buffalo.

Khan, Abrahim H. (1985) *'Salighed' as Happiness?: Kierkegaard on the Concept of Salighed*, Waterloo, Ontario.

King III, John Owen (1983) *The Iron of Melancholy: Structure of Spiritual Conversion in America from Puritan Conscience to Victorian Neurosis*, Middletown, Connecticut.

Kinsman, Robert S. (ed.) (1974) *The Darker Vision of the Renaissance*, Berkeley, Los Angeles, and London.

Kirmmse, Bruce H. (1990) *Kierkegaard in Golden Age Denmark*, Bloomington and Indianapolis.

Klein, Melanie (1988) *Love, Guilt and Reparation: and Other Works 1921–1945*, London.

Klemke, E.D. (1976) *Studies in the Philosophy of Kierkegaard*, The Hague.

Klibansky, R., Panofsky, E. and Saxl, F. (1964) *Saturn and Melancholy*, London.

Klossowski, Pierre (1992) *Sade My Neighbour*, trans. Alphonso Lingis, London.

Knox, Norman (1961) *The Word Irony and its Context, 1500–1755*, Durham, North Carolina.

Kojève, Alexandre (1969) *Introduction to the Reading of Hegel*, New York.

Kolakowski, Leszek (1981) *Main Currents of Marxism: volume one, The Founders*, trans. P.S. Falla, Oxford.

Kolb, David (1986) *The Critique of Pure Modernity: Hegel, Heidegger, and After*, Chicago.

Koyré, Alexandre (1957) *From the Closed World to the Infinite Universe*, Baltimore.

—— (1978) *Galileo Studies*, trans. John Mepham, Hassocks.

Kretschmer, Ernst (1936) *Physique and Character*, trans. W.J.H. Sprott, London.

Kristeller, Paul Oskar (1943) *The Philosophy of Marsilio Ficino*, New York.

Kristeva, Julia (1989) *Black Sun: Depression and Melancholia*, trans. Leon S. Roudiez, New York and Oxford.

Kuhn, Richard (1976) *The Demon of Noontide: Ennui in Western Literature*, Princeton, New Jersey.

Kuzniar, Alice A. (1987) *Delayed Endings: Nonclosure in Novalis and Hölderlin*, Athens, Georgia, and London.

Lacoue-Labarthe, Philippe and Nancy, Jean-Luc (1988) *The Literary Absolute: The Theory of Literature in German Romanticism*, trans. and Introduction Philip Bernard and Cheryl Lester, Albany, New York.

Law, David R. (1993) *Kierkegaard as Negative Theologian*, Oxford.

Lawson, Lewis A. (1970) *Kierkegaard's Presence in Contemporary American Life: Essays from Various Disciplines*, Metuchen, New Jersey.

Lepenies, Wolf (1992) *Melancholy and Society*, trans. Jeremy Gaines and Doris Jones, Cambridge, Mass., and London.

Lessing, G.E. (1874) *Laocoon*, trans. Sir Robert Phillimore, London.

—— (1956) *Lessing's Theological Writings*, trans. and ed. Henry Chadwick, London.

Lloyd, G.E.R. (ed.) (1978) *Hippocratic Writings*, Harmondsworth.

Llull, Ramon (1985) *Selected Works of Ramon Llull (1232–1316)*, trans. and ed. Anthony Bonner, Princeton, New Jersey.

Lönning, Per (1962) *The Dilemma of Contemporary Theology*, New York.

Lovejoy, Arthur O. (1960) *The Great Chain of Being: A Study of the History of an Idea*, New York.

Löwith, Karl (1964) *From Hegel to Nietzsche: the Revolution in Nineteenth-century Thought*, trans. David E. Green, London.

Lowrie, Walter (1938) *Kierkegaard*, 3 vols, New York and London.

Lukács, Georg (1974) *Soul and Form*, trans. Anna Bostock, London.

—— (1975) *The Young Hegel*, trans. Rodney Livingstone, London.

Luther, Martin (1967) *Luther's Works*, ed. and trans. Theodore G. Tappert, Philadelphia.

Lyons, Bridget Gellert (1971) *Voices of Melancholy: Studies in Literary Treatment of Melancholy in Renaissance England*, London.

Lyotard, Jean-François (1984) *The Postmodern Condition: A Report on Knowledge*, trans. Geoff Bennington and Brian Massumi, Manchester.

McCarthy, Vincent A. (1978) *The Phenomenology of Moods in Kierkegaard*, The Hague and Boston.

McClure, George W. (1990) *Sorrow and Consolation in Italian Humanism*, Princeton, New Jersey.

McEvoy, James (1982) *The Philosophy of Robert Grosseteste*, Oxford.

McFarland, Thomas (1981) *Romanticism and the Forms of Ruin*, Princeton, New Jersey.

Mackey, Louis (1971) *Kierkegaard: A Kind of Poet*, Philadelphia.

—— (1986) *Points of View: Readings of Kierkegaard*, Tallahassee, Florida.

Malantschuk, Gregor (1971) *Kierkegaard's Thought*, trans. and ed. Howard V. Hong and Edna H. Hong, Princeton, New Jersey.

—— (1980) *The Controversial Kierkegaard*, trans. Howard V. Hong and Edna H. Hong, Waterloo, Ontario.

Mâle, Emile (1958) *The Gothic Image: Religious Art in France of the Thirteenth Century*, London.

Manheimer, Ronald J. (1977) *Kierkegaard as Educator*, Berkeley, Los Angeles, and London.

Mann, Thomas (1983) *Reflections of a Nonpolitical Man*, trans. Walter D. Morris, Ungar, New York.

Martensen, Hans L. (1866) *Christian Dogmatics*, trans. Rev. William Urwick, Edinburgh.

—— (1873) *Christian Ethics*, trans. C. Spence, Edinburgh.

—— (1885) *Jacob Boehme: His Life and Teaching*, trans. J. Rhys Evans, Edinburgh.

Martin, H.V. (1950) *Kierkegaard The Melancholic Dane*, New York.

Marx, Karl (1973) *Grundrisse: Foundations of the Critique of Political Economy*, trans. Martin Nicolaus, Harmondsworth.

—— (1975) *Early Writings*, ed. L. Colletti, trans. Rodney Livingstone and Gregor Benton, Harmondsworth.

—— (1976) *Capital: A Critique of Political Economy, Volume One*, trans. Ben Fowkes, Harmondsworth.

Marx, Werner (1984) *The Philosophy of F.W.J. Schelling: History, System and Freedom*, trans. Thomas Nenon, Bloomington.

May, R., Angel, E. and Ellenberger, H. (1958) *Existence: A New Dimension in Psychiatry and Psychology*, New York.

Melzer, Sara E. (1986) *Discourses of the Fall: A Study of Pascal's Pensées*, Berkeley and London.

Mesnard, Pierre (1948) *Le Vrai Visage de Kierkegaard*, Paris.

—— (1960) *Kierkegaard: sa vie, son oeuvre avec une exposé de sa philosophie*, Paris.

Meyerson, Emile (1930) *Identity and Reality*, trans. Kate Loewenberg, London and New York.

Minkowski, Eugene (1936) *Vers une Cosmologie: Fragments Philosophiques*, Paris.

—— (1970) *Lived Time: Phenomenological and Psychopathological Studies*, Evanston, Illinois.

Moltmann, Jurgen (1971) *Man: Christian Anthropology in the Conflict of the Present*, trans. John Sturdy, London.

Montaigne, Michel de (1991) *The Essays of Michel de Montaigne*, trans. and ed. with notes M.A. Screech, London.

Mooney, Edward F. (1991) *Knights of Faith and Resignation: Reading Kierkegaard's 'Fear and Trembling'*, Albany, New York.

Moretti, Franco (1987) *The Way of the World: The Bildungsroman in European Culture*, London.

Muecke, D.C. (1970) *Irony*, London.

Mueller, William R. (1952) *The Anatomy of Robert Burton's England*, Berkeley and Los Angeles.

Mullen, John Douglas (1981) *Kierkegaard's Philosophy: Self-Deception and Cowardice in the Present Age*, New York.

Nemoianu, Virgil (1984) *The Taming of Romanticism*, Cambridge, Mass.

Neubauer, John (1980) *Novalis*, Boston.

Neuhouser, Frederick (1990) *Fichte's Theory of Subjectivity*, Cambridge.

Newton, Isaac (1931) *Opticks*, Introduction E.T. Whittaker, London.

Nielsen, H.A. (1983) *Where the Passion Is: A Reading of Kierkegaard's 'Philosophical Fragments'*, Tallahassee.

Nordentoft, Kresten (1978) *Kierkegaard's Psychology*, trans. Bruce H. Kirmmse, Pittsburgh.

Nordstrøm, Folke (1962) *Goya, Saturn and Melancholy*, Uppsala.

Olson, Alan M. (1992) *Hegel and the Spirit*, Princeton, New Jersey.

Onians, R.B. (1988) *The Origins of European Thought about the Body, the Mind, the Soul, the World, Time and Fate*, Cambridge.

Pannenberg, Wilfhart (1985) *Anthropology in Theological Perspective*, trans. Matthew J. O'Connell, Philadelphia.

Pascal, Blaise (1850) *The Thoughts on Religion and Evidence of Christianity*, ed. and trans. M.P. Fauger and George Pearce, London.

—— (1966) *Pensées*, trans. A.J. Krailsheimer, Harmondsworth.

Patrick, Denzil G.M. (1947) *Pascal and Kierkegaard*, 2 vols, London.

Pattison, George (1992a) *Kierkegaard: the Aesthetic and the Religious*, London.

—— (ed.) (1992b) *Kierkegaard on Art and Communication*, London.

Paul, Jean (Jean Paul Friedrich Richter) (1839) *The Death of an Angel and Other Pieces*, trans. A. Kenney, London.

Paulsen, Anna (1955) *Søren Kierkegaard: Deuter unserer Existenz*, Hamburg.

Perkins, Robert L. (1969) *Søren Kierkegaard*, London.

—— (ed.) (1984) *International Kierkegaard Commentary: Two Ages*, Macon, Georgia.

—— (ed.) (1985) *International Kierkegaard Commentary: The Concept of Anxiety*, Macon, Georgia.

—— (ed.) (1987) *International Kierkegaard Commentary: The Sickness Unto Death*, Macon, Georgia.

Petrarch, Francesco (1991) *Petrarch's 'Remedies for Fortune Fair and Foul': A Modern English Translation*, trans. Conrad H. Rawski, 5 vols, Bloomington and Indianapolis.

Peursen, C. van (1966) *Body, Soul, Spirit: a Survey of the Mind-Body Problem*, trans. Cornelius Anthonie, London.

Pfefferkorn, Kristin (1988) *Novalis: A Romantic Theory of Language and Poetry*, New Haven and London.

Pippin, Robert B. (1991) *Modernism as a Philosophical Problem*, Oxford.

Plato (1951) *The Symposium*, trans. Walter Hamilton, Harmondsworth.

—— (1973) *Phaedrus and Letters VII and VIII*, trans. Walter Hamilton, Harmondsworth.

—— (1993) *Phaedo*, trans. David Gallop, Oxford.

Pojman, Louis P. (1984) *The Logic of Subjectivity: Kierkegaard's Philosophy of Religion*, Alabama.

Price, George (1963) *The Narrow Pass: A Study of Kierkegaard's Concept of Man*, London.

Proust, Marcel (1983) *Remembrance of Things Past*, I, trans. C.K. Scott Moncrieff and Terence Kilmartin, London.

Quincey, Thomas de (1966) *Confessions of an English Opium Eater and Other Writings*, New York and London.

Reidl, C.C. (ed.) (1942) *On Light*, Milwaukee, Wisconsin.
Reimarus, Hermann Samuel (1970) *The Goal of Jesus and his Disciples*, trans. and Introduction George Wesley Buchanan, Leiden.
—— (1971) *Reimarus: Fragments*, ed. Charles H. Talbert, trans. Ralph S. Fraser, London.
Ricoeur, Paul (1986) *Fallible Man*, trans. Charles A. Kelley, New York.
Roberts, Robert C. (1986) *Faith, Reason, and History: Rethinking Kierkegaard's 'Philosophical Fragments'*, Macon, Georgia.
Roccatagliata, Giuseppe (1986) *A History of Ancient Psychiatry*, Westport, Connecticut.
Rohde, Peter (1963) *Søren Kierkegaard: An Introduction to His Life and Philosophy*, London.
Rousseau, Jean-Jacques (1911) *Emile, or Education*, trans. Barbara Foxley, London.
—— (1953) *The Confessions of Jean-Jacques Rousseau*, trans. J.M. Cohen, Harmondsworth.
—— (1973) *The Social Contract and Discourses*, trans. G.D.H. Cole, London.
—— (1979) *Reveries of a Solitary Walker*, trans. Peter France, Harmondsworth.
—— (1984) *A Discourse on Inequality*, trans. Maurice Cranston, Harmondsworth.
Rudd, Anthony (1993) *Kierkegaard and the Limits of the Ethical*, Oxford.
Saville, Anthony (1987) *Aesthetic Reconstructions: The Seminal Writings of Lessing, Kant, and Schiller*, Oxford.
Schelling, F.W.T. (1980) *The Unconditional in Human Knowledge: Four Early Essays (1794–1796)*, trans. and commentary Fritz Marti, London.
—— (1988) *Ideas for a Philosophy of Nature*, trans. Errol E. Harris and Peter Heath, Cambridge.
Schlegel, Friedrich (1971) *Lucinde and the Fragments*, trans. and Introduction Peter Firchow, Minneapolis.
Schilder, Paul (1964) *The Image and Appearance of the Human Body; Studies in the Constructive Energies of the Psyche*, New York.
Schiller, Friedrich (1967) *On the Aesthetic Education of Man*, trans. and ed. Elizabeth M. Wilkinson and L.A. Willoughby, Oxford.
Schleiermacher, Friedrich (1979) *On Religion: Speeches to its Cultural Despisers*, trans. John Oman, New York.
Schleifer, Ronald and Markley, Robert (eds) (1984) *Kierkegaard and Literature: Irony, Repetition, and Criticism*, Norman, Oklahoma.
Screech, M.A. (1988) *Erasmus: Ecstasy and the Praise of Folly*, Harmondsworth.
—— (1991) *Montaigne and Melancholy: the Wisdom of the Essays*, Harmondsworth.
Shestov, Lev (1969) *Kierkegaard and the Existential Philosophy*, trans. Elinor Hewitt, Athens, Ohio.
Shmuëli, Adi (1971) *Kierkegaard and Consciousness*, trans. Naomi Handelman, Princeton, New Jersey.
Shumaker, Wayne (1972) *The Occult Sciences in the Renaissance: A Study in Intellectual Patterns*, Berkeley and Los Angeles.
Simmel, Georg (1950) *The Sociology of Georg Simmel*, trans. and ed. Kurt H. Wolff, New York and London.

Singer, Irving (1987) *The Nature of Love, vol. 3*, Chicago and London.

Sløk, Johannes (1954) *Die Anthropologie Kierkegaards*, Copenhagen.

Smart, N., Clayton, J., Katz, S. and Sher, P. (eds) (1985) *Nineteenth Century Religious Thought in the West*, 3 vols, Cambridge.

Smit, Harvey Albert (1965) *Kierkegaard's Pilgrimage of Man: the Road of Self-Positing and Self-Abdication*, Delft.

Smith, Joseph H. (ed.) (1981) *Kierkegaard's Truth: the Disclosure of the Self*, New Haven and London.

Smith, Ronald Gregor (1960) *J. G. Hamann 1732–1788: A Study in Christian Existence*, London.

Smyth, John Vignaux (1986) *A Question of Eros: Irony in Sterne, Kierkegaard, and Barthes*, Tallahassee, Florida.

Solomon, Robert C. (1983) *In the Spirit of Hegel*, New York and Oxford.

—— (1987) *From Hegel to Existentialism*, New York and Oxford.

Southern, R.W. (1986) *Robert Grosseteste: The Growth of an English Mind in Medieval Europe*, Oxford.

Sponheim, Paul (1968) *Kierkegaard on Christ and Christian Coherence*, London.

Stack, George J. (1977) *Kierkegaard's Existential Ethics*, Drawer, Alabama.

Starobinski, Jean (1985) *Montaigne in Motion*, trans. Arthur Goldhammer, Chicago and London.

—— (1987) *The Invention of Liberty 1700–1789*, trans. Bernard C. Swift, New York.

—— (1988) *Jean-Jacques Rousseau: Transparency and Obstruction*, trans. Arthur Goldhammer, Chicago and London.

—— (1989a) *La Melancolie au miroir*, Paris.

—— (1989b) *The Living Eye*, trans. Arthur Goldhammer, Cambridge, Mass., and London.

Stepelevich, Lawrence S. (ed.) (1983) *The Young Hegelians*, Cambridge.

Stirner, Max (1971) *The Ego and His Own*, trans. Steven T. Byington, ed. John Carroll, London.

Strauss, Erwin (1966) *Phenomenological Psychology*, London.

Swedenborg, Emanuel (1909) *Heaven and its Wonders, and Hell*, London.

Swenson, David F. (1945) *Something About Kierkegaard*, ed. Lillian Marvin Swenson, Minneapolis.

Tanner, John S. (1992) *Anxiety in Eden: A Kierkegaardian Reading of 'Paradise Lost'*, Oxford.

Taylor, Charles (1989) *Sources of the Self: the Making of the Modern Identity*, Cambridge.

Taylor, Mark C. (1975) *Kierkegaard's Pseudonymous Authorship: A Study of Time and the Self*, Princeton, New Jersey.

—— (1980) *Journeys to Selfhood: Hegel and Kierkegaard*, Berkeley, Los Angeles, and London.

Taylor, Ronald (1970) *The Romantic Tradition in Germany*, London.

Thaning, Kaj (1972) *N.F.S. Grundtvig*, trans. David Holman, Copenhagen.

Thomas, J. Heywood (1957) *Subjectivity and Paradox*, Oxford.

Thompson, Josiah (ed.) (1972) *Kierkegaard: A Collection of Critical Essays*, New York.

—— (1974) *Kierkegaard*, London.

Thomson, J.A.K. (1926) *Irony: An Historical Introduction*, London.

Thomte, Reidar (1948) *Kierkegaard's Philosophy of Religion*, Princeton, New Jersey.

Thorslev, Peter L. (1984) *Romantic Contraries: Freedom versus Destiny*, New Haven and London.

Thulstrup, Niels (1980) *Kierkegaard's Relation to Hegel*, trans., George L. Stengren, Princeton, New Jersey.

—— (1984a) *Commentary on Kierkegaard's Concluding Unscientific Postscript*, trans. Robert J. Widenmann, Princeton, New Jersey.

—— (1984b) *Kierkegaard and the Church in Denmark; Bibliotheca Kierke-gaardiana, vol. 13*, Copenhagen.

Thulstrup, Niels and Thulstrup, Mikulová (eds) (1982) *Kierkegaard's Teachers; Bibliotheca Kierkegaardiana, vol. 10*, Copenhagen.

Tieck, Ludwig (1831) *The Old Man of the Mountain*, London.

Tillich, Paul (1967) *Perspectives on Nineteenth and Twentieth Century Protestant Theology*, London.

—— (1974) *The Construction of the History of Religion in Schelling's Positive Philosophy; its Presuppositions and Principles*, London.

Tocqueville, Alexis de (1968) *Democracy in America*, trans. George Lawrence, 2 vols, London.

Todberg, Christian and Thyssen, Anders Pantoppidan (1983) *N.F.S. Grundtvig: Tradition and Renewal*, trans. Edward Broadbridge, Copenhagen.

Trinkaus, Charles (1970) *In Our Image and Likeness: Humanity and Divinity in Italian Humanist Thought*, 2 vols, London.

Unger, Roberto Mangabeira (1975) *Knowledge and Politics*, New York and London.

Vicari, E. Patricia (1989) *The View From Minerva's Tower: Learning and Imagination in 'The Anatomy of Melancholy'*, Toronto, Buffalo, and London.

Vinet, Alexander (1843a) *An Essay on the Profession of Personal Religious Conviction*, trans. Charles Jones, London.

—— (1843b) *Homiletics: on the Theory of Preaching*, Edinburgh.

—— (1852) *Pastoral Theology: the Theory of a Gospel Ministry*, Edinburgh.

—— (1859) *Studies on Pascal*, trans. Thomas Smith, Edinburgh.

Vlastos, Gregory (1991) *Socrates: Ironist and Moral Philosopher*, Cambridge.

Wack, Mary Frances (1990) *Lovesickness in the Middle Ages*, Philadelphia.

Wahl, Jean (1949) *Etudes Kierkegaardiennes*, Paris.

Walker, D.P. (1958) *Spiritual and Demonic Magic: from Ficino to Campanella*, London.

Walker, Jeremy D.B. (1972) *To Will One Thing: Reflections on Kierkegaard's 'Purity of Heart'*, Montreal and London.

—— (1985) *The Descent into God*, Kingston and Montreal.

Wartofsky, Marx W. (1977) *Feuerbach*, Cambridge.

Webber, Joan (1968) *The Eloquent 'I': Style and Self in Seventeenth-Century Prose*, Madison and London.

Weber, Max (1930) *The Protestant Ethic and the Spirit of Capitalism*, trans. Talcott Parsons, London.

Wenzel, Siegfried (1960) *The Sin of Sloth: Acedia in Medieval Thought and Literature*, Chapel Hill, North Carolina.

Wernaer, Robert M. (1966) *Romanticism and the Romantic School in Germany*, New York.

Westphal, Merold (1979) *History and Truth in Hegel's 'Phenomenology'*, Atlantic Highlands, New Jersey.

—— (1987) *Kierkegaard's Critique of Reason and Society*, Macon, Georgia.

Wheeler, Kathleen M. (ed.) (1984) *German Aesthetic and Literary Criticism: The Romantic Ironists and Goethe*, Cambridge.

White, Alan (1983) *Schelling: An Introduction to the System of Freedom*, New Haven and London.

Wind, Edgar (1967) *Pagan Mysteries in the Renaissance*, London.

Wittkower, Rudolf and Margot (1963) *Born Under Saturn: The Character and Conduct of Artists*, London.

Wyschogrod, Michael (1954) *Kierkegaard and Heidegger: the Ontology of Existence*, London.

Xenophon (1990) *Conversations of Socrates*, trans. Tredennick and Robin Waterfield, Harmondsworth.

Yack, Bernard (1986) *The Longing for Total Revolution*, Princeton, New Jersey.

Yates, Frances (1964) *Giordano Bruno and the Hermetic Tradition*, London.

Zeller, E. (1885) *Socrates and the Socratic Schools*, trans. Oswald J. Reichel, London.

—— (1931) *Outline of the History of Greek Philosophy*, trans. L.R. Palmer, London.

Zimmerman, J.G. (1852) *On Solitude*, London.

Ziolkowski, Theodore (1990) *German Romanticism and its Institutions*, Princeton, New Jersey.

Name index

Subject index